THE BOOK

OF LOVE

AND CREATION

THE BOOK

OF LOVE

AND CREATION

A Channeled Text

PAUL SELIG

Jeremy P. Tarcher/Penguin
a member of Penguin Group (USA) Inc.
New York

JEREMY P. TARCHER/PENGUIN
Published by the Penguin Group
Penguin Group (USA) Inc., 375 Hudson Street, New York, New York 10014, USA • Penguin Group
(Canada), 90 Eglinton Avenue East, Suite 700, Toronto, Ontario M4P 2Y3, Canada (a division of Pearson
Penguin Canada Inc.) • Penguin Books Ltd, 80 Strand, London WC2R 0RL, England • Penguin Ireland,
25 St Stephen's Green, Dublin 2, Ireland (a division of Penguin Books Ltd) • Penguin Group (Australia),
250 Camberwell Road, Camberwell, Victoria 3124, Australia (a division of Pearson Australia Group Pty
Ltd) • Penguin Books India Pvt Ltd, 11 Community Centre, Panchsheel Park, New Delhi–110 017, India •
Penguin Group (NZ), 67 Apollo Drive, Rosedale, North Shore 0632, New Zealand (a division
of Pearson New Zealand Ltd) • Penguin Books (South Africa) (Pty) Ltd,
24 Sturdee Avenue, Rosebank, Johannesburg 2196, South Africa

Penguin Books Ltd, Registered Offices: 80 Strand, London WC2R 0RL, England

Most Tarcher/Penguin books are available at special quantity discounts for bulk purchase
for sales promotions, premiums, fund-raising, and educational needs. Special books
or book excerpts also can be created to fit specific needs. For details, write
Penguin Group (USA) Inc. Special Markets, 375 Hudson Street, New York, NY 10014.

ISBN 978-0-399-16090-5

Printed in the United States of America
3 5 7 9 10 8 6 4 2

Book design by Meighan Cavanaugh

Neither the publisher nor the author is engaged in rendering professional advice or services to the
individual reader. The ideas, procedures, and suggestions contained in this book are not intended
as a substitute for consulting with your physician. All matters regarding your health require
medical supervision. Neither the author nor the publisher shall be liable or responsible for any
loss or damage allegedly arising from any information or suggestion in this book.

While the author has made every effort to provide accurate telephone numbers, Internet
addresses, and other contact information at the time of publication, neither the publisher nor
the author assumes any responsibility for errors, or for changes that occur after publication.
Further, the publisher does not have any control over and does not assume any responsibility
for author or third-party websites or their content.

CONTENTS

Book Two

ALIGNMENT TO LOVE

Book Three

FREQUENCY AND CREATION

INTRODUCTION:
THE ROOF

One night when I was twenty-five years old, I climbed up to the roof of the building where I lived in Chelsea and asked whatever God there was to wake me up.

I had been raised something of an atheist on Manhattan's Upper West Side, and I had been taught that people who had a spiritual life were perhaps deluded, or ignorant, and not to be taken seriously. But I had come to a point in my life where the need for something else had become apparent. And so I asked.

I can't say exactly what happened on the roof. I wonder, still, if I didn't perhaps induce it myself in some way, but I had an experience that left me mute and paralyzed and swaying in an energy that seemed to come from the pit of my being and course through my body and out the top of my head. Shortly thereafter, I began seeing little lights around people, like fireflies.

I began studying a form of energy healing to gain a context for what I was now beginning to experience and found that when I had my hands on people, I began to hear things for them—names, fragments of information, phrases that seemed to emerge from the chatter in my own mind. What I heard made no sense to me, but made perfect sense to the client. In this way, I began to evolve as a clairaudient and later as a conscious channel. My guides, a consortium of beings from a higher level of consciousness, were here to teach.

I convened a small group in my apartment for weekly sessions with my guides and found that the information that came through me as I channeled was accompanied by an energy that was profoundly loving and physically palpable. This went on for many years, quietly, as I continued my life as a playwright and academic.

In 2009, my guides announced, quite unexpectedly, that they had a book to write, and two days later began to dictate the text of *I Am the Word,* which they described as a treatise on the manifestation of Christ in man. They stated that the book was an energy transmission that worked directly on its readers to bring them into accordance with the frequency of the Word, which they have defined simply as "the energy of God in action." The dictation took two and a half weeks. They promised that *I Am the Word* was the first book of three, the mission text, and that other books would follow.

The Book of Love and Creation was dictated shortly after *I Am the Word* was in the hands of its publisher. I had not wanted to channel another book so soon—a relationship that I had valued had ended badly, and I wasn't keen on returning to my role as a student of and channel for my guides, whose agenda seemed, at times, a bit loftier than my personal happiness.

Victoria Nelson, a colleague of mine at Goddard College, had been the "active listener" or audience for *I Am the Word* and was eager to learn what more the guides had to say. I reluctantly agreed to call her for a brief check-in to see what the guides had planned, and they took the opportunity to deliver the prologue of the book you now hold in your hands.

The Book of Love and Creation, although it bears my name, was not written by me. I am a conscious channel, and the book was dictated, verbally, often at lightning speed, over thirty days of sittings conducted over a month and a half. I called Victoria at her home in Berkeley at the appointed hour, closed my eyes, and spoke the words that were given to me until I was told to stop. The recordings were then transcribed and the transcriptions were proofread. The amount of editing was so small as to be completely negligible—a dropped word here and there, a misspoken syllable. What you have is the teaching as it was delivered.

I am a student of my guides' work, not the teacher. I have always been a somewhat private man, and now that my work as a channel has become known I am often called to work with others. As the guides promised, *I Am the Word* has found its readership, and I continue to receive e-mail from people around the world whose lives have been changed by its teachings and who claim the shared experience of being worked with energetically as they engage with the text.

I am grateful for the work that comes through me. I am grateful for the privilege of sitting in an energy that feels so loving and strong and can be felt by others—often those who have never felt energy or who were, like me, raised to believe that such things cannot be possible.

But it is possible. The work is here. As my guides continue to remind me, this is the time, we have choice, and we are being asked again and again to wake up and claim our divine birthright.

If you are new to the work of the guides, this book will be your introduction. If you have already worked with their teachings, you will find this to be a continuation and a deepening of them. There is more to come. Thank you for sharing this journey with me. May it be a blessed one for all of us.

Paul Selig
April 8, 2012
New York City

The following are transcripts of channeling sessions recorded between August 15, 2009, and September 25, 2009, in New York City. Paul Selig served as channel. Victoria Nelson was present via telephone from Berkeley, California.

PROLOGUE

Day One

We're going to talk for a little bit about what this has to be and what has to come to make this happen. Between this issue of fear and requirement for work, the requirement for work has to bring forth the notification to the self that the work that will transpire is the correct work, and that the self that stands in the way and watches from the hallway to make sure that everything's okay is put to use elsewhere.

This next book is a big one. It's a treatise, again, but it's a different kind of treatise. And it's about walking in the light, and how to stand in the light, and how to become yourself in congruence with the Divine Self that you are through your relationships, through your actions, and through your requirements of your knowing, and what is given to you through spirit through your consciousness as you walk forward.

Now Paul is already wondering, "Is this different from the first one?" And we will say it's entirely different in several respects. The annotation that we have asked you to do on Book One, which really had to do with questions, has been done, in a certain way, in our understanding, and many of the questions that were put forth in thought as the first book was transcribed will be addressed in Book Two.

But Book Two has its own mission, which is the jurisdiction of light in manifestation. What is the work of the light, what is the light to do, how are you supposed to respond to it, and how do you work with it for the benefit of your lives and for the lives of those around you?

Now this is not a personal text, it's not a self-help text, but what it is, really, is a caution against operating without the light and a creation that will enable those who read it to walk forward in the jurisdiction of the Creator.

Now what that means, really, "to be in the jurisdiction of the Creator," is to stand firm in awareness of your honoring the bypassing of the fear-based self to be in truth. In truth we mean, "I am Word." Now the basis of this book has been written already. Your first book is the basis, it is the mission text, and how this mission is put into action, both in daily lives and in planetary awareness, will be the consequence of the second book.

By "consequence" we mean when the second book is printed, and we say it will be, it will be seen *in consequence,* it will have *rapid* ramifications on those who read it. And Paul is seeing an image of a deck of dominos or playing cards falling down, one after the other in a tumbling effect, and that is correct. This book will have that kind of a ramification in its consequence, and that is a pleasure for us. And what we mean by this is that the work is taking hold and it is passed, in hand, from one man to the next as the world begins to replicate the intention of this book, which is to stand in the Word and to be operating from a planetary consciousness that will bypass fear.

Now we want to talk a little bit about fear today and the

requirement of fear. And Paul has said this already in other teachings, but it bears repetition. *The action of fear is to create more fear.*
Like produces like, and fear's intention, believe it or not, is to activate the grid of fear. And the war that is going on now, if you wish
to use that term, is a planetary one between the consciousness of
the light, which bypasses fear, and the fear that would like to hold
its name fully, and regarding itself as the provision for safety.

Now if you understand, first of all, that safety, as you envision
it, is about freedom from fear, than you can look at how ridiculous it is to look at fear as a protector. How can you have fear as
protection?

We are giving Paul an image of a Mexican wall where they put
pieces of bottle glass at the height of the top of the wall so that
people cannot climb over. The fear of the wounds is what keeps
people out. And we understand this. But imagine you as the one
trapped in the house trying to find your way out, over and above
that wall? Your fear is also keeping you in, and your belief in your
own safety and the requirements of safety have produced a grid and
a matrix of fear that is requiring now to break down, to collapse
and to disintegrate.

All of the investments in this fear, all of those things that have
been created to support fear, and to keep you in a place of fear, have
been held there and are now in abeyance to this trial. If you can
imagine the investment of the illusion of fear to keep itself as
seen as truth, you will be shocked at the creations that you have all
made in a belief in safety.

Paul is saying, what are these creations? And we will tell you
some of them now: War is the primary one. And defensiveness that
is based in fear has given you the opportunity as a global civilization to end yourselves rapidly. So your belief in your safety and
your need to protect things is what has created the instrument of
destruction that you are going to have to contend with.

Now if you can understand, very simply, that what has been created in fear must be dismantled and, on occasion, confronted fully in order to realize itself for its worthlessness, you can understand what you have to prepare yourselves for if you don't change consciousness.

Now consciousness operates on different levels. The self perceives the self as separate from others, and that is individuation. And a county, perhaps, perceives itself differently from the situation it is placed in on the map of the state. And the state perceives itself individualized from its country and the country is differentiated by the country beside it. These are all individuations, believe it or not, of how consciousness is out-pictured in this world.

Now the creations of consciousness that require separation must be looked at carefully. There are times when differentiation is radically important. Paul is seeing two people with two blood types who require transfusions. And it is imperative that they get the blood type that is important to them from the donor who has the appropriate gift and appropriate blood type. That is okay and that is required. When you get to issues of prominence and jurisdiction over others' well-being on a global level, you have to begin to look a bit differently at the creations of man.

If we use the image of a garden wall as a simple image that will keep you safe from your neighbor's theft—and you see that is a simple reminder, "My land ends here, yours is over there"—there are no complaints. The wall is simply a symbol of division. But if you go below the wall, you understand perfectly well that the ground continues and the wall is a manmade construct.

If you look at the world and how property is developed in civilization, you can understand that the walls have been redrawn multiple times over the course of the history of this plane and they will be redrawn. And if you look at all of the pain, and all of the suffering, and all of the bloodshed that has been happening for thousands of years over the placement of a wall, we do not understand why you don't decide, once and for all, to tear the walls down and greet your neighbor as your brother.

Once this is done by one man, in love, across a border of consciousness it will be done again. Now Paul is saying, "How impossible is this? Walls will not be razed." We will tell you this now: They will be razed, they will be razed, and they are being razed in consciousness first. Nothing happens in the physical plane without it occurring first on a level of consciousness, and that is the teaching of this book.

We say your neighbors are your brothers and your sisters, and your self-identification as a Divine Being is the archway that you pass through in order to know that this is true. As you know that this is true, what you contend with are the illustrations of separation that you will now be clear to see fully for what they are: a construct based in fear. As you have this information, as you understand that the fear is an illusion, and that which is built in fear is built in fear's intention to protect itself, you can begin to dismantle it through your choice to be embodied as the Christ, as the Word, as the wonder of God embodied.

Now we will tell you again by definition: What the Word is is the anchoring and the manifestation of the Divine Self incarnating as you. You operate from your divinity with an awareness of your unification with Source. You become a demonstration, walking and talking, of love. And the identification of the self as Word, as the Christed Self, is the way this is done in fullness. So you will say, "I am the Word," and it will be wonderful, and it will be true, and it will bring forth those changes that will align the matrix of fear to the dissemblance of itself once and for all time.

Now we say fear, and what you must understand now is that the requirement of fear to create fear is an unconscious action. It is not a plan. It is how the breed grows itself. If I fire somebody from my job because I am frightened of what they do, I have created fear, and the ramifications of that choice will contend to bring about more fear. So when you see this as an operational system that seeks to realize itself, you can begin to work with it as a construct. And once you can see something as a construct with attributions and laws and practices and rules, it's a lot easier to understand them.

The crucifixion of the self that you each fear will come to you if you realize yourself as your Divine Self is a promise of fear. There is crucifixion of the lower self, and the lower self has the investment of self-identifying as separate and creating constructs of separation. So you see, the war that is happening, if you wish to use that illustration, is between two different planes of awareness and self-identification: the self that is in terror of being seen for what it is, which is a fear-based construct, and the self that knows that it is free but has not had the primary rule to be able to fulfill itself.

If you can imagine a babysitter who allows the children to run about and do as they want until they get tired, that is a semblance of this. You are not allowed to override your will with an outside force. No one is allowed to come into their Christed Self if it is not through their own choice and awareness. So that said, the idea of free will comes into play here in very, very direct ways.

Now Paul is wondering what we are talking about and we will explain it to him. You have the privilege of running around and creating all the destruction you want to. You can do that as a child, you can do that as an adult, but you are doing it through your free will. Your Higher Self is intervening only through the permission it is allowed. No one will tell you, at a certain point in your life, that you have to go to bed and get the rest that you need. That is your requirement to give yourself. And, conversely, until you decide on a level of consciousness that you are willing to ascribe to the teachings of the wisdom of your own Christed Self, you will do what you want. And the division between these two selves in operation, in a funny way, is the consequence of operating in form while you are spirit.

The teachings of this book and the book that has preceded it are about embodying in consciousness. And when you are embodied in consciousness, you are in your awareness of your Christed Self. And that self is running the show.

The self that self-identifies as separate from this still operates on a certain level that is supported by you for protection of practical ways. "I know my blood type is O positive" is separation. "I know I wear a size thirty-two jean and that I have paid my taxes and that my name is such and such." All of these things are supportive of the requirements of the individual. But to the extent that you are operating from selfishness and an unawareness of the self in conjunction with the larger matrix of humanity through their own divinity connected as you in one grid of light, you are creating separation.

So we are going to congratulate you each today for embarking on a new tour, a new journey, a new way of operating in ambition. And by ambition we mean you stand in your own knowing and you create from the space, "I am in my knowing," and you align to the possibility that you will be taught.

As we teach you, we remember who you are in truth. And as you are remembered by us, you remember yourselves. We are working with you. This will be an energetic transmission. No one is without the love of the Creator and we will bring this to you on every page as we can. We will give you thanks now, and Paul will stop. This will be the end of the prologue, and we give thanks for your participation in the work that is to come.

"Word I am Word through this intention to allow this second book to come into its perfect form in perfect ways and in perfect timing. I am Word through this intention to be of service through this manual of love and creation. Word I am Word through this intention. Word I am Word."

Thank you and stop.

Book One

AWARENESS

ONE

AWARENESS IN CONGRUENCE WITH THE DIVINE SELF

Day Two

We're going to talk today about things that have to do with differentials and what differentials mean. Now in your last session, Paul, we spoke to you about light and the requirements of light, and the jurisdiction of light, as it were. And today we want to talk about differentials between light and what stands outside of the light.

Now the responsibility for you in this session is to allow the words to come. The placating of the self that fears the information that is to follow will happen clearly and responsibly through our light. We want to give you information today that is new to you and will have to withstand the counsel that you bring to it that states that this cannot be so, and that the words that you speak cannot be in truth.

Now the reason you are having the resistance to teaching in this manner is threefold.

The first area of fear has to do with your issues of truth. And the fact that you are requiring truth to be at the center of anything that comes through you is a great thing, and we support you in this. But the fear that you could be misled, or that you are misleading the self and thereby misleading others, is the thing that has to be contended with now. This is actually a creation, and it's a symbolic one, because it amplifies fear. And we want to talk about fear today. But we will get there soon.

The second area of creation that you contend with in your resistance is the ideal of what *should* come through you. "This should be wonderful," "This should be coherent," "This should have information that others will require." And we will say yes, those are all accurate desires but, in a funny way, they have nothing to do with you. To the extent that you resign the self to being participatory to the channel as the vehicle for the information and not the designer of the book jacket, as it were, we will tell you what this book is as it is written.

This is a different kind of book. And the reason you have not been given the information about what is required from it is because it would precede a level of resistance on your behalf to the information that wishes to come forth. Now the alignment to the new information that we will bring through you is going to happen very rapidly. The dictation will be fast and spontaneous. And the regard for chapter headings and things like that will come into place as it is required, but that is an afterthought to the content of the book.

The content of the book that we wish to write with you is about amplification of creation, how light is worked with, how you work through yourself and how you govern yourself from a place of Creative Source. Creative Source, we will say, is another word for the Christed Self. You can operate from your Creative Self and you will be in your Christed Self. We are using this word "creative" not as a replacement for Christ but to bypass fear of a readership that may have resistance to a configuration of consciousness that they have already labeled to be uninhabitable, for whatever reasons, to their lives and to their ability to access. So the interchangeable words, Creative Self and Christed Self, will come into play in this book.

Now the second thing we want to tell you about the book is about responsibility to it through the response you have as the dictation occurs. You cannot allow yourself to become involved with the information as the information moves through you. And we are going to do our best to keep you in abeyance as this process happens so that you can remain accurate to the intention and to the vocabulary that is handed to you. And this is important: The requirement of this book to be in translation from your vocabulary to a vocabulary that will be held in higher frequency is part of this process. We will explain this later.

Now the third issue you contend with, as the dictation occurs and your resistance to it, is your responsibility to yourself. What does it mean to be in this position as a human being who holds forth and brings through a consciousness of the Divine Self, an aspect of the Creator, into language and design that will support others in the manifestation of themselves as their Christed Selves?

"Who are you to do this?" becomes your question, and the relegation of your fears respond happily to that statement because you can always find reasons why you are not worthy of the mission you have been given. You have been chosen, in a funny way, to support this work partially because your resistance allows for a declaration of independence for the information to come through accurately and with a predisposition to come forth honestly.

The design of the work is not yours, but your temperature rising whenever you have a response to the work in a way that does not feel truthful is a healthy thing. So in a way you can allow yourself to have a bit of resistance because it calls to it honesty. But to the extent that you design the book in your mind is the extent that we cannot work through you to bring through the book that is required.

So in this case we will say that, "What am I? Who am I? Who am I to do this?" is not your responsibility either. You are simply the vehicle for the manifestation of this book. And this book, we will tell you now, is going to be a long one. It is a bigger book than the last book because it will be relegated into three parts.

The first part, which we will begin today, has to do with awareness, an awareness of the self and awareness of that which is around you and all things true. Now you can ask yourself what this means. What are all things and how am I to be in contact with them? And we are going to tell you something very funny right now. You are all things. All things come forth from you through your thoughts. Now the radical idea that man creates his own reality is nothing more than language given to something that has been at play since the beginning of creation. And we have spoken about this in the previous text and we will describe it again.

There can be nothing created in this land, in this existence, in this plane of consciousness without it being thought first. Now the simplicity of this idea is something you understand, but is not something that you navigate with in awareness on a day-to-day basis. "I didn't create the subway system." "I didn't create the blemish." "I didn't create the tree." Well, in fact you did. You all did, on a collective level of thought.

The world around you has been created in order to give you an experience of yourselves in reality that will come forth and bring about the change of consciousness that you require. Paul is seeing a kindergarten classroom where the walls have been painted with colorful figures. And those are paintings, out-pictured, meant to appeal to the level of maturity and consciousness of the people who tend to stay in that room all day, which are very small people who have certain requirements.

The planet that you exist in, in many ways, operates at the same level. The designs that you have created around you are there to support an experience that you are intending to have as a human being operating in a body on a physical plane. Now the transmission of change into the physical is a process. It does not happen in the twinkling of an eye, but it does happen. And if you can understand that a hundred years ago much of what you take for granted today was not even at play here, you can understand how rapidly thought becomes reality.

Now if you choose as a culture to become aware of your creations, those things that you have invented, for good or for evil or for whatever intent was behind their creation, you will begin to get a sense, in truth, of how powerful you truly are.

Now the consciousness that you have been given by your Creator, that aspect of the self that is you, that operates in its Creative Self, is in congruence with its design as an aspect of the Creator. You are each a piece of the Creator congruently operating with the Great Creator to the extent that you become congruent with that frequency. And the design that you are, then, can out-picture in consciousness a changed reality.

Your reality can transform to the extent that you bring forth a new ideal of awareness of yourselves as the creative force in the world. You do this intentionally, individually, as you claim, "I am Word." "I am Word through all that I see before me. I am Word through my designs. I am Word through my choices. I am Word through all that I know."

These are the things that you perceive yourself, now, to begin to have some control over. And that is a truth. You do. And as you have been working in frequency with an awareness of this, you have begun to experience yourself as frequency. And as you engage in frequency as the self, you engage with everything else as frequency and you understand the flexibility, the plasticity, the malleability of that which is in your dominion as an individual creation in consciousness.

As you do this individually, what you have created through consciousness resonates with the intention that you have placed before you. "I am choosing to create from a Divine Self that already knows

what is required for my highest good" will bring you into an alignment with those creations that are, indeed, made for you by your
Higher Self, by the divine aspect of you, in accordance with your
highest good.

Now if an individual is capable of creating change in her own
reality, in her own awareness as what can happen in her life can
change, she can say, "Yes, I am the creative force in my life, and
what I bring forth is required for my growth in healing and in
truth." Now if you can do that individually, you can do that collectively as a group energy, and as the group energy begins to change
in consciousness, the changes then can be magnified. There is no
fear, ultimately, in transformation, when you understand that the
requirement for transformation will be different for the individuals
as they operate in group consciousness to bring forth collective
change for good. The choice you make as a group energy to divine
the future in a positive way can bring forth positive manifestation
on this plane.

Now group collective thought is already in operation. Everything that you see around you has been created by a collective
source that agrees on certain things. We can do this individually,
we can do this collectively as a group, as a culture, as a country, as a
place to inhabit that we call this planet. We can do it as one group,
as factions, but it is all being done through collective intention.

Now when you walk down the block and you see a sign on the
wall that tells you to purchase something, that is a directive that is
being given to you by someone else who is operating to inform the
collective consciousness through a description or an idealization of
a thing, a "thing" meaning what is advertised on that wall. When
you choose to describe what you want to see on that wall from a
higher perspective, believe it or not, what you will find on that wall
will be transformed by your requirements.

Now Paul is asking, "Is this individual? Is this as individual jurisdiction of a creation?" And we will explain. If you have always wanted a pair of blue jeans, or a certain bottle of wine, and this is what is placed on the billboard, you will go into agreement with it, and the culture, essentially, goes into agreement with what it has been given and handed on a level of belief and matrix. You all believe that the bills come every month. You all believe that nice guys finish last. Or choose a belief that has been encoded into culture, and then you will begin to see how your creations have been made to support those choices that have been idealized, for better or for worse, by group consciousness.

So the billboard we describe on the wall is simply an example of something that has been created in manifestation to meet the requirements of those things you have agreed upon, either because that is what you wanted, or because that is what was told to you and you decided, for lack of anything better to do, than to go into agreement with it, and there it is, out-pictured for purchase on the wall. Now if you want to design a new billboard that will bring to you the change of consciousness that you desire to be in awareness with your world in a new way, we say it will be done. And we will design it with you.

We want you each now to take a moment to decide that what you bring forth in your life has been created by you, with no excuses. "I can no longer blame my mother for the terrible things she told me," or "I can no longer blame my boss because of his temper," or "I can no longer blame my schooling, or my lack of schooling, or my body. I have created what I see before me."

Now to the extent you accept this as a truth, you become empowered to change that which you see before you. "I am Word through all that I see before me" is your command to be in demonstration of your power in dominion. We say "dominion" because your fear of being in dominion, in your power, is what is keeping you small and unaware of how powerful you truly are and allowing you, then, to relegate the creations of your life to someone else's authority.

"I can't be that powerful. I don't have what I want. I don't even have what I need." Well, if you believe that, that is what you are creating from. And if you do this as a culture, to examine that for a moment, you would begin to see that what you have brought forth culturally, for better and for worse, are things that are about the abnegation of individual authority in creation.

You are all being told what to do on a basic day-to-day level. You all inhabit a world that you have created that gives you a set of instructions about what you are to do, and how you are to behave, and how you are to think, and how you are to greet your neighbor. You have chosen this and it has been a way of abnegating power and relegating authority to other sources.

Paul is wondering, "Well, am I listening to another source? Am I relegating my authority now to a disembodied frequency that is telling me one thing while my own intention is to hear something very, very different?"

We are never commanding our authority override free will. This is very important. You have been gifted with free will. You do not use it when it comes to issues of creation that you have been trained to believe that you have no authority over. You don't believe that things can be changed that are out of your jurisdiction as an individual self. And therefore you do not change. You accept, you are docile, and you move about willingly accepting your fate as a being that is experiencing only one-fiftieth of her, of his, inherent creative power. You do this in agreement with your brothers, with your sisters, and everybody shakes hands at how small you really are.

Now Paul has many questions about this and we are going to attempt to answer some of them. You have been gifted with free will, and it is your choice to operate from it. So as Source embodying in a physical body, you have to begin to realize that what you are capable of trumps any outside power that you could ever possibly contend with.

Now Paul is seeing the image of someone getting evicted from a house, and he is saying, "Oh no, the person who is evicting this tenant has all the authority." And in a way, that may be true, but on another level that person only has the authority that he has been gifted with through cultural approval. And once that is changed, everything begins to sort itself out differently.

Now the demands of creation, what it means to be in responsibility of your creations, is a responsibility that you each have to choose, now, before you read further.

"I am now choosing to stand in my awareness as the Creative Source that brings about the change that is required in my life. I am doing this through this intention: I am Word to begin to identify myself through my choices as the one empowered to create change. I am Word through this intention. Word I am Word."

Now once this is decided, you have to go through a process of discernment. When you decide something in consciousness, you have to become very aware of the aspect of the self that you are choosing to create from. Is it in the jurisdiction of the Creative Self, the Christed Self, or is it born out of fear? You can ask this question any day because, frankly, those are really your two choices. Am I creating out of love, out of the light, or am I creating out of a fear-based reaction to something in my world?

Once you understand where you are creating from, you become aware of everything in your world that has been created out of fear. Now we want to work first with a level of identification that the individual holds. Look around the room you live in. What have you purchased that you did not want, or bought because you thought you were supposed to have it, or because you feared that if you didn't have it, something might happen to you?

Now we will explain what we mean. You are in the purview of your environment, and it is very easy for you to accept that everything in your space was chosen by you if, in fact, you live alone. If you are in a partnership or if you are in a shared space, you can still accept your responsibility for your landscape on this small a level. So search the room. Where did I make choices and bring things into manifestation out of a place of fear?

Now this can be as simple as saying, "I bought the rug that was on sale because I was frightened I couldn't afford the one I really wanted," or, "I have the keys hidden in that special place in case somebody robs my apartment; I will know how to get back in and have the locks changed." Do you understand? They can be very small symbols, but if you begin to understand quickly, on a level of consciousness, that what you have created is your choice, you begin to make other choices.

Now if I realize that I only married a man because he said he loved me and I was terrified no one would love me again, regardless of the fact that he is not the one I chose to love, you can see that much of your life was based on a decision born out of fear of lack. If you have a fear of lack, believe it or not, you are creating from lack. And as you try to counter lack with fear, you end up creating from fear and not changing the consciousness that will bring about the prosperity that you require. We will devote a chapter to this later. But at the moment we want you to see that what you have created in your landscape was chosen by you.

Now we will extend this, now, beyond the walls of your space into the neighborhood that you live in. You chose to be here, on a certain level. You are existing here and your reality extends as you look around you. "My store," "My post office box," "My . . ." whatever you want to name that is in your jurisdiction.

Now Paul is already saying, "Please don't say that we create the post office box." Well, you did. You chose it. It is a part of your reality and, consequently, you have power over it. Once you understand that it is a creation of your own, you suddenly imagine that there may be other possibilities outside of the framework that you choose to exist in.

Now yesterday when we spoke about walls, we spoke about them as barriers. And we want to speak about a dimensional barrier right now, that which holds your reality in place through a dimensional barrier of your cognizance of who you are in a body. As you experience yourself in physical form, you begin to have an experience in this dimension, and you operate from this place in a comfortable way, because it is what you are trained to do.

Now if you can understand today that what is actually available to you through your consciousness can exceed the limitations of this dimension, you will begin to open to a new ideal. And the ideal that we speak of has to do with the awareness of other worlds, other aspects of the self that are available to you through frequency at a higher vibration. Now as you call these things to you, the boundary of the dimensional shift begins to change and what you do is expand your consciousness to extend beyond your room, and your neighborhood and your dimension, to extend to higher realms to access those aspects of the self that are about to be brought into form.

Now Paul is saying, "What is going on here?" And we are simply saying to him this is a brief introduction to a concept that we will return to down the road when the preparatory work for it has been finished. This first book of this three-parter is about awareness, and your cognizance of what is in your landscape will come into consciousness for you to begin to see what it is truly made of, and that is thought.

Now Paul wants to know, "Is this the chapter on awareness or is this title of the book?" We will tell you this. The chapter is called "Awareness in Congruence with the Divine Self" because that is going to be the intention of this chapter: how each individual comes into an awareness of her reality through individuation and then through congruent awareness and symbiosis with the Divine Self that you are created in. As you begin to create from that aspect of the self, which is the Christ, which is the Creative Self, what you manifest happens rapidly, can only be for the good, and can make itself known to you as a manifestation of your own divinity expressed in material reality.

Now we want to talk about two things, and the first thing is awareness of what is in your physical reality and what that means. What you touch, what you see as physical or material, are all of these things that we are going to be talking about. However, what is created in consciousness is transformation. You are really not creating a toaster in consciousness, although you may be manifesting that in the material, if you wish to say it that way. When you are transforming consciousness, what changes is consciousness. As consciousness is altered, the physical reality that you exist in and the material matter that you encounter must be transformed in obligation to the change in frequency and perception that has brought you to this new alignment.

You can understand this very simply. If you are a wealthy man, you have an expectation to a look at a bank statement and be proud or be aware of the abundance that presents itself on that picture of a statement that you receive each month. If you are a poverty-stricken person, you look at that with fear because the statement has a negative balance.

Now when we speak of consciousness, we speak about the change in consciousness that aligns you to a new creation that will bring forth different results. If your consciousness is liberated from a semblance of poverty in its self-identification, there will be no low bank statements. It cannot happen, because it is no longer part of what you can call to you in frequency. So the consciousness that changes, in fact, transforms the material experience that you embody here on this plane. If you want a house but say you can never afford a house, you probably will never afford a house until you decide to expand your consciousness to a place where that image can be held as true.

Now Paul is asking, "Is this going to be about creating in the physical? Didn't this book think that it had bigger fish to fry in consciousness?" Well, yes and no, and that was an ill-stated quote. If you can think of it this way: The consciousness that you have is creative, and what you create from consciousness first is out-pictured in the physical reality that you have. If you look around your room and you see things you don't like there, ask yourself why you created them and then you will get the answers you need.

If you look at this as a group consciousness and what you create as a group, look at your neighborhood, look at your country, look at your planetary issues and you will see that they are out-picturing of collective thought. So it is actually perfectly correct to begin with something small like a bank statement as an example of what you create to show you that you have other options in consciousness that are available to you now.

Now we want to take you forward a little bit in time so you can have an experience of amazement. And we want you to do this with us:

We want you to imagine for a moment that your life, as you choose it, pictures outwardly all of those things you say you want. "I am feeling good about myself." "My body is healthy." "I am with the partner I desire." "I am in the work I love" or "I am no longer working because I no longer need to support myself that way." Create in your mind the image that you say you want from this level of consciousness that you are today. We want you to do this now.

Imagine your perfect life and take a moment and decide that this is now available to you.

Now if you start with your own life and you are able to begin to make changes on this level of individualization in your world, we can amp you up to the next level to do the group work that this will happen with once this work is in progression as we describe.

So you have seen yourself in an idealized future life. And we will tell you now that those creations that you just chose, however well intentioned, are also born out of fear that you will not have them. If you already had them in your lives now, this would not be an issue. But those things that you say that you want, that you do not have, quite simply mean that your consciousness, at this stage of development, today, does not require that you have them. And we will tell you this: The likelihood of why you don't have them would be because you don't believe you deserve them, or you are afraid to have them, or you believe that if you did have them, something terrible would happen to you.

People stay alone in their lives for very different reasons. And solitude in a life can be a wonderful thing and partnership is certainly not a requirement. But many of you who are alone believe that is where you deserve to be because you are frightened of deciding that if it were otherwise you could have what you wanted and perhaps experience pain. So you keep yourself safe by staying alone, and then you say, "I guess no one wants what I have to offer." So your reality has been designed to protect what you say you want, which is, truly, not to be harmed.

So if you see that those things that you say you want in the future are not in your present reality because you do not believe that you can hold them, or you are frightened of them, you will see that what has been created out of fear is your poverty, is your loss, are those things that you cannot out-picture because you don't believe you can have them. So today's exercise, we will say, is going to be about awareness.

As you go about your day, we want you to begin to imagine that everything that you encounter you have chosen. Every smile from every stranger, every piece of dirt on the street, every telephone call, every mailing in your mailbox, everything on the television, everybody's face at work, on your children's faces, everything is created by you. We want you to do this as an experiment so that you can begin to understand the idea of your jurisdiction.

Now we talk about differentials today and we will do this very simply. There is a differential between how you feel and how you are. And we want you to understand this and this is important. Paul has had this lecture already, but it will be repeated for you because it will be important for the reader to understand this as part of the process.

As you embark on a journey of change, that which you create will become conscious to you in ways that you have not experienced before, and as you do this, you may choose to experience discomfort on a little bit of a level as your reality changes. So how you feel when you feel good might simply be because everything is in its proper place and where you expect it to be and you feel a sense of comfort in that space that you have created that you are safe in.

As we are expanding you, which is the work of this book—expansion in consciousness and awareness of your jurisdiction as a Light Being—you can begin to see that as you move through this, you move from room to room and you have to identify those things in your world that no longer serve your good.

Your choice to do this may incur uncomfortability. And as you do this, we will say that what you will experience will be a differential. You will feel terrible, half an hour, because what's going on is good.

Now Paul is worried. He just heard us say, "You'll feel terrible." Well, in fact, perhaps that is an exaggeration, but you will feel the discomfort that comes with no longer being able to say comfortably, "I know what I am," when what you have self-identified with up until now is a lesser aspect of the self that wishes to come into form.

So "Awareness" is the title of our chapter today, and Paul is wondering what the title of the book is and we will tell him when we tell him. His worry about this is actually a selfish mandate. He wants it to be something that he can feel comfortable with. And he will have to get through this quickly because there may be discomfort not only in the title but in the content, as we are taking him to a place of new ideals that perhaps bypass those things that he can be comfortable with in life.

As you change, your landscape changes and you cannot expect to know what goes on in a frequency that you have not yet inhabited. And we aspire as a group endeavor to lift you in frequency to a new vibration where you are in congruence with your Divine Self.

Paul is asking, "Wasn't the work of the first book to do that?" Absolutely. It was in the manifestation of the Christ within man, "I am Word," that this is made possible. It is not possible without that awakening of the self in his divinity, in her divinity. However, learning to operate through this place as your true self in a creative way, which means you are operating from and as Christ consciousness, is where we are taking you now.

So we want to say this: The work of the first book, yes, was not only foundational, but a prerequisite for what is to come. And of course, we will give you the energy and the experiences on a higher level that you require to support you in bringing about this change. But you must allow this passage to come in its own form without relegating it to familiar patterns, familiar structures, even familiar ideals, because we may want to break some rules as we go forward.

Part of the issue we have had with work in consciousness that has been written in recent years is it does not allow the individual's life to begin to see fully what it is created through. You have the belief now, through many sources, including this one, that thoughts are things and are creative. But the extent that you still don't believe that you are a manifestation of the Creator in form keeps the lid on everything.

Now Paul is wondering, "Is everybody going to get this? Are people going to walk around believing themselves to be the Creator? What a mess that sounds like."

Well, Paul, you have it backwards. Everybody already is the Creator and the mess that you see is the forgetting of that that you have been held to in lifetimes since the beginning of incarnation. It is time to put an end to the rule that says, "You are not allowed to know who you are." And that rule was put in place by a false self that seeks to control and to diminish the light that you truly are in manifestation. You are always this thing, regardless of your memory of it.

"Now is there magic in this book?" Paul wants to know. And I suppose we mean to say in response to this that there is magic only in the extent that a miracle could be called magic. But we are not magicians. We are consciousness, and we do not conjure with you. We decree. And what a decree is is a statement of truth that brings about manifestation of change. So Paul's real question, we would say, is, "Will there be miracles in conjunction with this book?"

We will say this: Yes, there will be miracles, and they will be of two kinds. The first kind is a personal miracle. And once the personal miracle occurs, and by this we mean that the individualized consciousness expands beyond this system of creation to embrace the possibility of Christdom inhabiting this plane to bring about global manifestation of change that will be happening, we will say, yes. The second kind of miracle will be one of change of scenery and how your physical life will begin to alter through your perceptions of it. And becoming aware is the first step to this part of the miracle.

So today we have asked you to see what happens in your world as you identify things as your creation. Why do I choose this? Why is this here? What do I think that I created this? If this feels like a silly exercise, do it anyway. Because it is only through becoming conscious of that which is already here that you can begin to make changes.

Paul is seeing the image of a room where things have been left so long that they have become invisible. That photograph on the shelf that requires dusting that you don't even notice anymore because it's been sitting there so long. Or that stack of newspapers by the front door that seems to always be growing. These are the things in your lives we are asking you to see. Now these two little examples were, perhaps, symbolic, but they were good examples for what is being out-pictured in your world. And as you do this on a larger level, you will learn what your environment is created with and how you now have the opportunity to create change.

(Pause)

We want to give you permission now to design a life that you want. But we want this life to be in construction with the needs of your Divine Self. So much of what you've created in your life, thus far, has been created out of patterning that you have designed in response to the cultural mandates and the familial requirements that you were embedded with through your raising. And we will tell you this: The alignment to those doctrines, to those beliefs, to those requirements that you have chosen to create your life through will be coming up for examination as part of this process.

If we were to give you full permission today to say, "I can have this exactly as I want it"—and we are talking right now of a future creation, a future life you would design for yourself, it would be ninety percent born out of those beliefs of what you think you should be, you should have, and you should want. This is a promise to you.

So you are going to be very surprised as you revisit the exercise you did earlier to discover that what you will create in your new identity as your Christed Self, the Divine Self, will be a radical departure from anything you could have imagined. You each wonder why you don't have the things you say you want. In fact, you have everything you've created, and you have designed that thing, that creation, that life, in response to those requirements that you have been given by your parents, by your society, by everything you've ever inhabited in consciousness and believed to be true.

So you say, "Why don't I have the thing I want today?" Well, we're going to give you an example: "I want the perfect partner who is going to give me all these things, and take care of all my needs." You can each ask for that, but in fact, that is a requirement that is being born out of lack, that your needs are not already being met, that you are not already loved or in possession of companionship. So you will be creating this idealized lover out of a place of lack or out of a place of a diminished idealization of who you truly are. What you choose in manifestation from your Divine Self will be markedly different from what you would create from the fear-based self that is going to be releasing through the process of engagement with this text.

We will say this again because Paul is wondering if he heard us correctly: The creation of the self that is born in fear, that was created in fear, will be dismantled and released through the dictation and the process of engagement with this text.

This is a text that will leave the reader without an aspect of the self that has controlled her since the beginning of her creation. We are saying this in a matter-of-fact way to bypass the resistance of our channel. We are saying that what you will be through the experience, through the discipline, and through the response to your engagement with our words, both on the page and through structures of frequency that we are bringing forth to support the group and individual readership of this text, will align you to a self that will no longer require that she be dictated to by a frequency of fear.

How this manifests is the action of this book. And how you choose to engage with it is going to be your choice. "I am in my knowing," is the decree we offer you.

"I am Word through my knowing of what I need to know to bring me to a new awareness of the requirements of my engagement with this text. Word I am Word through this intention. Word I am Word."

You have now embarked on the first stage of this journey, which is to be standing in awareness. As you stand in your awareness, you see what you have created and you can begin to look at the consciousness that produced these creations. Where was I in lack? Where was I in frustration? And where was I responding in fear as I created these things in my world? Once you can see them for what they are, the process of disengaging and removing and releasing will commence. And we assure you that it will commence in a way that you can understand and triumph through.

We have no investment in teaching people how to fail. We have no investment in speaking through Paul in a way that will not be clear and in the appropriate engagement with the reader to bring about wondrous change. We have no desire to amplify fear or to give you messages that would incur fear.

We are teaching you. We are the teachers. We have come to teach. We have come to heal. And we offer you Divine Love. As we see you through your journey, we will give you the information and we will cheer your progress. We will amplify your light and we will bring you love to see you through the passage of creation that you are now choosing.

We are going to say something now, Paul, and it will be something that you need to pull back from so that your awareness is not engaged. And we're going to ask you safely if you would go look at a book on the bookshelf in your mind's eye while we are speaking so we don't get tampered with through this dictation.

We want to give you the title of the book. And the title is *The Book of Love and Creation. I Am the Word: The Book of Love and Creation*. We are giving you this as a present. It is a journey book, it is a passage book, and it is a book of great insight that will achieve within its work the designs that are required to bring you each into fruition as a manifestation of God embodied. We honor you each and we give you your love and your tethering to the past so that you can release it fully and say, "Yes, I am present. Yes, I am ready," and "Yes, I am Word."

We will finish this chapter now and we will ask you to convene in two days for the next session. We are amplifying Paul's frequency and working on his systems to ensure that he is ready to incorporate this next level of information into his field. The information we bring through Paul is first impressed into his frequency, and then it is heard, and then it spoken. We are working with his system to improve reception, to improve clarity, and to allow him to trust that the work of this book is the book that is intended for the highest good of all who would encounter it.

We are blessed through your attentions. We are Creative Source. We have come in peace, we have come in love, and we have come with an encouraging Word.

Goodnight.

TWO

AMPLIFYING LOVE

Day Three

We're going to talk about love today, what love is, why you love, what love can bring to you, and what you need to understand to navigate from a position of love.

The ideal of love, as out-pictured culturally, has enormously little to do with the actuality of love. The actuality of love, as understood by the love scene we would bring you, has much to do with the quality of expression in frequency of the action of the Divine Self as the Creative Self manifested in this realm. The action of love, we would like to say, is to be *in love.* And as one is *in love,* one creates from the aspect of the self that is love. That which is created as love brings forth good. And that which is brought forth in good creates good again and again and again.

So we spoke yesterday[1] about fear and how fear creates. And today we wish to talk about love and the creations of love that you

---

1 Actually two days previously, as the guides indicated in the previous transmission.

will begin to understand can be made manifest through your lives, individually first, and then through group action as love.

When an individual loves, the individual has an experience of love, and a private experience, in many ways, of the blessing of love. It is another country that the lover stands in when the lover first experiences her love. And the magnification of this love as a shared construct can be seen when people marry, or couple, or have children, and the frequency of love is larger and holds in tandem several identities engaged in an action of love.

The ideal of out-picturing love in a collective level comes forth through the intention to marry a great group of people in consciousness through united effort and awareness. And this can only come about when the individual resigns herself to the abrupt change of systematizing the self as individualized in love, to understand fully that love, as an action, is always active.

Anything that is selfish, frankly, is not, could not, will not be love. "If I love you so much, you will never me leave me," is not love. It is fear. "I love you so much I would never be with anybody else" is fear, and it is a projection on the other, the object of love, as leaving you. These are all manifestations of fear that you conjure and create with to bring about a distortion. And love will not be distorted. It cannot be. It cannot be tampered with because it is a high frequency. And a high frequency, so you see, will always stand in congruence with the Creative Source.

So we will tell you this: When a group loves in marriage—and we use the word "marriage" not in any other way than to say "in agreement"—when a group is in agreement in love, the group's power to manifest as love becomes paramount, and the changes and the ramifications and the spontaneity of the action of love in movement will transform structures at a larger level than you can believe.

Now we will talk about this in several different ways. The ideal of an individual lover loving those she sees without discernment of their qualities, only to say, "I am in love with those I see before me," from a place of consciousness that will support this creates individualized change and group change.

What you focus on in your intention, regardless of the emotional impact you imagine you are creating, is impacted by your focus. That is clear. "If I am focusing on something with the intention to be angry, the subject of my focus is changed and is altered by the frequency of my intention." That is a clear ideal that you must begin to understand as you evolve in your own frequency.

Energy interacts with other energies, and as you energize an emotion and you send it out, you are impacting that thing which you are intending. And we will say that this is done intentionally and unconsciously, depending on where you are operating from in your awareness of your surroundings and your interactions with those you encounter. You can be passive or active, but you are still projecting your emotion on the object you focus on.

Now if you are operating at a high frequency and someone is sending you negativity, believe it or not, you will not be in congruence with it. It cannot hurt you because you are aligned at a higher frequency that will not accept a distortion of frequency at a lower objectification in energy. So this is very simply understood to say that when we say, "Love cannot be distorted," we are saying love, in its truth, is a high frequency, and the high frequency will ennoble itself to support a system from negativity.

Now the individual who sends the energy and the frequency of love to that which is before her is, of course, benefiting the subject of her focus through this intention. Now this has always been the case and, to an extent, what we are saying now is an explanation of what has always happened in your experiences, but you have not been given language for.

As you are loved by someone in a true way, you are healed by them, and this has always been the case. When you love someone from an objectification and a support in love as "I am seeing the one before me as love. Word I am Word through this intention," that person is changed through frequency. Now we will give you simple examples so that you can understand what we mean. When you have a toy and you are young and you invest that toy with love, the toy becomes different. It has endowed properties in your imagination because you have embedded it in the frequency of love. When you have a person in your life who is operating in frequency who you are in love with—and we will say "in love" not in the romantic way, but in a way that is about frequency and an intention to love—you understand that that person may be transformed through this exchange.

Paul sees himself before his class and his students are all very lovable. And they are transformed through the exchange of frequency as much as they are transformed through the exchange of information.

Now when you have an object that you are endowing with love, the object transforms. You give it value; you give it the responsibility of your creation to be in love with it. Now you can do this with your pet, with anything you choose to state, "I am in love." But you understand that how you have identified love in the past—as an idealized directive that you would gift yourself with—has very little to do with the actuality of love. And that is what we will work on this morning with you as we speak about frequency in love.

Now once you understand that when you love someone individually, the individual is transformed, and once you understand that when a small group is engaged in love, the group had the ability to transform its work in the world, the larger group that operates in a construct of love and from an authentic frequency in love can impact matter. And this is done through a collective focus to transform that which is seen in love.

If you can understand that on a very basic level, much of what you call healing in a true vibrational sense is the action of love transforming matter and healing through the intention to see the subject of the healing in its perfection, in its perfect healed self, you can begin to understand how structures can be realigned through the focus of love.

Now we will give you an example of this: When you have a church who holds someone in prayer and that is the ambitious agreement of the group, to hold someone in healing, the vision of the holding and the action of the holding supports an endowment of frequency to the one who is in reception of the energies. And that subject can be transformed through this action if the action is in alignment with the requirements of that soul's needs.

For example, people operate from a place of presumption that one who needs healing, in their estimation, *should* be healed. And that is actually a wrong idealization, because it puts the subject out of her own free will, and people choose their dilemmas or their sicknesses for very different reasons, and they can be wonderful teachers. That is not to say that someone who chooses illness should not be healed. We are simply talking about the presumption of the one who decides what someone else should need without understanding the requirements of the soul's journey.

So when you suppose that the one before you needs fixing in love, you are actually operating from your ego and from a place of control, and that is not love. But a group effort to send love to someone who is in a requirement of the need for love is a blessed action.

How that soul and the frequency that is that person operates in the new frequency of love is that person's decision on multiple levels. If the soul says, or the Higher Self says, "Yes, I receive this and I am integrating this frequency," it will be integrated. But decisions are not always made at a personality level, which is why when you decide that someone needs fixing, they may not require it at all, because their learning is unfolding exactly in accordance with their soul's dictates for their evolution and healing in ways that are unseen by you.

So the group frequency can and does impact an individual frequency regardless of how the frequency is assimilating. Someone can be gifted with the frequency of love and do something very different with the frequency of love than the sender would intend. And that is as it should be.

Now we want to give you some examples of ways that you can begin to operate in love and activate yourself through love to bring about change in your world first. And then we will go on to collective energies as they are out-pictured operationally in love.

"I am in my love." This is a simple statement. To state that you are in your love activates you as your frequency in the field of love. "I am in love" states that you are in the frequency of love.

Now Paul is sitting here going, "I don't feel it, I spoke it, it didn't do a thing." Well, we are speaking on a frequency level, Paul. And you are actually looking to have an emotional response that is familiar to you through the description of love that you have imagined it should feel like. When an individual states, "I am in love, I am in my love," the individual is activating herself as frequency, and the object of that frequency is to do it, to be in the frequency and action of love. As this happens, what the manifestations are in that individual's world begin to support the frequency that she is. "I can be in my love and I can have an experience in love, in my experience of myself in action in my world." Period.

Now when we say this, we are speaking of intention and as you understand already, "I am in my Word, I Am Word through that that I see before me" is stating intention and aligning in frequency to the causal action of the Source to be in creativity and interaction with matter. And with experience and with consciousness, you can understand that to state "I am in my love" will do something very similar in frequency.

Now we want to describe what love is in a way that you can hear and work with. The energy of love is uncompromised by love, as love, in love, and is the action of the Creator in this frequency. Now Paul was expecting a Hallmark card, a saying: "Love is a tenderness." Love is not a tenderness. Love is a frequency that only knows itself in love. And as it is in love, what it creates is more love.

Now you have an imagination that we would like to use for a moment to set this up for you in a way that you can begin to hold. If you can idealize love outside of a valentine to be an ocean, a veritable ocean of wonder, and of goodness, and of clarity, and of perfect union with the aspect of God that is goodness, you can begin to get a semblance of what we mean by the action of love. And what we are saying to you is your aspect, individualized as love, is in the ocean and creating through that wonder, through that frequency that is God in perfect compassion and love.

We will give this to you again. You have made love small. You have made love an ideal that is stuffed with candy and rests in a box. You have made love a discerning issue. "I will give my love to this guy because he's got what I want," or "I will give my love to my child because my child deserves my love," or "I will love the couch I just bought because it's a great couch," or "I will love my job because if I don't, somebody else is gonna take it from me."

Guess what, everybody? None of that, in truth, is love. They are all aspects of ego seeking to control or to dictate a frequency that, in truth, cannot be dictated. You can no longer create love from a cookie cutter that excludes the fabric that is around it. You can no longer love John and not love Fred. You can no longer love Frances and hold Jonathan outside of love. You can no longer hold your culture in love while claiming that another culture cannot be in love because you disapprove of their actions. You cannot do this, anymore.

Now how you stop doing it, in several ways, are things that this book will discover with you as you continue to read. But we will tell you this: The decision to love, to be in the action of love, in the truth of love as the water, as the ocean, as an aspect of that frequency and the conduit of it realized in form, is the manifestation of Christ consciousness.

If you can understand this, that what you are truly doing is embodying Source and acting as Source in the action of love, you will understand that you are indeed a vessel. And the love that flows through you cannot be contained by a seal, by a decision, by a mandate that anything or anyone is excluded. If you exclude in this frequency, you turn the faucet off, and you put yourself, ultimately, in a kind of separation from the frequency that is, in fact, ever present and always there.

We are speaking of an ocean of love that is present now and, in a lot of ways, the work that we do with you is to unblock, un-create the resistance to aligning to that frequency once again to remember who you are as an aspect of the Creator. When you work in love, what is changed is the frequency of your energies. The energies that you operate from design themselves, and redesign themselves, based on your consciousness.

Now Paul is already thinking, "It is too overwhelming. I could never realize this. I am a failed lover in this regard. I still don't love myself enough. How am I going to love the world?"

Now let's talk about this very directly. Not to love the self is an act of selfishness. Period. It is an act of selfishness because you have decided on some level that the self that you are is not worthy of love. And frankly, who are you to decide that, in truth? It makes you God. And as we said to you earlier, the aspect of you that is God is part of the larger Source. But to differentiate yourself by saying, "I don't deserve love," is saying what you said to your neighbor who you don't feel deserves love, either. And as we explained already, the object of that is to turn off the faucet so that the love does not flow.

You are keeping yourself out through a decision, a false belief that you are not worthy, and that you are so terrible, or so changed by your experience on this plane, that God could not work through you.

Now this is true for everybody who has decided, for whatever reasons, that they cannot be in love, and that they cannot be blessed, and that they cannot be aligned in truth to the Creator. We have some news for you now. We said it was selfish, and that is accurate. But you have to understand that it is a motivation of fear that keeps you in this belief in your separation from Source. And whatever it is, be it guilt, be it a belief in unworthiness, be it a belief in past patterning or cultural dictates that say "Because you are this kind of person, you could not be in love," you have to understand that this is all fear being created with the intention to stop you from your realization of yourself in Christ, in Divine Love, in the movement and in the action of the Creative Self that is inheriting the kingdom through this choice to embody.

So, Paul, if you were to say, "Yes, I am worthy of love, and I understand now that the belief that I am not allowed love by myself is an act of fear, and is the ego seeking to maintain jurisdiction of my light to prevent me from full realization of my Divine Self and all of the wonder that it would bring to me," you can say, "I am free of this fear as I say it. I am free. I am free. I am free."

Now we want to give an affirmation to all of you who hold yourselves as unworthy of your love. And we say this with you now:

"I am Word through this intention to release any and all creations that have kept me from my belief, and from my knowing, and from my honestly accepting my worth as a child of the Creator. And I am now aligning myself to new belief systems that will align me to my own ability to love, to be loved, and to allow myself to serve as a transmission of frequency as love. I am Word through this intention. Word I am Word."

So we go back to our original ideal: Once you have the faucet on, you are in your energized state and you are operating from this aspect of the self as and through love in order to transform and recreate that which you see before you in frequency. We said you would be winning the prize with this one, and you will be. You will begin to identify yourself through your discernment, as you understand it, that you are an aspect of the Creator in love and honestly expressing herself, himself, as this frequency.

The action of love in this life to become itself and to be realized on this plane is long overdue. It is being done always, and there are many who walk around in their ability to recruit others into their frequency because their love is that powerful. When you seek to be in love, you have to believe that the worth is present, and that your alignment is present, and that that which keeps you from your alignment will be revealed to you in order to release it in fullness.

Now we are not going to tell you that you will manifest as love and walk around healing people without engaging in a process of doing the work. And the first thing you have to do is to become one with your frequency as it is today in your awareness. So we would do this with you:

Ask yourself right now to close your eyes, and when you do this, discern in your own frequency what you feel. How do you feel now?

Now we want this experience to be energizing to you beyond your physical form. So we are going to ask you to radiate your frequency, to feel yourself as frequency, as you sit. And we want you to begin to feel what you feel like as energy. Now we want you to do this:

"I am now offering myself to that aspect of myself that is in alignment with the Christ, with the Creative Source, to bring to me my own knowing and my own experience of love as divine frequency. I am now offering myself to my Creator in the way that I choose to bring about the transformation of frequency that is required to align myself to the action and to the jurisdiction of the frequency of love. And I do this in alignment with my highest good and through my own free will. I am Word through this intention to offer myself in love, as love, and to be realized as love. Word I am Word through this intention. Word I am Word."

Now Paul is feeling his frequency shift because he has made this offering. And what this shift actually means is that his frequency is being realigned in accordance with the offering that he has made. And what it means to say is that those aspects of the self that are not in alignment will come into congruence to be cleared, or to be restructured, so that this work can commence in its perfection.

Now Paul is doing this decree as you are, too, and you are being worked with on a level of frequency and intention by Paul's system, by the systems and the intentions of the authors of this text, and we are divine aspects of the Creator. We are masters in our work and we are willing to be in full support of this change, not only to benefit you, but to benefit this plane of existence, which is now transforming itself for the new millennium to commence in truth.

So we will say that this work is done with us through your intention. As you idealize your own manifestations through the action of love, your life changes radically. Paul is saying, "How so?" And we will tell you.

When you walk down the street and you are in the frequency of love, your frequency, which is a high frequency, counterbalances that which it encounters and you become an active force healing and supporting the frequencies of those that you encounter. Paul has a woman he works with in his group who was instructed last week to walk down the street as if she was dancing in frequency with all that she encountered. In fact, what she was being told to do was to be engaging in frequency with all she encountered, as and in the vibration of love that she has successfully begun to anchor into her consciousness.

So as you do this, as you walk down the street and you encounter others, you bring their frequency to a new level of enlightenment. Now this does not mean they will stop on the street corner and break into song or blast off in a beam of light. What it simply means is that, on a frequency level, their systems will now be attuned to this new awareness that blesses them and gives them the opportunity to renegotiate their own frequency to bring it to the higher plane. This is always done when the higher frequency meets the lower. The higher frequency has the ability to shift the lower and this is not done necessarily through conscious intention, although it will be enhanced through your understanding at this stage of your development that it can be so.

Paul is seeing the biblical woman who said that she would be healed if she touched the robe of the Christ. And in a funny way, that is a metaphor for what transpires in frequency. When one operates as Christ, as a manifestation of God in action, the energy system that you are has many opportunities and will find them.

Paul sits in his room today dictating through our frequency this information to support the readership who will then take this work and engage it and, ideally, gift themselves with a transformative process that is intended for them through this reading experience in frequency. However, your work is not to be sitting in your room. It is to be out there as consciousness, and to be transforming consciousness as love.

As you are this thing, your landscape has to reflect it. So not only are you walking down the street having this experience and aligning others to it through your vibrational level, what you call to you in action will support this new ideal. This new frequency calls to it that which is congruent with it. Period.

So you no longer attract those things that you have attracted through your obligation to your fears. And so much that you have attracted in your life, that has always been your experience of yourself in your world, has been the result of the fear that you have created with. Period.

Now once you are no longer operating as fear and you are operating as love, what you act on transforms. You are no longer acting on selfishness because selfishness is entirely born out of fear and the fear in lack that there will not be enough for you, so you have to shield or horde your life, your goods, and your love and your energies and your intentions. Once that is gone, you become infinitely available as a tool, as a symbol of the action of Christ embodied and doing the work as love.

Now we are not talking "symbol" in an iconic way, we are talking frequency and consciousness. And what we say is, your energy system in its amplification as love brings about that which it requires in order to do what it needs for the highest good of all. Period.

Now you can understand this. So you can wonder, "Does this mean, I am doing all these boring things, and do I have to become a saint, and what does it really ask me?"

Well, we will tell you this: It demands that you become the self that you truly are. And how that self realizes herself is in regard to the self's mission and purpose in this life. One man may have a purpose to help the poor while another may have an intention to design a system that will help millions through technology. And someone else will paint the picture that will give wonder to a whole generation. So you see, who you are as you, realized as love, is the perfect you, is the you that you are without fear and without your actions being dictated by fear. Why would you want that when we are offering something better? Can you offer yourself the ability now to honor yourself to the extent that you can now say:

"Yes, I am worthy. Yes, I am in need, and I honor the need by accepting the gift I am being given. I am Word through my intention to honor myself as my Divine Self. I am Word through my obligation to love myself as a creation of God embodied. I am Word through my love of myself, and I allow this love to extend to all that I see before me. My consciousness is changed through this intention. I am Word. I am Word. I am Word."

We thank you both and we will stop now for a moment. We have other things to talk about.

(Pause)

Let's talk again. And where we left off was in your awareness and your recognition and our plea and our decree on our behalf that you embody as love. The work of the book is, in fact, the embodiment of love, and that is why we gave it the title *The Book of Love and Creation.* We are going to say that the title of this chapter is "Amplifying Love" and we will talk now about what this requires from you on a daily basis of engagement with this text as a manual for your awareness and through the actions that you are now required to take in order to bring this into fruition.

The job you have today is to stand in your awareness of all that you feel—"I feel this, I feel that"—and to come into discernment about where you feel what you feel, and then ask yourself why you feel it. This will give you information about how you operate in consciousness. No, this is not about love, Paul, this is about learning who you are so that you can begin to choose love where you have chosen other actions in the past. And you have to understand now that so much of what you do is predicated on an emotional response that you have that gives you a feeling that causes you to take actions in response. And of course, as we have stated, fear is the primary responder to those things that make you feel uncomfortable.

So we are going to give you some answers about how to process your feelings and how to bring yourself first into an awareness of what you can experience in a changed way and then how to bring yourself up in frequency to align to love and to God and to the Christed Self or Creative Source in a perfect way that will handle each situation you might encounter.

As you walk down a street and you monitor your emotions, as you walk into your job or your school of your family dinner and you say to yourself, "Okay, now what's going on?" we are simply asking you to become aware of what has always gone on that has fallen below the radar in habit. You have always asked yourself questions about what you feel when you have been confused about something, perhaps, but you don't do that when you are being passed the peas at the dinner table for the three hundredth time. That just happens. The action that you take, which is to pass the peas, may well be informed by "I hate peas. Why am I doing this? Where am I in my life that I am still passing the damn bowl when I wanted to be doing something else?" But those things go by you invisibly because, of course, it's just a normal thing that you have been doing for years.

Yes, we spoke a few days ago about a dusty picture sitting on a shelf that you no longer see because it's just ignored. And we asked you to bring that into your awareness. Now we are saying the same thing for that behavior and the emotional responses that come in your life so that you can begin to discern what they are. As we work with this, you will become aware of how much waste you engage in and how much negativity you actually impact your reality with through this choice to remain unconscious to your feelings.

Now we will say to you this: Love is not a feeling. Love is frequency. And when we work with love, we invest you in frequency that transforms your feelings because the feeling of love that you might think is a feeling is actually the expression of love through you.

Paul is saying, "I'm not quite following," so we will discern this explanation and try it again. When you are experiencing love, the frequency of love *is you*. And of course, because you self-identify through feelings, you assume that love itself is a feeling. But love is not a feeling. Love overrides feelings because it is an expression, an active expression of the divine operating as and through you. So as you align to the frequency of love, you call to you love.

So we are telling you this: You may be passing the peas, but when you are in love and the peas are passed, you experience yourself, your peas, and everybody around you in this creation, and it is quite wonderful to know.

Now get this: When you become love, you forget who you were without love. This is important. You forget who you were in fear. The amazing thing about the frequency of love is there is no fear in love. And, consequently, when you are love, you are not fear. And when you are in the frequency of love you don't remember the frequency of fear because it cannot align, it cannot exist in this way. You have transformed. You have become love. And in love there is only love, and all that is called to it co-resonates with love or is seeking to be in resonance with love. That is why you call to you those who need what you have. And you will frequency-wise support them in their transformation, either through choice or through unconscious frequency exchange. Both are fine.

Now Paul is asking, "Didn't you say you were going to give us something to align us to a higher frequency?" We are, in fact, doing this now. And it is happening on two levels. The book that you are reading actually has a frequency in it that supports the changes that we speak of. It is as if there is a grid impressed into our language and our intentions that operates concurrently with the reading and the intellectual assessment of the information on the page.

So it's already happening on one level, but we want to give you an exercise that you can operate from, simply as an exercise in your frequency in order to change it from low to high.

As you accept that your frequency is your choice and is your responsibility, you can work with it. Imagine that you have hair on your head that you like to change colors of, or patterns of decoration. You do this without thinking because it's the hair on your head and you know you have control. Well guess what, everybody? Your frequency is yours to operate from. And just because you can't see it certainly doesn't mean that you can't work with it.

Now Paul is saying, "Can they start to see their frequency? Can we work on seeing?" And yes, we will, at the proper time. But feeling frequency and simply acknowledging frequency and that this is who you are will support you now more than the interesting stuff that begins to occur as you evolve in your consciousness in psychic ability and conscious awareness.

So we say to you: Each day your intention needs to be to align your frequency to the highest level available to you. And we will say it can be done in two ways. Here is the first way.

"I now set the intention to align my frequency up to the highest level and octave available to me in my consciousness at this time. And I set the intention that I will monitor my consciousness through my feelings and through my expressions as the day goes on, so that I may become accountable to my experience as an energy being operating in consciousness and through frequency. I am Word through this intention. Word I am Word."

Now what this exercise does is put you in the hot seat to be the one monitoring your frequency, which is when you have to say, "Oh, why did I feel that? I felt the dip in my energy." "I'm feeling great, I am seeing the truth in all I pass." "I am becoming aware of my own divinity and, consequently, my world is out-picturing in accordance with this new system of self-awareness."

These are the benefits, but you are the one in charge. And we ask you to do this every day for two weeks to get into the habit of it. It is an exercise. As you become engaged with the honesty in your own responses and you become shifting in frequency in ways that you can begin to discern, it becomes more ambitious. But for the time being, setting the intention and staying in conscious awareness will give you what you need.

The second thing we will ask you to do is commit to vibrating at a higher level in a way that you can feel. And we will do it as such:

We are going to ask you sit and close your eyes and go into the heart center and activate the Christ within, the consciousness that is the self, that aspect of God that exists within the heart. And we want you to align this light in intention to the Great Light.

> "The light within me is in congruence with the Great Light. The God within me is in congruence with the True God. The God within me is a light that I can experience and connects with all the light there is."

As you do this, you set the intention to activate the Christ into its fullness and allow its frequency to emerge, to encompass, to enfold in frequency, in vibration, through your body and through your energy field. And you align to this through this intention:

> "I am now choosing to align my frequency to the indwelling Christ, to the Creative Source, to the Inner Light, to the God within to become manifested in my full realization of myself as an aspect of the Creator embodied in love. I am Word through this intention. Word I am Word."

As you do this, you change frequency and you realign to Source through an intention to bypass lower systems of self-awareness to bring you into true self-identification. Period.

Now this is an exercise. As you walk about your day and you have expressions, be conscious of your energy system. If you can walk around in your frequency, in your light body expanded around you in this joy, in this love, in this intention to be in embodiment, your experience of your life will transform in ways you cannot imagine. And it will happen fast.

But again, it is your choice to stand firm in the requirements of this. We help you, we align you, we will answer you in your questions through this text and the texts to follow. However, we tell you that your coming into your own ownership of your divine information is far more important than anything that we could tell you or that Paul could transcribe.

You are each aspects of consciousness identifying in physical form. And as you remember who you are—"I am in my knowing. I am Word"—you align, again and again, to the self that knows who he is, that she is, and this brings about triumphant change.

God bless you each as you continue on your journey. You have two assignments. We recommend that you keep a notebook of your own experiences as you work with this material. It will become important to you as you move on to be able to demarcate the differences in how you respond, frequency-wise, to the different situations that present themselves in your work with this book.

Now Paul, we have two things to say to you before we go farther:

The work of this book has to come into manifestation in a very fast way. And in order for this to happen quickly, we want you to begin to work with us to dictate directly without as much repetition of information being heard and spoken, one in succession to the other. We would prefer that you begin to speak directly as channel with no repetition. In order for this to happen, you need to give us permission to begin to realign your system to negotiate the seals that have prevented you from hearing in fullness in past incarnations so that they may be released.

In a funny way, we are saying we are uncorking the remaining bottles that have prevented flow of frequency. We are very pleased with the work thus far: that is not the issue. However, as we continue in our pace, we would be aligned to a shift for the reader that will come more effectively as we work directly. Do not put pressure on yourself. As this happens, it happens, and you will align in perfect timing. So we will say to you this:

> "I am Word through my intention to bring forth the information of this text in the most fluid and appropriate way available to my energy systems for the highest good of all who encounter it. I am Word through this intention. Word I am Word."

The second thing we wish to say is that what you will encounter through the manifestation of this book will be what you have required of yourself to learn who you are without fear. And of course, this requires you to decide now that you are no longer willing to engage with it on a level of frequency.

Now the reader will do this with you, and we will do this as a group:

> "I am now choosing to realign my energy field to a place where I no longer vibrate in accordance with the requirements of fear. And I give permission to my Higher Self, to my Christed Self, to my Creative Self, and to those teachers and teachers of teachers who align me and my readership to this frequency of love to disengage me fully from all the energies of fear that I have held to me in the false belief that they were my protectors. I offer these

to my God, to the self in me that knows in truth that he is free to do this in the ways that are perfect for my evolution as a Divine Being encountering himself in fullness and in frequency. I am Word through this intention. Word I am Word."

And yes, Paul, we will assure you that this release is done in safety and in peace and alignment with the highest good for all, yourself included.

So we gift you each now a blessing as we close this chapter.

"I see before me a world where love is the predominant frequency. I see before me a world where I am safe in my knowing that my worth is good and in allegiance to the Divine Love that is gifted to me and to all through the love of the Divine Source that I call God. I am Word through my knowing of myself as loved. Word I am Word."

Thank you and good day. Period.

THREE

AWARENESS OF THE SENSES

Day Four

We're ready to talk, and about navigation of your own senses, your senses being what you see, what you hear, what you feel, what you taste, what you experience in your job as a human being accessing information through the senses.

Now we will tell you why we want to speak of this. The senses are the gateway to your perception. How you sense, how you see, hear, feel, taste, touch are the ways that you access information. And once you understand that the limitations that have been placed on the senses in your matrix allow you a minimal experience of that which is truly around you, you can begin to expand them to access information at a higher level. We will say, you will be expanding your system to experience yourself beyond the physical and into the frequency of the Christ awareness we speak of as Word.

Now once you understand that what you are is a systematized being, a being that operates through a system of creation, of rules, and expects those rules to be met each time she opens her eyes, or touches a wall, or smells a broth burning on a stove, you will understand that that which is experienced is expected by you. One thing smells one way, one thing looks one way, and this becomes the way you access yourselves in your placement of yourselves in your world.

You walk around as if you know what is before you, because in fact you expect what is before you to look and sound and feel like what it actually is. This is not a criticism. Of course not. It is an explanation of why your experience is so predictable in terms of that which you encounter through the acquisition of information by the senses.

Now you can understand that if you had an ability to see a million miles, into the future, into another state of consciousness, what you would be accessing would be entirely different. And you can expect your experience now to begin to alter through the acquisition of available energies that would sort through the disability you have experienced to allow yourself full manifestation of your gifts in touch, taste, sight, and hearing.

Now we will talk about sight first, and what you see. What you see, in many ways, is an out-picturing of a creation that someone else thought and that you have gone into agreement with. That is what you see when you go to the store, when you shop for your clothing, when you turn on a television or sign on to a computer. You expect to see a manifestation of someone else's identity and construct that you have gone into an agreement with and therefore are co-creating.

Now you can choose the limitation of what you have had, or you can begin to understand that by bypassing systems that tell you "what you see are what you see are what they are," you can begin to negotiate new vision, new availability to your senses to provide you with other information beyond that which has been agreed upon culturally through a system, frankly, of control.

Why we say control is that the belief that you are not able to access information through your clairvoyance has been systemized into you through your childhood upbringing and through the cultures that decided that it would be a negative experience to allow people to Know, and we say capital "K," their information through their psychic awareness and capabilities.

Now we will not speak of psychic abilities as if they are something mystical, because they are not. They are simply an amplification of what you are already doing without the limitations that you have placed there in your agreement with cultural availability to expected norms, or through a self-identification of limitation, which says, "I am not allowed," "Because it doesn't have to be so, I don't believe it can be so." Period.

Now once you understand that what is before you is in psychic prosperity, which simply means an expansion of what you can see, you will begin to understand that the worlds are larger than they are experienced in this dimensional construct, the one that you are all in agreement about.

Now there are many, many people who operate through multiple dimensional experience as a matter of course. And, in fact, each one of you already has enormous experience with navigating other dimensions through your consciousness. However, you dismiss it as impossible. "That was a coincidence." "I really didn't have that precognitive thought. It was coincidental." "Well, that *dream* was precognitive, but I must have imagined because, of course, I cannot access those abilities that are offered to the few." The belief that psychic ability is awareness that is gifted to a few is one of the limitations that you have created and gone into agreement with that keeps you from accessing your psychic ability. Period.

Now when you see a child who has an awareness of an imaginary playmate, don't think for a second that that's an imaginary playmate. Become aware of the possibility that the psychic ability of the child has not yet shut down to the experiences being proffered. It is there to be experienced, and the child experiences it naturally because it is present in his reality. There is nothing to argue with because it's right in front of his nose.

But a repetition of telling the same child that it is their imagination will actually dismantle the construct and the ability to access multidimensional information and thereby suppress a natural, innate, and God-given ability to see: "I see all that I see before me." If you can imagine that the limitlessness of this statement far transposes anything that you could claim it to be in its magnificence, you would begin to see that what is capable of any man through the witnessing of his experience goes beyond the limitations that he has held until now.

Now we will talk to you about sight and the seeing that we speak of. When a child sees something and claims it to be true, and that self that governs the child does not agree with it—the parental self, the person guarding the child—the child supports the will of the authority and relinquishes his belief systems. When you understand that authority has many different forms, and that the way authority rules is always through control of the senses, you will begin to understand that what that child's experience is is still the experience of everyone who has been told to believe that she cannot see her future, her aura, the aura and frequency of her child, and operate with the information that is available through this psychic discourse that she can have with her own soul's knowing—K, capital K, "Knowing."

Now we speak of knowing in different ways at different times, and one of the decrees we have emphasized so far is "I am in my knowing." "I am in my knowing" states that what I know, I am claiming in truth, and I am operating from a higher claim of knowing that has been available to me through my appropriation of my divine knowing. Period.

Now we will tell you that when you are in your knowing through your senses, you have to then navigate with the senses to do the work that the work can bring forth. To claim, "I am standing in my knowing and I am moving beyond the constructs that have limited my availability to see all that is before me," will create a possible interaction of the self and those obstacles that have been made so through matrix. But the matrix can be collapsed when you understand that it is born out of the need to control a system, to keep it at bay and out of its divine authority. Can you understand this?

The reason that you do not see, and you have not seen, is because you were burned at stakes, you were told it was damnation, you were told it was crazy, or impossible, or the gift of a few. If you look at the gifts of the Holy Spirit in the Bible, the gift of knowing and the gift of prophecy are spoken of directly. Now of course you have to understand that all that is good is in alignment with Source. And there have been abilities used by man throughout time in ways that have not been for the highest good.

If you understand, frankly, that prayer is concentrated psychic thought with an intention to applicate to the divine, you will see that application in negative ways occurs just as readily when someone sends out a negative consciousnesses to bid energy to change. So we are not speaking about anything fearful. We are simply giving you an example so that you can see that the rap psychic ability has been receiving is simply a way of controlling you from your own innate ability to be in manifestation.

Now we will tell you this. The requirement to open up in this regard is in the manifestation of your own soul's discourse with you. You do this in conjunction with your soul. We will give you the opportunities through this manifesto, *The Book of Love and Creation*, to begin to discern what your abilities are and how you can begin to navigate them, but you must work with your self in jurisdiction of your own soul's intention for you to bring this into fruition. There are no magic wands here. We do not work that way. We teach you and we support you in your work through our frequency and our aid.

Now sight, we will say, is how you learn where you are, who you are standing with, where you need to go, and what you have to do. There is one way that you can see that will direct you, and you have been working with that every moment that your eyes have been operation since you were born. If you can understand that second sight, or clairvoyant sight, can manifest in different ways and support you in this work, we will give it to you as a teaching that you can use systematically to serve you in your own understanding that all you see before you is a property of vibration and is God vibrating in frequency.

If you can understand that walking down a block and seeing everyone as perfect, which was a teaching we have given you in our first manifesto, you can now understand that the vibration that you are in frequency has abilities to alter perception through active intention. "I am claiming the good in all I see before me," states you are claiming your vision of what you see before you in goodness.

Now to see psychically involves your understanding that matter, what you see before you, is transitional and vibrating in frequency. And if you can believe for a moment that everything shapes itself in out-pictured ways based on its requirements, you can begin to understand that things are created and made in frequency that moves.

Everything at one time that you see was once another shape. An infant will grow into an adult. And a table was once a tree, and a brick was once mud, and that which you eat was once in the ground or grazing in a field, and that which you drink was a grape or was water in a lake somewhere that came from a raindrop or a glacier melting. Everything you see before is transitional in form.

So the idea right now is to break away from the sense of permanence that you have become aware of on your journey on this plane. That everything is supposed to look a certain way. Nothing looks the way you think it does under a microscope, and the closer you get, of course you know, the more you see that everything is frequency. Everything is alive and vibrating in its way.

So now we want you to do something. We want you to pick a person in your life and we want you to make an appointment with them to sit and to see them. And you will take notes and we will give you the instructions for our exercise with this partner now.

"I am sitting beside my partner. We are sitting beside each other with our eyes open. And we are seeing what we see before us in its permanence. We are seeing the brick as the brick in the wall, we are seeing the bench as solid, we are seeing the tree as bark and leaves rooted to the ground."

Wherever you are, you see what is before you as if it is in its permanence.

Now you will claim this: "I am Word through that that I see before me" and in this intention what you are doing is you are claiming that what you are seeing is in alignment with the divine vision you attain through the decree.

"I am Word through that that I see before me" decides that you are seeing the divinity, the God in what you are perceiving. And you do this now with what is before you, and you see what you see. You see how your perception magnifies the perfection of what is before you through the intention, "I am Word through that that I see before me."

And you stay here and you do this and you claim it and you write what you notice in your notebook so you have a written record of your perceptions. That is step one. Then take some time to share with your partner the exercise you have done together.

And then you will face one another with about four feet between you. And you will look at your partner and you will see her, see him, as they are in the body. And you will look at the body, and the face, and the eyes, and the ears and the hands as what they are: flesh, skin, bone, padded with fiber to make an operational being. You are simply looking at the system that the body is, without operating from a place of consciousness. You are looking at the system. For example, we will say, you are looking at the house, not what lives inside the house. And you will hold this vision. You will look at them objectively as a thing, as a body, as a person sitting opposite you. And you will notice what you see. Period.

Now this next step is repetition for those of you who have done the work in our earlier text. But you will now look at your partner and you will say, "I am Word through the one I see before me. Word I am Word through this intention, Word I am Word." And as you do this, you will allow your vision to see the beauty and the divine perfection in your partner: a being realized in her own divinity, in his own divinity. And you will see how your perception begins to alter.

Now understand that when you claim, "I am Word through the one before me," you are bringing energy to them and you are amplifying their frequency. And now we want you to hold this vision. "I am seeing the one before me in her perfection. Word I am Word through this intention. Word I am Word."

We will recommend now that when you begin to work with your sight, you learn how to use your eyes. To relax them, not to stare with sharpness, but to relax them, will allow you to begin to see the frequency and the energy field of your partner. "I am Word through my availability to see the energy field of the one before me" will claim this possibility for you and state the intention that that is now being so.

"I am Word through my availability to see the energy field of the one before me. Word I am Word."

Now again, watch what you see. Imagine for a moment that the one before you is a frequency and vibrating in her frequency. And that frequency aligns to your frequency, and together you are expanding your energy fields around you so that they can be made visible to the eyes, to the third eye, meaning the pineal gland chakra, sixth chakra, of your partner.

Correct, Paul, we use language you are not comfortable with, and therefore you are going to have to pull back.

Now once we say you are seeing in frequency, we want you now to turn around again and see what you are watching the first time—the wall, the tree, the bench—and see it in its expanded state. Now we want to tell you something. We are not conjuring with you, and we are giving you an exercise in beginning to expand your vision to hold clairvoyant sight in one regard. But there are many, many ways to begin to access information through sight and many of them have nothing to do with your physical eyes whatsoever. We are starting here because it's the way you are used to operating.

Each one of you has a mind's eye, a place in your mind where you visualize, where you imagine how you would look in that outfit, or when you imagine yourself being late for work and you picture the reaction there of your boss. We want you to become familiar at this time with that aspect of the self that sees in the mind's eye and become aware of what you see. Now we will speak of Paul for a moment to give you an example of sight.

Paul's ability as a younger man was to see energy with his eyes open, but he always wondered why he couldn't access information with his eyes closed. He did not have an active third eye screen that he could work with. Well, in fact, he did, but he assumed that what it was was something other than simply accessing the visual information that the mind is given.

So if you can begin to experiment with your own mind's eye to see what information is currently being made available to you through this system, you will begin to see how much information you can access. We are not teaching you right now. We are explaining to you that you are already in possession of the vehicle for your clairvoyance.

So imagine now for a moment that you are seeing a flower. And see this flower in your mind's eye. Close your eyes if you need to as you complete this paragraph and complete the exercise we are giving you with your eyes closed.

Imagine at your forehead is a flower, and the petals are closed. And now allow this flower to begin to gently spin at the forehead, cycling around. And as it does so, the petals gradually begin to unfold making a perfect flower at the forehead. This is the sixth chakra that you are now in operation with. And we are going to teach you, as this book continues, how to access visual information in consciousness through the acquisition of your higher senses.

So we go back to the idea the senses are how you navigate. They are how you operate. They are how you know who you are when you look in the mirror, or when you touch your skin, and how you know what you taste and what you smell. And you have been operating with these systems in the quietest way possible. Which is to say, the lid has been on the box and the music has not been allowed to play fully.

So today we are going to take you through a little tour of the opportunities that will become available to you through the senses as you expand them in your higher awareness.

Now Paul is saying, "I'm not there yet." Paul, you actually are, and the ability that you have to bring this book into form is the acquisition of the feature we speak of known as clairaudience, which is clear hearing. And we're going to conduct the audience of this book now in an exercise so that they understand what this means.

You each have the ability to hear your thoughts. And you hear your thoughts generally, in your own voice in your head and you think nothing about it. Now some of you, like Paul when he was younger, have a very active head, a lot of noise, a lot of discussion, most of it criticism of the self in voices that had been integrated through your parental arguments.

For example, when someone hears their mother's voice saying, "You're never gonna marry if you dress like that," or "You'll never be a success because your father was a bum," those are voices that people integrate and then acclimate to and they become their own. So first things first, you have to understand that you are already accessing a lot of people in your head when you walk around day to day and you are listening to yourself.

Now the attribute and the ability to begin to hear clairvoyantly comes in different ways to different energy systems. We will tell you this: When you can imagine that you are a tower, a radio tower, and at the top of the tower is a beam of light that calls to it other light, that beam will be met with and call to it the higher frequencies that would support you. Now Paul is saying, "Do people need to do this? Not everybody needs to hear Spirit or to operate through their clairaudience." Of course not. But what we are speaking of is the ability to hear yourself at a higher frequency.

Now you have multiple levels of the self, and you can understand this. You have the child who always wants what he wants. You have the adult self who governs the child, and you have the parental self, those voices that you have integrated, and you have the societal voice, those voices that you walk around with telling you what you are in association with the next guy, or the job, or the bank account, or the cultural mandates that you attribute as the way you should be. All of those voices are in operation.

Now when you begin to hear yourself in a higher frequency, frankly, what you are doing is releasing the lower voices in order to hear the higher. When Paul got through the level of dictation that was being given to him by the self that was a crucible or a critic, he began to open up to the higher voice and then to the spirit guides and teachers who made themselves available to him through his work as a healer.

Now Paul opened up through a system of healing, but the gift that he was given in energy of that work was the availability to be in service. So believe it or not, the only way Paul opened up to hear was to help others. It was not about playing the horses or getting the date or playing the stock market or anything like that. He had his hands on somebody's neck and he would understand through this process of clairaudience what the problem was because he would hear.

Now this is a very simple system, if you understand that what you are really doing is being in discernment to the higher voice that you already possess. And all you are really doing through this process of acquisition of higher frequency is clearing the obstacle that has been there, that has precluded the gift or the skill from becoming fully manifested.

If you have a well, but you cannot lift the bucket from the well because of the obstructions, you are never going to taste the beauty and the richness of the clear water that is available to you. What you have to do is clear the obstruction that stops you from accessing what is already there and waiting to be tasted, as it were.

Now when you understand this, that this is already present, you begin to operate from your knowing. "Okay, you're telling me that I already have the ability to hear myself in a higher frequency." And yes, we say, we are telling you this. What happens then is your system begins to renegotiate its promises to itself in order to make this so. So, for example, you would have to tell yourself, "Yes, this is possible," and then you have to claim it as a divine birthright.

"I am now claiming my availability and my honoring of my own information through my higher consciousness and my ability to hear myself in higher frequency. Word I am Word through this intention. Word I am Word."

Now once this is stated, what begins to happen is a de-acclimation to the prohibitions that have stood in the way of your availability to hear. It's that simple. You can hear. You can hear yourself. You can hear your voice without hearing the yelling of your parents or your culture. And you can also hear the aspect of yourself that is your Divine Self manifesting as you. Period.

Now Paul is asking, "Is hearing the Divine Self the same as hearing your spirit guides?" Absolutely yes and no. Your guides access you through that aspect of the self that is your Higher Self, so you are working in tandem. It is part of a linkup, as it were. Paul used to hear his guides say, "You have a telephone call," when they were trying to introduce him to another frequency. And in essence, his guide was serving as the gatekeeper or the telephone operator to ensure his safety and availability to access the information clair-audiently. The difference now is that Paul's system has integrated this such that he is able to access information without that kind of a hookup. In a funny way he is the hookup embodied because we can work with him where he is. He does not have to go elsewhere to access his information, nor do you once you understand that who you are is a Divine Being operating in her frequency.

So we work with Paul's system very, very directly. And we can do the same with anyone who escorts themselves through the process of acclimating to their Divine Self through the willingness to serve others, and through the willingness to disengage from the patterning and from the cultural mandates of prohibition that have kept you from sourcing yourself in this regard.

Paul is no more gifted than the next guy. He has put some time in and he has some good ability inherently. However, everyone has the ability to serve. And as you serve, what you call to you is that which is required for you to be in service. And of course, operating from your full spectrum of the senses will align you to greater ability to see, hear, feel, and taste and you will understand more of what is required of you.

Now we will give you an example. If you have a hearing issue and you understand on a certain level that what somebody needs is the ability to listen to themselves more, you can begin to work with them to do this through your intentions. However, you cannot access the information of what they need unless you are able to access it through your own system.

Now certainly you can be able to sit with someone and say, "Wow, this person really needs to hear themselves," and then say, "I am Word through this intention that the one who sits before me is able to hear herself in her fullness. Word I am Word through this intention." However, you are doing that from a place of descriptive decision-making. You are saying, "Wow, I think this what this person needs."

Get this, everybody: This is not about thinking. This is no longer about thinking. This about being in your *knowing,* and your *knowing* is what you must honor. If you are going to act on the behalf of another, you do not operate from your presupposition of what someone needs, which is actually based on your own requirements, and your own upbringing and cultural mandates, about what is appropriate for somebody. And that's mostly about control. Do you understand this? Most of what you aspire to in your lives is what you have been told to aspire to out of a place of control. And even the freest man, the man who believes he has achieved his dreams, has been achieving dreams based on constructs that were inherited and systematized out of a need to control.

So how can you hope to heal your brother or to help your sister if what you are operating from is ascribed by external requirements that have nothing to do with the individual's needs as a soul aspiring to realize herself in her fullness? Do you understand this?

So when you operate from your knowing, you are able to do this systemically because you will know. "I know that the one before me has a problem in her liver." "I know the one before me is in fear of her own majesty." "I know that the one before me is still fighting with her mother who has passed many years before." And once you understand that, you can be in service in a way that is appropriate to that situation.

Guess what, everybody? None of this is about being a busybody or accessing other information that is not for the highest good of those you sit with or those that you serve. This is simply about knowing, and being in your knowing means accessing information, and how you hear your knowing, how you understand it, is a God-given ability.

Now clairaudience manifests in different ways, as does sight. People hear differently. Paul hears through his crown chakra, whether or not he is aware of that. This is where the energy is entering to support him. There are other people that hear voices as if they are disembodied and are in the room. That is not how Paul operates. His gift is different.

Now we want to make a distinction between high hearing and low hearing, and this is actually important. When one begins to develop his senses as a clairaudient, one is able to access information at different levels of consciousness. And it is imperative that if you do this work, you set the following intention:

"I am Word through my intention to stand in my protection as a Divine Being and only access that information which is of the

highest source available to me for my highest good and for the
highest good of all around me. Word I am Word through this
intention. Word I am Word."

That was one way of stating the following: "I am protected in my
light and I am now choosing to access information from a high
source." Are there other informations available to you at a lower
level? Absolutely. Imagine a television. You can turn the channel to
the news, or to the horror movie, or to the vista of a valley. What
your choice is depends on the channel that you tune in to. And
there is no reason to access lower frequency whatsoever. The information that you will be receiving at a higher frequency will be in
alignment with your requirements for your growth.

Paul is saying, "Are you talking about ghosts?" Absolutely not.
That is not even part of this discussion. We are quite simply saying
that when you access frequency, you need to be in your discernment. And as you are standing in your discernment, you are protected through your intention only to bring forth that frequency
which is for your highest good. It's not about having something to
fear. It's quite simply deciding that the channel that you operate
from brings forth the light that is in congruence with the work that
we are doing here. And the work that we are doing here is about
manifestation of the Divine Self embodied.

(Pause)

We're going to talk about things now that have to do with the
requirements of activating your clairaudience. The first thing that
we want to talk about is understanding that it is able to activate.
Once you understand that you are able to do this, we put into the
construct what is required for this to happen. And this will happen
on a frequency level and it will happen through your intention.

"I am now choosing to realign my energies in order to make myself available to my own clairaudience and my own availability to hear my Christed Self clearly with the discernment that is required of me to stay true and in alignment with the light that I am in truth. Word I am Word through this intention, Word I am Word."

As you claim this, you put into gear the systems that are required to shift you to this next level of awareness.

Now we are going to take a break today and not continue this chapter. We have done what we intended to almost completely. And we will tell you this: The title of this chapter is "Awareness of the Senses," and we will call it Chapter Three. We are very pleased with the availability of the channel today, which was much clearer as a result of this work. We are working quickly. We will commence with this chapter tomorrow. We have things to discuss about sight, about touch, and about how you offer your physical self to your daily experience in wonder. We thank you both for your attentions. Word I am Word.

Good day. Stop now please.

Day Five

We'll talk about where we were yesterday in terms of your adaptability to the gifts that are going to be made available to you through your consciousness transitioning in a higher frequency. Once you begin to understand that the reality that you exist in is malleable to thought, you can begin to transition into a higher realm that you are creating through your intentions in frequency.

"I am Word" sets an intention of dominion that states that

which you see before you can be held in the frequency of the Divine Self. When you claim, "I am Word through this thing," this thing is impacted, and not only that, your creations, those things that you bring to you, adapt and shift to become what is required.

Now we will explain this: When you have a pencil in your hand that writes, you say, "Here is my pencil," and that is what this thing is. When you claim, "I am Word through this pencil," you are not endowing the pencil with magical properties, you are actually stating the truth that this pencil is actually an aspect of frequency. The pencil is frequency as what you write on the page is an extension of your consciousness, which is also an out-picturing expression of your frequency.

So the pencil only becomes what the pencil truly is. By stating, "I am Word through that that I see before me," you bring into manifestation that which resides in the same frequency that you are resonating at, and the Word is high frequency. So Paul is saying, "What happens to the pencil?" The pencil is the pencil, but in actuality it is a bunch of frequency in form. And if what you require to be holding is something grander than the pencil you will get it, it will be called to you because it will be what is in resonance with your frequency.

Now if you can understand that everything in your environment was created by you through your intention to bring it into being on the most practical level—"The curtains in my window and the pillow on my bed were chosen by me or for me in a way that I accepted"—you understand that dominion is very practical. You are in it already. You just don't take responsibility for it.

"I am in my space." Each one of you reading this book can claim that: "I am in my space." Your space may be the subway, or your bedroom, or a park bench, but you are in your space as you are reading it, and consequently as you claim this, you are stating your dominion over your environment: "I am in my space."

Now once you extend this beyond the practical, that which you see with your senses in the most immediate way, you begin to understand that what is brought to you is also an extension of consciousness. And that which comes to you is created by you with your intention. Regardless of whether or not you are consciously saying it is what you want, it is the frequency that you are putting out there that is calling to you these things.

Now we will say that when you are in dominion and you claim it, you become responsible for yourself on multiple levels. And the easiest way for you to understand this is to state this intention:

> "I am now accepting that I am in dominion of all that I see before me. And everything that I see is out-pictured by my consciousness to bring me the experience that I have required for my soul's growth."

Period.

Now if you claim this and self-identify as the one in dominion, and that your circumstances, whatever they may be, are here to herald your own soul's growth, you are no longer victimized by your surroundings, your circumstances, or that which would come to you. You are no longer in a place where this can be perceived as possible. Your consciousness has embraced a new paradigm that aligns to everything coming to you as part of your soul's journey. And that journey, you can claim, is to your benefit and towards your realization as your Christed Self in full manifestation.

Full manifestation. What does this mean, really? How do the senses play into this?

Well, we explained to you yesterday that your senses are how you experience yourself in your frequency. You smell it, you see it, you touch it, you taste it, you hear it. And you consequently are one large organ of receiving information. Your skin receives, your eyes receive. Your touch, your hearing, everything is about bringing forth information that is then processed by the system you call your brain, and integrated into experience.

But that is the only way you bring about the experience of receptivity. Beyond that physical frame and structure, the system of the physical body, you are an organism of receptivity and your auric field, the egg that surrounds you, is what holds the information on multiple levels that you respond to daily, informationally. Period.

Now once you understand that tactile experience is only one way to access information, you can begin to understand that the activation of the senses in higher frequency brings about other ways of accessing information. Now we are showing Paul the image of a television. And in the old days, when he was young, there were four channels on the TV set. Then somebody got the idea that you could program more channels through a cable system. And now there are hundreds of channels and much, much, much more programming and consequently more information available to the receiver through the television set.

Guess what, everybody? You are the television set. You've been operating with four channels. We're about to multiply that by twenty as you become engaged with accessing information through your subtle bodies, which comprise your energy system or your aura.

Now once you understand that how you impact reality is choice, you can begin to get the sense that what impacts you is your choice as well. And if you decide today that what is available to you in consciousness is a full spectrum of programming, you can align your system to be the receiver for it. We gave you the image yesterday of a radio tower which is you, with a beam of light at the top, which is your Higher Self, which is your crown chakra extended into infinity to access Source. As you begin to call this energy to you, you align to the higher frequency and what you call to you will be the premium channels as it were, the good ones, the ones you would like to hear.

We gave Paul the metaphor in his group two weeks ago of someone walking down the street who had the opportunity to hear those people that he passed, and we said, one could have the option of hearing the wise man or the dirty old man muttering to himself on the corner. When we speak of a premium channel, when we speak of high frequency, we are empowering you to hear the wise voice in counsel who would support you.

Now that aspect of the self that is available to you to hear we will call your Christed Self or your Higher Self, but it is the self, that aspect of you, that is already in his realization with an awareness of his placement and his divinity. By "placement" we mean in the order of things. This self is conscious, is aware, is not frightened, and knows what he is here for. As you begin to align to that aspect of the self, that aspect of the self can call to it other frequency that will supply you with the frequency you need in understanding to benefit in growth and learning. Period.

Now this is a process and we need to be clear with you. As we open you sensorially, and as we give you the instruction to begin to align to your hearing, you must begin to accept that you are going to engage in a process of change. To think that you can be passive to your spiritual growth, and consequently to the gifts that make themselves known through accruement of higher frequency, you would be wrong. To believe that you do not have to change your consciousness to align to high frequency would say that this is just about reception. It is not. It is action as well. And we will have to explain this to you because it is the process of embodiment.

When you see a place you want to go to anywhere on this planet, you have to make a decision: "I am going to take the bus." "I am going to take the plane." "I am going to walk there." But you assess the distance and then you create a map that will bring you there.

You don't expect to arrive there in a nanosecond. You expect the process to be the required one depending on the distance you need to traverse.

Now we will tell you this: When you decide on a level of consciousness that you are going to begin to hear yourself and the divine aspect of the self that is accessible to you, the same process is engaged in. However, there is a difference. You are not the one who will design the map of how that happens and comes into manifestation. If you were to do that, you would mess it up. You don't have the information and you would be operating from a place of control. You have to imagine that that aspect of the self, the Creative Self, if you would, knows the way and will bring you there in the speediest way possible, but also in the way that is appropriate to your learning. And as you go there, the process of divestment—and by divestment we mean the process of eliminating those things which have hindered this from coming into being in the past—will come up to be cleared.

Now understand this, everyone: When you deal with a blockage in your creative process of unfoldment, it is a real blockage in terms of your experience. Paul is seeing the image again of a tree trunk laid across a path in the road that is stumbled upon on the journey forward, and the body stands there and says, "Oh my God, I'm never gonna get past this trunk. It is blocking my way."

Well, the tree trunk is a block, but the block will be contended with through your own Divine Self and through this process of engagement. And the only reason it has presented itself is because it is an out-picturing of your consciousness, and your consciousness is showing you what you need to contend with to move forward.

Now the problem people face when they manifest anything is that what has hindered the process in the past—by that we mean, what has prevented you from accessing what you have stated you want—comes into play, and you think that's all you're gonna get.

It hasn't happened. There is a block in the road. So what you do is, you make a little campfire in the road and you set up house in the belief that that roadblock, that tree trunk, that boulder if you would, will never be transformed. The boulder is there, the block is there, the tree trunk is there, specifically for you to see it, to contend with it and to move on with it. Period. And this will indeed happen.

So we are giving you this understanding now so that you can understand that this is not mumbo jumbo, nor is this something that is handed to you on a pillow with a key on it that says, "Here is the key to your clairaudience and to the manifestation of the gifts of the spirit."

Some of you may have that experience, and frankly, those of you that do have already made the agreement, on a higher level, to bring this into full manifestation prior to incarnation. And this book is serving as a gateway and a reminder to what is already present in your consciousness. It already exists. You just had to be told that the elevator went up to a higher floor than you believed it could. And suddenly you are on the high floor having this experience.

For others of you it is more of a process of construction in consciousness: elevating consciousness, creating through consciousness. And when the blocks make themselves seen, we honor this, and we will support you and honor you with the information you need to contend with it perfectly and in accordance with your soul's growth.

Now Paul is sitting here trapped in the image of somebody sitting on the roadside by a little campfire humming to themselves while they face this block in the road. And he is saying, "How is this block to manifesting my gift proceeded with? How do I get off my stool and contend with it?" We will give you some answers soon, but we want to continue now with an elaboration of what it means to come into dominion in your fullness. What does it mean to stand in your embodiment as your Christed Self in awareness?

Now to say you stand in your awareness means, very simply, that you are in congruence with what you see before you, and you understand what is before you from the highest perspective available to you. When you come into full manifestation or embodiment, you are in your ascension. And by "ascension" we mean that your energy field is vibrating at a high frequency and has carried with it the physical form that you stand in.

This is not about going someplace else. This is about being here now, as yourself, as the Christed Self you were intended to be, and that is the self that understands her self, his self, to be an aspect of the Creator, and therefore in congruence with the will of the Creator in its dominion. We will spend time on what it means to be in will in accordance with Divine Will as we proceed in this journey.

And now we will tell you what you are going to do with the tree trunk on the road.

"I now stand before me as my Realized Self, the self that is perfect and conscious and aware. And as my self in this perfected state, I choose to transform and transmute that which stands in the way of my soul's purpose. I am now clearing the blocks in the road of my realization to bring me into manifestation with my awareness and with my ability as a Divine Being. I am choosing to release this block in accordance with my highest good and in accordance with the Divine Will. Word I am Word through this intention. Word I am Word."

Now what will be contended with in your consciousness is the resolution that that which has stood before you is also malleable, is also a creation, and therefore can be uncreated. In our last book we discussed very clearly the idea of boulders. And what boulders are are those things that have been created by you that have been so invested in that they appear to be immobile and immutable blocks on your path, or in your experience of yourself. And the system for transmuting boulders was given to you very clearly.

So the example we are giving you now is actually specific to being on a journey towards your own awareness of your divine gifts and then having to contend with some form of resistance or obstacle that stands in the way of your movement. Now please understand that some of what you will contend with will be extraordinary. And by "extraordinary" we mean out of your realm of experience. As you begin to transform and access higher frequency, you have paths to take and transitions you make that will take you to a new place.

Paul is seeing *The Wizard of Oz*, the movie that he liked when he was a boy. And there was forest to contend with, and there was a witch, and there were winged monkeys. But all of these things presented themselves as passable interference for someone on her journey home. And your journey, everyone, is to go home, to your own Divine Self, and to your own self as completely aware of who she is, who he is, as a Divine Being operating in congruence with the Divine Will.

"I am one with all that I see before me" is the decree we give you now.

"I am one through all that I see before me. Word I am Word through this intention. Word I am Word."

Now we are going to stop and call this the end of Chapter Three. We want to move into discussion of the other senses and give you more information on dominion, which we will do in the subsequent chapter. Thank you each. If you wish, take a break and we will move forward in our work together tomorrow.[2]

---

2 Although the guides invited the reader to take a break, Paul and Victoria were asked to continue.

FOUR

AWARENESS AND PERCEPTION

Day Five (Continued)

Now we will talk about feeling today, and feeling through the senses, and what energy is, and what the constructs are, and how you can begin to discern what it is you feel when you feel it. Now we spoke in our last book about empathy and operating as an empath. And we are going to expand on that. But we are also going to give you some instruction in your availability to serve as an energy field in ways that will benefit others.

If you can begin to understand that much of what you experience is actually bypassing the physical senses and coming quickly into consciousness, you will begin to see that you are a receptor beyond the physical form that you stand in.

So we will give you an exercise right now. We want you to sit where you are and begin to feel yourself in frequency. Where am I? What is around me? What do I feel in my aura? What is my aura? Does it extend around me? Can I experience this?

Now what we are asking you to do, very simply, is to begin to expand your awareness beyond the physical form: to realize that you are larger than the body that you exist in and the field that you operate is larger than you assume it to be.

If you are walking through a door, you assume that the parameters of the wall around the doorframe are the things that keep the wall in place. In fact, there are beams and structures supporting the wall that are much larger and go unseen by the physical eye. And we will say that your energy field operates like that as well. You assume that the bones in your body are what are holding you together, the sinew, the muscle, the tendon. But frankly, all of those aspects of yourself are frequency vibrating at a certain level.

Now your energy field is around you and encompassing you. It is not apart from you, it permeates you and extends around you and it is also vibrating in frequency. When you understand that the information that is accessed through feeling through the auric field can endow you with information that is productively used in service to others and in service to your own growth, you can begin to access it succinctly. And by "succinctly" we mean in ways that you can feel.

Now Paul doesn't understand the system that he operates in. He knows he has a frequency and he knows when he feels things in his body he is really feeling them in his auric field when he works with a client. However, his experience of a bum shoulder, when he sits opposite someone who has a bum shoulder, is one about congruence of frequency, and it need not be much more scientific than that.

When you operate in frequency you are meeting others in frequency, and the exchange of information that happens on a level of frequency is done silently. However, you are always feeling it. You have become attuned to accessing information visually and auditorially through your energy field. And this simply means if I am in a meeting with my boss, and he looks down at the table and he rolls his eyes, you know you may be in trouble. If I am sitting opposite someone who I care about and they look at me with love, I know I am being loved. Now you can understand this practically on a level of the senses. But please understand that the visual cues that you are responding from can be accessed without the eyes in frequency. If you were to try, for an afternoon, to learn what you felt through frequency alone, without access to visual stimulation or auditory stimulation, you would be surprised at how much you were able to feel.

Now no one is asking you to deprive yourself of your sensory awareness. We are simply stating a fact: that what you are in frequency has much more wisdom and is available to you on much higher levels than you have imagined previously.

Now we want to discuss feeling and what feeling is. And when we talk about feeling we are not discussing emotional responses. We are speaking in terms of sensory experience.

When someone touches you, it sets off a system through the chemistry in your body and the brain and consequently you are able to process it in terms of what it means. Now as you access information through feeling in your auric field, it's operating a bit differently. The information is entering your frequency and you are processing it in consciousness and then activating in accordance with the appropriate response.

Paul is asking, "Do you mean that the brain is bypassed here?" Well, Paul, you already understand that the brain is the computer that the information is downloaded into and processed. So the brain is not bypassed, but the brain is not the system that is being encountered when you are working through your clairsentience, and "clairsentience" means "clear feeling."

When you walk into a room, the room that you stand in actually holds memory. The memory of that which has lived there, which has happened there, is actually etched in physical space that can be cleared, that can be understood. And there are psychics who are able to step into a space and read the frequency of the room. An energy field of someone opposite you has the ability to give you similar information. So we have an exercise for you.

Earlier in the chapter preceding us, we told you to take a partner and sit opposite her and see her in her perfection. Now we want you to do this again. We would like you to choose someone to sit opposite and align to the frequency of them through your intention,

"I am Word through the one I see before me."

And as you do this, we want you to begin to feel what you feel in your own body and in your own energy field. You are not being anything other than being receptive to frequency. You are not going on a hunting expedition. You are not looking for anything. You are simply allowing yourself to be in your receptivity to what you begin to feel. As you open up to the possibility that information can be accessed through feeling, you can begin to observe the differences and the gradations of feeling you experience in your own field.

Now the reason we ask you to start by feeling your own energy field all around you is so that you understand what your field is, and what it needs to feel like on any given day in order to be able to feel what is going on with somebody else.

If Paul sits opposite somebody and he sees them in their perfection and then he feels a pain in his liver, he is tracking the energy field of the person opposite him through empathy. If you are sitting opposite your partner with your eyes open or closed, and you are in your energy field and you claim, "I am Word through my partner" and you allow yourself to begin to feel what you feel, track what you feel, how do you feel emotionally? How do you feel sensorially?

What is your experience of your body? Do I get a pain in my big toe? Do my eyes ache? Am I thirsty? Do I want to cry?

Now please understand that all that you are doing now is accessing information in congruence with the energy field of your partner. You are not fixing them. You are not doing anything. And we will admonish you not to take in the energy that you feel, just to simply let it move through you as you would a breeze. You are not staying for the long term; you are simply seeing what is there as you feel it.

Now once you have felt it, you may begin to understand what you feel by having a discussion with your partner. "When I was sitting opposite you, I went into your energy field in congruence and I felt my liver ache, or my left knee had a pain in it," and your partner will respond with their own feelings of what is going on in her body or her energy system.

In order to do this effectively, you have to get used to the fact that you are accessing information in a new way. You are not operating through the old system, and your own body and your own frequency is simply there to give you the mirror of what is happening in somebody else's system, and you are doing this through empathic feeling.

Now once you see what's going on, or you feel it, you can talk about it and assess the experience. Some of you may find that you're a quick study and that you've been doing this your whole life but you didn't realize it. You will suddenly realize that you've been feeling people's energies all over the place, and that's why your life has been a bit of an emotional roller coaster. You are feeling their frequency and assuming it to be your own.

Now we will tell you something. There is a need when you work with frequency at this level to operate with what we will call protection. And protection is not to defend you. It is no different than taking an umbrella out when you walk into the rain. You only want to shield yourself from those frequencies which are not for your highest good in order for you to serve as a clear channel for frequency and divine information. So this is not born out of fear, it is a tactical procedure.

So when you operate as empathic force, when you are in your empathic self, you'll be feeling lots of stuff. But it's extraordinarily important for you to be able to discern what is yours, what is hers, and what is the next guy's. So you've had your partner, you've felt the frequency, you've had your conversation, you've learned whether or not you were feeling anything that was accurate to their frequency system and, consequently, you can begin to build on this experience through intention.

"I am now choosing to develop myself as an empath through the refinement of my own energy field, and in doing so I change my frequency to the level required to support this work in accordance with my own highest good. Word I am Word through this intention. Word I am Word."

Now Paul is sitting here saying, "Why would somebody want to do this?" Well, we have answers for that. First thing to say is that you are doing it already, but you are operating unconsciously. Each one of you, on a level of frequency, is picking up information through the subtle bodies on a moment-by-moment basis. But you are totally unaware of what it is, and why it is, and how to deal with it. You can be a mess and you can be in a situation where the frequency around you is extremely negative.

Now you can learn how to defend yourself by realigning yourself to a higher frequency that will not be impacted by the lower energies, or you can do whatever you like, but it's always happening. So we are giving you vocabulary and simple tools to align you to your ability to feel, to use your energy system as another skin, as it were, that will be able to support you in accessing information that you require to support others in their availability to their own growth, or to give you what you need in terms of information to support the self on her journey in her ascension into manifestation as the Christed Self she is.

Now when you feel, you must be in your discernment. We gave you an example a moment ago of negativity. What does it mean to be in a space of negativity? For example, if you walk into a room where there are people angry at one another, that energy fills the air. It is in the frequency. And people are sending anger to one another in frequency whether or not they are saying anything. It is like walking into a boxing ring, if you can say it that way.

Now what you would do in this situation, first off, is to claim your power in manifestation: "I am a Divine Being. I am Word through all that I see before me," and in so doing, you are bringing frequency at a higher level to support the balancing of the energies that are being thrown about in anger. You are not going to change the anger, you are going to change the emission, and you also are going to support yourself in frequency by claiming your dominion over your own energy field.

"I am Word through my being" sets the intention that your being is in activation as your Divine Self. "I am Word through my body" sets the intention that the physical body is unified in frequency as Word. "I am Word through my energy field" or "through my vibration" affirms that your aura is in congruence, and your consciousness, which is to say, "I am Word," is in congruence. Another way to claim this is to say, "I am Word through my knowing of myself as Word," which establishes you as the one in dominion in frequency.

When you are operating at this level, believe it or not, you are actually breaking an agreement that you are going to be a receptor for the lower frequency. You are moving up an octave, or two or three, in frequency through the intentions that you have set and you have realigned to a higher level that will no longer go into agreement empathically with that which is around you.

Now there are ways to serve as an empath, and those of you that wish to heal through frequency will be given instruction in how that happens. However, we are not going to move to that yet; we are still in awareness as a subject, and being in awareness of frequency is the point of the lesson today *as you feel it*.

So as we have told you, you are always experiencing yourself as a frequency engaging with others in frequency. And the information we are giving you is in support of your feeling what you need to feel in order to understand what is actually going on in your frequency so that you can make choices. So we'll go back to the journey that you're on in embodiment.

Some of what we are saying to you is that the way that you operate unconsciously has precluded a way of self-identifying as the Divine Self. And as that self is offered to you, "I am Word," you begin to claim your own abilities in awareness through your touch, through your hearing, through your sight, through the other senses. There are ways to access information through smell, through the olfactory senses, and through taste. You may feel these as well as you work empathically. It is not possible to feel everything at the same time; your system would go on overload. But we will give you an exercise.

Imagine for a moment that there is someone that you care about. Now we want you to do this:

"I am Word through my body. Word I am Word
I am Word through my vibration. Word I am Word
I am Word through my knowing of myself as Word."

And now we want you to travel in consciousness, only to say, that you are going to set the intention to "tune in" to your friend: "I am

Word through the one I see before me. I am feeling my friend in frequency."

See what you feel. What do you feel like in your system? Now sometimes you can smell, sometimes you can taste. Paul has had the experience of tuning in for clients to loved ones, and he can taste cigarettes in his mouth and he will know that he is tuning in to a smoker. The energy field of the one being tuned in to will supply you with the information. You can smell as well. Most of you, actually, will find out that feeling, because it is the sense that is most highly developed, will be the one that comes forth first, so we are concentrating on it now.

"I am feeling my friend. I am Word through the one I see before me." As you begin to feel them, make notes about where you feel what you feel. How do they feel emotionally? What is going on in the physical body? Are you tired? Do your teeth hurt? Are your eyes strained? Become impressionable in this regard, and then note the impressions in a notebook. When you next speak with your friend, do a check. How were they feeling at the time you tuned in? You can do this with a partner.

Now like anything else, this is a muscle, and the more that it gets used, the more effective you become as a barometer. We have taken you through an exercise, initially, where you were first asked to see things as permanent and then to understand how they were all malleable and how they were all frequency. And now you are working with yourself and your fellows in this regard.

"As I become frequency in my awareness, my awareness allows me to access information through frequency. As I operate through frequency, I gain information and insight that can serve my friends, my fellows, and my own awareness of where I need to send the light. I am Word through all that I see before me. Word I am Word."

As we said, it is a muscle, in a way, only in that as you develop it, it refines and your system allows it to integrate. Now Paul feels this is important, and we are going to support him in this statement: It is important that you understand that you are the one in charge as you operate in frequency and that you are in your safety through this intention.

"I am Word through my knowing of myself as protected in my work in frequency. Word I am Word through this intention. Word I am Word."

Now in fact you are safe, and all is safe, and the Word is high frequency. But the dilemma comes when those of you who have had fear of the unknown encounter experience that is outside of your three-dimensional reality. When you begin to access information, and when you go on your journey in ascension and have to move through those things, or those fears, or those habituated beliefs that have kept you from yourself, what you will encounter may be extraordinary to your experience.

Now you always knew in *The Wizard of Oz* that Dorothy was safe and no harm could come to her. In your heart, you knew that that is true. We will tell you this: You are as safe as that. You are on your journey home in your awareness, and you are being escorted on this journey by the authors of this text and those guides who are supporting us in the individual alignments of the readership to bring that into congruence with the manifestation of the frequency we call Word.

This is a collective effort. You are being worked with. And as those who read the book share their information with one another, they will find that their experiences are congruent with one another. The dreams are similar. The waking moments of revelation are identical. However, you must understand that the growth that you each seek will be individualized in its requirements of manifestation.

If one of you holds a belief that to do this kind of work could result in some form of punishment in an afterlife, you have to understand that that is a belief you will contend with in its clearing. It is a common one. But believe it or not, that is about restriction and control. What you are doing here is accessing yourself in fullness. And if you can understand that it is a sin, to use no other word, to stand in the way of one's own growth, you will see how ridiculous it is to keep yourself stunted in your experience because of a doctrine that was established to keep man outside of his knowing.

As man ascends in consciousness, the species comes into knowing. And the gifts that we speak of will no longer be seen as gifts because they are the birthright and the next manifestation of the species come into form. This is the time of the new revelation. And those who are being born are born in attunement with the agreement that they can access their own capabilities in fullness in ways that previous generations have not been aligned to.

Now to understand that the growth that you are seeking is actually paving the way for those who will follow in your footsteps should give you a sense of the transitional nature of the times that you stand in. You are on the brink. You are in the doorway of an infinite knowing that is going to be made available to this planet through great changes in conscious awareness. You will see, in time, that telepathy is common. And that is what is being demonstrated by Paul, other mediums, and anyone who has begun to develop an attunement to these abilities are simply partaking in the gift that is now being made available to all.

The lid is off the pot. The rules have changed. You can change in your choices in manifestation through realigning yourself to your own self as Word. "As Word" means as your Divine Self incarnated in a body. "I am Word through my being. Word I am Word."

Now as you change, you bring about change. And as your field changes, you redesign your experience to meet the new needs of your frequency, and the frequency that you endow others with supports them in their changes of redesigning and realigning their own frequency. It is about propagation of frequency and alignment. And if you can think of popcorn popping, that is much what it is like. Everyone is popping. And the first one does it, and then twelve more, and a hundred more, and a thousand more, and then a million.

This is the awakening that is being promised to each man through the significance of this time. This treatise is one effort to support this global consciousness shift that is happening as we speak. And we spend time on awareness so that you can see and feel and know what is in this reality for what it is, so we can take you to the next one and you can know what that one is as well. We are talking about dimensions in consciousness and you are waking up to yourselves as inter-dimensional beings having a new kind of experience of himself, of herself, through divine alignment in frequency.

Now we want to talk for a few minutes about fear. And we've talked about this again and again, and we will return to it as a subject throughout this manifesto because it is choosing to make itself known again and again throughout the journey.

The belief that you are not allowed to progress beyond a certain point keeps you at a certain point. Now why would you hold that belief in spite of what we are telling you—that it is a construct, that it has been born out of control or a need to control, and it is a dictate that is born in fear. So you have this explained to you, but we are still seeing you poised at the starting point ready to run the race. But you have not broken through the first ribbon at the sound of the gunshot that would herald the race is begun.

Guess what, everybody? You're scared. You're scared of breaking the rules, but more than that, you're frightened that if you become this thing you say you are, you will be frightening to others. They will not understand you, they will blame you, they will think you ridiculous, or they will move away from you because you are now embarking on an experience that they cannot identify with.

Now can you understand for a moment that as you choose to grow, you outgrow certain things, certain situations, and a certain populace that would hold still while the water is moving forward? You are in the river now, you are journeying forward, and what you will meet on this journey are the fellow travelers who are incarnating as themselves in this frequency. But all are welcome. And the belief that you will be frightening is just another tactic that the ego has to keep you from experiencing yourself in your ability to manifest as a Divine Being in incarnation as Word.

So get this, everybody. It's time to quit the battle. And we can tell you this: To engage with the ego in a battle over rule always means that you are engaging in the ego's wish to support it in its strength. So we will do this with you now:

"I am now aligning to the reality that as I move forward on my journey, my experience will change and my experience of myself in manifestation will bring me to those I need to know to support me in my journey. And that I am bringing with me all that I need by way of love, by way of support, and by way of reason to know fully that I am not in agreement with any rules that state that I am in my limitation. I am free of limitation. I am knowing myself as free. And I am aligning now to my willingness to experience myself as the one who is in alignment with his freedom. Word I am Word through this intention. Word I am Word."

The realization that you are allowed to go now, and to stand firm in your awareness of your willingness to experience yourself through your senses in a new way, will bring you to a new goal. And the new goal is:

"I am knowing myself as a manifestation of the Divine. Word I am Word through this intention. Word I am Word."

(Pause)

We will talk about now about love and choice. And you have the choice now to bring your sensory experience into an agreement with the frequency of love.

"I am now choosing to bring myself into an awareness through my senses of the experience of love. And as I do this, I bring into alignment with me my experiences as expressed and informed through my senses. Word I am Word through this intention. Word I am Word."

Paul is saying, is that silly? We will say, of course not. Everything that you experience right now you are processing through your frequency. But your main way of experiencing yourself in this dimension that you operate from is through the senses. So endowing that, and aligning that into the frequency of Divine Love, will support the love that you are experiencing as navigated through and processed by your sensory awareness.

Now we want to talk again about *feeling* and what you feel. We asked you to sit with a partner and to have an experience with her. We asked you to tune in to someone at a distance and have an experience with that person as well in frequency. Now we want you to tune in to yourselves:

> "As I sit here, I become aware of my frequency. I feel my bones, I feel my skin, I feel my teeth, my hair, my lungs, my lips, my eyes, my mouth, my back, my spine. I am feeling my entire being in form in vibration. Word I am Word through the physical body that I inhabit. Word I am Word."

Feel this, please. You will feel the shift in your frequency as you claim this, as your physical body realigns itself to the frequency of Word. Now we will take it out:

> "I am Word through my subtle bodies. I am Word through my etheric body. I am Word through my experience of my mental and emotional selves through my energy field. Word I am Word through this intention. Word I am Word."

As you do this, you will begin to feel the frequency around you begin to shift and to alter as you bring the emotional body, the mental body, the etheric body, the causal body into alignment with the Divine Light that establishes itself as Word. "I am Word through my being. Word I am Word."

By claiming this, you bring the Word in full unity through the physical, psychic, spiritual being that you are on all levels. "I am Word through those I see before me" brings that energy in perception and awareness to those you see before you in a way that will allow you to experience them in frequency as well.

We have taught you today and we have given you assignments. We ask that you keep a record of your experience. And we also ask that you continue to commit to working with the frequency when you are not reading the book in practical ways. You do not get a muscle operative if you sit in your chair and you don't exercise it. Now understand that you may have resistance and you may not want to do it, and it's easier to read on than to stop and do the homework that has been offered to you.

But in fact, you are in a course on instruction in your own awareness, and you are your own teacher through your experience of this text. This is the manual, but you are the relationship with the course of study. And it's not that you get a diploma at the end of the class. You get your own information through your consciousness as amplified by your own ability to stand in your knowing and in your awareness as Word.

We thank you both for your attentions. We leave you now, and we leave the readers now with this praise:

"We bless you for your forward action. And we honor you through your creations, that which is created for your good, and what is which is created for your learning that will now be clearing so you can move forward on your path in love. Word I am Word through this intention for all who read this book. Word I am Word."

Thank you and stop.

FIVE

AWARENESS IN RELATIONSHIPS AND CONSCIOUS STRUCTURES OF LOVE

Day Six

We'll talk about love, we'll talk about knowing, we'll talk about responsibility, and we will talk about the awareness you need to embody yourself as the Divine Self that you truly are.

The consequences of your actions in your life thus far are the things that you contend with when you realize yourself as the one in charge. Everything that you have created has impacted you on a level of creation. Those things in your environment, and also those things that you characterize as the personal life that you have, have, in fact, been created by you. And these things have had consequences.

Now we will talk about what consequences are. And what consequences are are the ramifications of things thought. And we will say "thought" because thought precedes creation. Now if you have a relationship that is not operating well, the thoughts that you have created prior to entering the relationship are the things that have created the situation that you are in now.

The moment you understand that the consequences of past

thought are the reasons you don't feel embodied in this moment is the moment you become aware that you can embody, because those thoughts that were created in knowing on a higher level can bypass and can recreate your emotions, your responses, and the relationships that you have in your personal life.

Now we will talk about a "personal life." What a funny way to say something! Everything is your personal life because you are the one inhabiting it. But, in fact, what is being talked about is your emotional private life in relation to others. And here is what the work is today: We want to discuss your relationships with your fellows in terms of your awareness.

Now strife, in a personal relationship, is a reflection of a need to control on one part or on another part. But if there are two people in a relationship and there is strife, you can understand very quickly that control is the issue at hand. And if you can understand that all control and requirements of control are born out of a need from fear to be in charge, or whatever you want to say will be incurred by *not* being in charge, you can understand that fear, once again, is the culprit.

When you have a relationship that is operating well, and in your awareness you can state, "I am in my knowing in this relationship, and what this relationship brings forth is creative and wonderful and loving," you can clearly understand that there is no battle of control, because the relationship is in congruence, and the benefits of the relationship are making themselves known very, very clearly through positive impact.

Now once you understand that every relationship you are in is your teacher, you can begin to see what is available to you through your own information about what you need to manifest yourself through your knowing as the one party to an aware and healthy relationship.

Now Paul is saying, "Is this going to be a chapter on how to have a healthy relationship?" Yes and no. This is a chapter on awareness in your relationships that will support work that will come later in the book that will speak of how to be in creation on a higher level through all your interactions. But this cannot happen until you see clearly what the availability is, today, to your own understanding about how you engage with your fellows.

Now we will talk about different kinds of relationships today. And were going to start with the big one. You. Your relationship with you. Until you understand that you are the basis for every relationship that you have, you're going to be in trouble. And the ignorance of this simple fact has destroyed more relationships than you can know.

People assume very, very quickly that they are not the one in authority in any given time, when, in fact, the only way you cannot be in your authority is to abnegate your authority. And then if you do that, you are still in choice. And that means you are still the one in authority. So please, everybody, first things first. You are at the center of all of your relationships.

Now the relationships that you manifest in your environment are created by you to know yourself, to see yourself, and to believe in your own worth through activation and transformation. Now we will explain this: If you have an authority in your life who you are frightened by, you have created a situation where you have to learn your own relationship to your own authority. The outrage that people experience at authority figures is usually outrage that is meant to be directed at the self for not being the one in authority, and the mirror is effective, but only to the extent that the individual sees what is truly happening.

When you don't believe that you are the one in charge, you are leaving yourself out of the picture and out of the relationship. Now Paul is wondering what this means. "What happens if you have a friend who is not speaking to you?" Well, that's an example of choice. You are in authority. Do you pick up the telephone, do you walk around the corner and shake his hand, or do you let sleeping dogs lie? But whatever you choose to do, you stand in your authority and you are the one in choice.

Now understand this: Becoming aware of yourself in your relationships does not require anyone else to change. They will change in response to the change of your consciousness. And as that change happens, what you create has to change. So if you are a female who has believed herself to be controlled by men and holds great anger at a paradigm that supports that kind of imbalance, and you realize finally that this gives you a great excuse to remain disempowered, you can then change your consciousness. And as you are empowered through this transition in your awareness, the paradigm changes to support your requirements for a new identity that will be reflected back to you in your relationships.

You are still the one in charge. You do not change the ignorance of others by combating their ignorance. That actually enhances the ignorance because it supports a requirement for protection. When you realign to your knowing, and others can come into their knowing through the congruence of intention, you can then change the self, and the self will then create others in their landscape who will reflect back the new choice, the new awareness, and the new reality.

Now to understand, once again, that you are the one in charge of all of your relationships forces you immediately to abandon the idea, the belief, and the investment in being one who is being victimized by anyone for any reason. Now we are not talking about physical experience right now. If you are walking down the street and somebody hits you in the nose because they are out hitting people in the nose, yes, in fact, that was created by you on an experiential level, but at the same time what we are really speaking of is the way you self-identify as a victim that brings these experiences to you.

Now it's much easier to blame someone else for your issues than to take responsibility for them. But to the extent that you have the investment in blame, you become the victim who then cannot help to transform the circumstance that she says she wishes she would, once for and for all, change.

Now the limitations that you have in your requirements for your freedom in relationships are about judgment and fear and a belief that you have to adhere to certain paradigms of behavior that have been entrenched and made so out of a need, yes, to control you.

Now if you believe that if you do not behave a certain way you will not be met with love, you are creating situations where your behavior is being dictated by fear. And those people who were raised to be extremely polite were told that if they weren't, they would not be welcomed. And, consequently, they have created fear based in behavior that dictates how they will be received by others.

Now we speak this and we hear how obvious it sounds. But at the same time a relationship which is party to several people—the individual at the center of the relationship and those she chooses to interact with—has been created by these systems for too long. And the only way to change is to become aware in your investment of what you create, how you create, and why you keep it in place to the extent that you do regardless of the fact that it no longer serves you at all.

Now when you have a marriage, and that is an agreement between two people—and we will talk about marriage as "agreement" and not as a piece of paper, which is also just a contract made to support systems of fear and control—you will begin to see that the agreement is made to support the individuals choosing to engage with each other.

Now we are not knocking marriage as an agreement. We are all for it. What two can achieve through united will and in their learning as coupled can be quite wonderful. But a contract that limits behavior and is for the reasons of taxation or rule over another essentially has been created in a doctrine, historically, that was a requirement of control.

Now Paul is sitting here going, "Oh no, they just said there should be no marriage, this is too much." We are not saying that. Marriage is an agreement between two parties who elect to conjoin to have certain experience. And if a contract supports that, so be it. But do understand that the contracts that you sign are always about control and a perceived belief in safety.

"If I marry my husband, he will never look at another woman." Oh well, how often does that happen? "If I marry my husband, I will get all the money when we divorce." Well, that's another way of looking at something, but of course understand that's what contracts are for, and nothing about human experience as interchanged, interfaced, interwoven, and linked through consciousness is available in a legal contract about marriage. It does not exist there. A ceremony can be held that evokes and states all of the truisms about partnership and agreement, and that is marriage we endorse heartily, because union and availability to that in commitment is a wonderful thing. We are speaking of contracts.

Now Paul is saying, "Well, a contract and a commitment are two very different things." Actually, they are not different, but they can be operated very differently. A commitment is a choice, but it is not binding, and a contract is a binding thing that has ramifications to it if it is broken. It is a protection and it is a threat.

When you sign a lease on an apartment, you are stating that apartment is yours and no one else's for the duration of the lease. It gives you permission to do what you want only within the parameters of the time you have made a promise to pay for it contractually. Nobody cares, frankly, about paying rent on a home they do not live in.

Now if you look at a marriage, an agreement between two people where there is shared information and love, the idea of signing a contract "until death" is a wonderful idea, but it's also a big threat and invites problems. Because when you state something is finite, you actually have resistance to it as well. Now if you understood that the choice to be in an agreement in a relationship or marriage that was born in consciousness was not tethered contractually to a basis of fear, you would find that that marriage was enhanced through the awareness that the individuals involved were always choosing to be in commitment through their consciousness and not through the dictate of an external authority system that states, "This is how you will now behave, this is what is appropriate behavior, and these are the repercussions you will have if you do not live up to the contract," which is divorce or anything else that you can think of that can be incurred through the violation and dissolution of a contract.

The free will of individuals to be in relation to one another always has to be made in an identification of conscious choice, aware choice, and not through systematized jurisdiction by external authority.

So to go back to our original idea of what it means to be the one at the center of your relationship, what we want you to understand is that there is no one else finally choosing your life but you. And if you are welcoming others into your experience in any real way, you do this through identification, consciously, with your choice to be in relation. Period. When you are in conscious choice, you are always aware.

Now Paul is saying, "What is the difference between conscious choice and unconscious choice? I am not in unconscious choice in any of my relationships." You absolutely are. Eighty percent of the interchanges that you have you are doing through programmed behavior that has very little to do with your own needs and awareness.

When you make an agreement to walk down the block and have a conversation with someone, you are in mutual agreement and awareness of what you are choosing to do. However, when we say unconscious behavior, what we are really speaking of is the way behavior is informed by the patterning that you have inherited in your culture and through being raised with certain requirements and dictates about what is appropriate. And as you operate from that place of unknowing of what is conscious, you can delude yourself to the end of your experience by saying that you are choosing it in a conscious awareness of choice.

Here is an example. You have a child that is raised to believe that she must get married one day and have children. And that embedded belief informs her choices and she becomes aligned and goes into agreement with a self-identification that states that her worth is tied to behavior that has been created for her. And she believes it and, consequently, she creates from this place, and perhaps is happy because she is condoning expectation by others. Or perhaps she is miserable because her true self wants to be living on a cliff with a young man who eats grass and drinks out of a coconut. It doesn't really matter what you choose as long as the choice is made in inherent accordance with your Divine Self. And to understand what the Divine Self requires in its relationships has to come through an awareness of what in your life now has been created for you in unconsciousness, in lack of awareness, through cultural dictates, parental requirements, and now, we will say, religion and systemized ways of controlling everyone.

Now we will talk about what that means. Everybody has a belief that they are free. And this is true to the extent that you acknowledge that at your essence you are absolutely the one in control. But you have gone into agreement about everything, for better and for worse, that you have created around you. And to the extent that you believe that the ceiling is low, that is the low ceiling that you all engage in experiencing. What we would intend to do with your consciousness through the experience of this text is raise the roof. Raise the roof high so that you can see the limitlessness of creation and experience that is available to you.

But if you are operating out of systems that tell you, "This is appropriate, this is not, and the taxes are due, and the toll needs to be paid, and the contract needs to be signed so that I can be in accordance with others' beliefs," you are operating through mutual agreement that actually is based in control.

Now Paul is saying, "Are you preaching or teaching anarchism?" No, no, no. Don't be silly. We are teaching awareness. And we are not telling you not to sign a contract. And you should pay your taxes to the extent that you are in agreement with that. However, you must understand that what we are asking you to do is to become conscious that you are doing these things, and not be on automatic in the disciplines that you believe, falsely, to be your freedom. "Is it my freedom to pay my taxes?" does not make a lot of sense. Well in fact, it's true, you write the check, you put the stamp on the envelope, and you are in choice and in freedom. But the cultural choice to engage in this system is finally one that is about agreed control.

Go back to the founding of this country, which was a country that was born out of retaliation against an existing authority that decided how people should be taxed and thereby controlled. Now we will say to you that the identification of the self as the one who is in choice in her relationships, in his relationships, will actually begin to make you aware, and underline "aware," of how you are not free in your relationships.

You are going to begin to experience yourself as operating through certain dictates that have been given to you that you have been previously unaware of, and you have ascribed your own behavior in relationship to this. When you are free of those things, those creations that have limited you, then you can call yourself free. But the coming of awareness that we are promising you is about seeing where that belief has been tainted, been constricted, and not been truthful. And in order to do this, you have to become aware of your present landscape in your relationships.

Now Paul is wondering how this is done. He's feeling weary. "There is no need to analyze all of your relationships," he says. "Is there?"

Yes, there is, and not in the way that you think. This is not as much an intellectual exercise, it's an energetic one. First things first. Begin to understand that every relationship you are in has an exchange of energy attached to it. Where are you liberated in the energies that you experience in this relationship, and where are you depleted? Where do you feel constricted, and where do you not feel honored? Now if you can begin to ask yourselves these questions, you can begin to discern why this is so. And then you can understand why you choose to be in engagement with others in ways that make you feel constricted and depleted and not free.

Now when you do this, you become conscious and aware of things that have always been there. "I am always polite." "I always open the door," "I'm always cranky when I don't get my way," whatever it might be, is what you need to understand about the capability and the structure of the relationships that you have created. And yes, we will say again, your relationships have been created for you in order to learn who you are.

That sounds selfish, but in fact, everyone is doing the same thing, and it is a construct that is agreed upon, and everybody is being taught through their interactions.

"I am listening to myself, now, in a new way that will support my awareness of myself in relation to my fellows. I am seeing clearly where I am required to learn from the mirrors that are presenting themselves to me in my relationships to others. I am Word through this intention. Word I am Word."

Now the responsibility has just been relegated to your own Higher Self, the Creative Self, to support you in bringing this to you in your awareness. As you stay in your awareness, you begin to understand what is before you, how you create what you create, and what the investment is you have in the dynamic that you have created.

"I always feel weak in my relationships." "Nobody ever loves me the way that I want them to." "I am always in control and everyone acknowledges this even though they don't like it." Whatever it may be that you call to yourself in the form of experience will be brought to you in your discernment. And what you require now is the *awareness* that will support you in processing this information and making it operate in ways that will be creative for you in your experience of appropriation and acclimation as and to your own Divine Self.

Here's a little thing to know: When you operate from your Divine Self, and we will get there eventually, the relationships that you create will be in congruence with it. Every relationship in your life right now, without exception, is in congruence with your vibration, with your frequency and the constructs that you have created that are now being out-pictured. This is what you call to yourself through your consciousness. And when your consciousness changes, your relationship changes in accordance with it. Period. Period. Period.

Back to today. You each have relationships in your lives that you feel are not working, that you would like to repair. And we want to give you a little bit of instruction in frequency about how to begin to work with this:

> "I am now choosing to be in alignment with my own knowing, my own higher knowing about what is required to bring this relationship into perfect order. And I am now seeing and understanding and becoming aware of that which is required of me in order to make this so. I am Word through this intention. Word I am Word."

This will bring about a configuration and a change in frequency that will support your ability to realign to the possibility of what is required to change and transform the relationship. It will not fix it. We do not fix. This is not about fixing. If you think about fixing, it's usually about control.

"I want the relationship to go back where it was when it was working." Well, that means going back. It does not mean going forward, and many times relationships change, restructure, and reform based on the conscious requirements of those who are involved. But when we say it brings you to a new awareness, we mean what it will do is give you the required information you need in order to navigate and to be in party to whatever level of change is required in the relationship you are asking about, or you want healed or changed. Now here's another one, and this is a good one:

> "I am Word through the frequency that exists between me and my fellow. Word I am Word through this intention. Word I am Word."

When this is stated, what transpires is an activation of frequency in the fields and in the place that exists between the fields, or the interference between the two parties to bring the fields and the frequency into congruence with divine frequency. Period.

Again it does not fix, it realigns. And if you can understand that there is a need for relationships to realign in new ways, you can accept this as a healthy tool that will sponsor and invigorate the process of transformation.

Now, everybody, get this:

> "When I am claiming my own dominion in my life, those things
> that I have created that no longer serve me will be made known
> in order to be cleared, changed, and transformed. This is a
> requirement for my change."

Now understand that when you say this, you acknowledge your worth as the creative force in your life. But we have spoken a lot in this book so far about congruence, and that is the key here.

When you are stating an intention in congruence with the Divine Will, you are operating as an agent, as an aspect of the divine in manifestation in consciousness. That is extremely different than operating from control or to fix something because you would prefer that it be the way that you think it is supposed to be.

Remember, we recently told you that this is not about thinking. This is about knowing. Now you can delude yourself and say that you know that this relationship is meant to be, or that you know that this child is meant to behave in a certain way that does not harm my feelings. However, you don't know that. You are wishing that, you are intending that.

Now we will tell you something. When you are in your knowing, that aspect of yourself that knows accepts and does not question. Paul has been told things that on a conscious level he has no agreement with whatsoever. However, he knows, he accepts, there is an aspect of him that is unable to argue because the information resonates and bypasses the thinking mind. He goes into acceptance.

If each one of you now would once again go back in your life to a place where you knew something: You knew you were in love. You knew you were getting that great job. You knew that your parent was passing, or the dog was sick, or the move would have to happen. But on a deep level of resonance, you knew. Can you do this now? Can you go into this place of knowing in your own self?

When you remember this—and we say re-member, reconnect to that memory—you will go into resonance with it and this will be the touchstone for you. It is very different to know that you have been fired from a job than to think it. So go to your knowing. Your knowing will invigorate you and it will be your teacher.

So when we tell you this, don't trick yourself that your thinking is your knowing. We are inviting you to bypass the self that invests in other things from a place of control or from a place of fear: fear that you will not get what you want, fear that it will be taken from you, fear that if it doesn't happen the way that you decide, something must be terribly wrong with you or your world.

So knowing, again, is the placement for your consciousness when you are in response in consciousness. Now we will talk about love and the need for knowing in consciousness.

(Pause)

When you go into love and awareness, and you understand that the congruence of the actions that you take that are born out of love will always be for your highest good and the highest good of those around you, you can begin to trust more effectively that the reason you are in charge of your congruence is because you have become one with your own knowing in love.

Now, Paul, we will stop. Word I am Word.

Day Seven

There is discussion coming to you today about needing people. Why do you need people? What does it mean when you have requirements of others to fulfill your own requirements? When we get into this information, we want to tell you that we will be using examples from your own life and from the lives of people you have encountered. And we will be doing this carefully, not in a way that is invasive. We will be discussing things to make very clear points about issues of love as they relate to others in systems based in fear, and systems that are about fear in relation to others in general.

Now to discuss fear in a relationship must signify that there is a relationship to discuss. So we will take two people right now and have a little talk about them. There is a young man and a young female who are existing together in a relationship. The female desires the male to stand by her when she has issues that she does not like. And she requires him to support her through these issues in order to feel safe, to feel defended, to feel right. Now he can say, "I am standing by you," and he can stand by her. But for him to go into agreement with her issue is to compromise himself in frequency. Now we will give you an example of what this means. This young woman has a job where she hates her boss, and she never likes what he says to her. She wants his approval, he never gives it, she works harder to get the approval, and she gets angry at how hard she has to work to please this man who will never be pleased. And she comes home at the end of the long day of efforting on someone's behalf and says to her partner, "You have to agree with me that he's a terrible boss," or "I work too hard for him for not enough money," or create a scenario in discussion that that scene we provided you could concur with.

Now he could say to her, "Yes, I know, you do work too hard," and then he is in his authority, and he is stating a truth from his place of understanding and knowing. To the extent that he says, "You have a terrible boss, you are too good for the job, you should get out of there," he is actually condoning her in her behavior, which is wrong minded. Her first effort is to contend with her own issue of requiring others' approval to feel validated. And once she does that, she will be in the right job, the boss will not be the issue. But to require of a partner that he goes into an agreement with her issues creates congruence in absolutely the wrong way.

If you are in a relationship with someone and they say, "You have to convert to my religion to be in a relationship with me," and the other person says, "That's wonderful, I would love to do that for you, that's a wonderful religion," and makes that choice, there is no issue. But when someone else sacrifices their own identity or those things that they require to make them feel true to themselves for the benefit of another, you are not supporting integrity in your relationship. Period.

Now Paul is saying, "Okay, I get all this. What is this about really?" This is about truth. This is about claiming truth in your relationships. In order to claim truth, you have to see what is there already and then you have to move from it. So today, if you would, look at your primary relationships in your life, the big ones, the partnership, the children, the boss, the friendship, whatever makes itself apparent to you first, and isolate the ways that you have compromised your own knowing to go into agreement with someone else's issue. By "issue" we mean construct of their requirements for their reality to be out-pictured in a certain way.

Now if you have a friend who engages in behavior that you know is self-destructive, you can choose to love that person with the behavior intact. That is the appropriate thing to do. You do not withhold love from someone because they are being destructive. However, to *agree* with a behavior—"I understand why you do that,

that must be okay, because it's you and I love you anyway"—is a horrible thing to do to someone that you love. And we say "horrible," because you are supporting them in a lesson that they are choosing that is self-destructive.

Now if someone is about to throw themselves down the stairs, you can grab them, you can let them go, but how awful to say, "What a lovely thing, to throw yourself down the stairs." It is dishonest, and frankly you are engaging in that behavior through your own fear of being released by the one you say you care about.

"If I tell him to stop drinking, he's not gonna be happy, so I'm not gonna say that." Well, telling him is one thing. Deciding within yourself that you are no longer going to be in a relationship where you are having to go into agreement with someone else's behavior that you cannot ideally support in truth is the right thing to claim. And from that position, you can begin to heal yourself.

So Paul is saying, "Are you only asking us to discern what relationships we have that are destructive to us?" We are not saying that, really. We are asking you to discern about yourself where you move out of truth, where you move out of your integrity, and where you align to someone else's truth in a way that bypasses your own sense of truth. Period.

Once you understand this, then you can recreate the relationship in your consciousness. Now what this means is:

> "I am now choosing to remain in my truth regardless of what is presented to me by way of interaction with this person I care about. Word I am Word through this intention. Word I am Word."

Now Paul is saying, "Does that mean we don't have Chinese food, because I never liked it and I always agreed to have it?" Well, on a very simple level, yes, but it's not about Chinese food, it's about honoring yourself and being in discernment. There is nothing wrong with compromise and there is nothing wrong with doing for another. You know this well. But where there is a problem is when someone distorts their true self to get it to fit a mold that will embrace the requirements of another.

Now this is always done when two people engage in courtship, there is always a kind of navigation that happens back and forth through dialogue and through frequency about whose needs are going to be met, and how they are going to be shared, and where there are going to be compromises, and there is nothing wrong with that to the extent that everything is done in truth and in consciousness.

When you abnegate your authority from a belief of fear—"He will leave me if I do this," "She will not love me if she knows this," "I will not be allowed home if I tell her that I did that"—you are creating new constructs that have been born out of fear. And as you create out of fear, you create more fear. And this misaligns, misinterprets, and demands more fear. Because that is the action of fear: to create fear.

So to the extent that you stay in your truth and you operate from your knowing, you can be in your choice. So Paul is saying now, "Does this mean we never lie in our relationships?" We are going to tell you this: You should never lie at all. Lying is always, without exception, based in control. And that control is born out of fear or selfishness, which is of course a creation of fear. So when you lie, you create a new structure, born in fear, that will then have to be un-tethered, uncreated, before it moves on and does more damage.

We will tell you this: A white lie is not white. It is a lie being disguised with something pretty. Now we will not tell you to be harmful. To say, "I'm sorry, but I don't want to go out with you because I find you unattractive," is not a nice thing to say, and there is no need to be directly blunt in that interaction. You can just as easily say, "I'm sorry, I'm not going out with you, I'm not available." You are not available. You are speaking the truth. However, if you say, "You know, I'd love to, but I'm really busy and I actually think I might be going on a trip that week," you are being ridiculous and you are also being harmful. You are sending out an energetic construct to this other person that is born in deceit and asking them to accept that.

So Paul is worried now. "How about talking about things that are not available to discussion normally?" Now Paul, what you are really saying through that question is: "How do we talk about the hard stuff in honesty when we are frightened of the ramifications of the results of the discussion?" How do you tell someone that you are leaving them in a way that is not harmful? How do you tell someone you do not feel in alignment with them in order to move forward in a relationship?

Now lying, of course, is not the appropriate way to be in discussion. The way to be in discussion always is from an awareness of the Divine Self within you and within the partner, or the person, or the friend, or whoever you are discussing this with. When you can move into truth at this level and witness the divine perfection in that one that you see before you, you can begin to engage them in a level of divine truth. And the ego, which is that aspect of the self that would control, gets bypassed. You can be wonderfully honest in love and not in fear. This sounds hard, but in fact, the doing of it is very easy.

"I am in my knowing. I am in my knowing of what is required of me in this conversation. I am in my knowing of my truth, and I am expressing my truth in ways that are loving and honest. And I am doing this with a true awareness of the requirements of the one I am discussing with. I am in my responsibility as I choose to discuss, to speak, to say what my heart requires that I say. I am Word through this intention. Word I am Word."

Now Paul thinks that is a copout. That's a nice way of avoiding a hard discussion. Imagine, Paul, that you have a husband who is leaving a wife for someone else. That's an awful thing for people to go through. It's painful, it's disgusting in the emotional charge that can be released to the one being left. But there are ways of having this discussion as well that are high, and not about fear and not about release.

But if you can understand, please, that if there was deception in this relationship that supported the affair, then you have a big issue that has been undermined by a lie. So of course, if there had been honesty operating all the way through the system of the relationship up through the ending and dissolution of it, the issue would not be that awful. It would be understood. And both parties would have had the opportunities to be in their awareness, to be in their congruence with their knowing, and then make choices higher than they would have if the cat was let out of the bag a year into a process of deception of a mate. Do you understand the difference?

You are always trying to protect what you have, and sometimes the need to protect someone else's feelings is extremely selfish. Now again we are not talking about discussion that is cruel, is overly blunt, but to tell the truth in a loving way will support growth. To keep someone in a position of illusion, or of being disempowered in their own choices because they are being dealt with through deception, is much, much more difficult.

Now we will talk about something else for a minute. And this is about knowing in terms of who you are with. There are signals being approached between two people in any interaction. And when one person is speaking their truth, and another person is navigating from a place of self-deception or deception of others, you have an incongruence in the merging of the energies.

If one person is saying, "I love you," and another person is saying, "I love you too," but really they want to run for the hills, that's not a very healthy situation. If someone saying, "I love you but . . ." and the "but" goes unexpressed, it's going to create a new energy. And this is an energy that will build until it is addressed directly. So the point we want to make right now is, how you learn to talk with your partner, with your friend, with those close to you must now be informed by the proposal we gift you with:

> "I am now choosing to stand in my knowing and to speak only truth in my interactions. I am now choosing to know my truth and to honor my truth in all of my relationships. I am no longer willing to compromise my integrity for the sake of making someone else feel safe in their illusions, or feel better about themselves at the cost of a truth that needs to be told. I am learning now to heal the requirement to engage in deception on *any level* that presents itself in my life, and I am doing this through this intention: I am Word through my honesty. Word I am Word through this intention. Word I am Word."

The responsibility now becomes yours. And please understand that as you go about your business and you feel inclined to engage in old patterns of deception, whatever they may be, you will feel very, very uncomfortable. And this is the situation that causes it: When you bring about new behavior of any kind, the habituated self, and the self that believes that she requires the behavior, goes into response and attempts to hold at bay the change that you would incur through the decree you have stated.

If you have always gone fishing on Sundays, you are used to getting the rod out and going over to the water and throwing the pole and the line in. You do this naturally. If suddenly on a Sunday you learned you had to do something different, your body and your system would still be attracted to the old. It self-identifies as the old, and it believes itself to know itself through its behavior. So in a funny way, we only mean to say that as you go forward and change, you will now have to deal with the consequences of those changes through periods of uncomfortability.

Now we told you, Paul, that we would use you as an example in some ways, and we are going to today. And we are going to withdraw you a little bit so you can hear this more after the fact.

When one decides that one is going to be in a relationship with someone and makes that decision in their truth, that truth will bring forth results. But there is always free will in relationships. And parties come together and then they disassociate for whatever reasons when energy changes or requirements of energy change. So when you know yourself fully in your power, you can relearn how to be engaged in love with people that will support your frequency.

When someone holds you in love, they are holding you in a vision of themselves in perfection. There is no harm in love. But you must understand, still, that people use the word "love" in very different ways. And there are people, still, that use the word to simply state affection or control. If you tell someone that you love them as a way of keeping them close, you are simply tying them to you for a reason that may be unconscious. When we say, "I am in love," we are always speaking of this: "I am in the frequency of love, I am learning my love in frequency."

Now the lesson for you, Paul, and the lesson for the reader is to now disengage with the romantic belief in love as something that will call to you a certain kind of experience. That is an experience that is blessed, it can come, but if you narrow the scope and the frequency of love to a limitation, you will not be happy. How love comes in frequency is how love comes.

We will give you an example: If you are sitting on a hill, and you decide to call to you love, and you say "love," you can claim love comes to you, and the form that it comes in will be the perfect form for you. You can call the love of an animal, or a friend, or a partner.

Now if you decide that what you really require to experience in love is mutual partnership, you can call that to you as well, but that is only one form that love takes. And to discount other forms of love that come when love is called, because it does not look right, or feel like or seem like what you thought you wanted, actually creates a dam, and that dam blocks the love that would touch you at your heart in a real way.

So we say to you, all of you now who are desirous of romance, to release the structure of love as a paradigm that looks a certain way, to allow the water to flow, to be in the ocean of love as we stated, to merge with the frequency of it, and then to begin to align to the possibility that what you call to you will be in love, and what you ask for may be there already. You just have not been able to see it because you expected it to look a certain way.

> "I am Word through my ability to be in love. I am Word through my ability to align to the frequency of love. I am Word through my knowing of myself as in my worthiness of love. Word I am Word through this intention. Word I am Word."

Yesterday we spoke to you after the session about this book, and we will speak of it again in terms of congruence. This book that you are engaging with is a living organism. It is made up of consciousness in an awareness of the needs of the reader. And you experience this book on multiple levels. The first level you experience it is as a text with printed word on a page, and this book exists there and you can call it to you in physical form any time you wish.

This book also exists on an energetic frequency and it has its own properties in consciousness. The example that was given, and will be given again now, as if the words on the page extend off the page and you can touch them as you would Braille and be learning in silence without visual sight the information that is required to bring you into new awareness. We say this to you so you understand that the process you are engaging in now is one in frequency. And as you choose to engage it, you are engaged. At the level of willingness, you allow. We are honoring you each.

Now we will talk a little bit more about relationships before we end this chapter. We began by saying you are at the center of all of your relationships, and what is created by you must be responsible, because you have chosen it. Now when you choose from a higher place, you will change in your awareness of what you need. And you will move into a passage that will change those things in your consciousness that have brought to you relationships that have not supported your knowing of yourself as a Divine Being. So we would like you to state this with us now:

> "I am now choosing to bring my consciousness into alignment
> with those relationships that would define me in the highest way
> and support me in the recognition of myself as a Divine Being. I
> am knowing this is so. I am Word through this intention. Word
> I am Word."

We are going to title this chapter "Awareness in Relationships and Conscious Structures of Love."

> "I am Word through this intention to move forward in this book
> in perfect alignment with the dictation being given to me. I am
> Word through this intention. Word I am Word."

Stop now please. Take a ten-minute break. You can talk. Thank you both.

SIX

CREATION
IN AWARENESS

Day Seven (Continued)

We're ready to talk about love, and how you have love come to you when you require it. And this is a joyous chapter, because it's about the gift of love that is available to every man the moment he says, "I am in my knowing as a Divine Creation worthy of the love that is available to me now."

When you choose love, what comes to you is love. And if you have anything that stands in the way of your reception of love, any belief in unworthiness, undesirability, belief that you could not be loved for any reason at all, it will become clear to you.

Now understand this, everyone, this is *extremely* important: When something comes up in your consciousness, it is coming up to be addressed and to be cleared. In order to clear it, you have to accept it as it is: a creation, an embodiment of thought that you have made to fulfill a promise of your own consciousness based on dictates that you inherited or ascribed to. "No one will ever love me the way I look" creates that situation. You know this and you perpetuate it. And you perpetuate it every time you look in a mirror and affirm that you are not lovable.

Now that is one way people create a system that will deprive them of love. However, the examples are so voluminous that we could not begin to list them here. It would take ten books in very small type of the reasons people believe they could not be loved. And this goes back to the initial separation, that which you believe to be the Fall of Man, the disassociation of man from his Creator. That belief that has been created that you are separate from, and apart from, and have to appease a Creator who is enraged by your existence, or your behavior, or your desiring of your own knowledge. This is born in your collective consciousness, it is a way for you to be controlled, it is a way for you to continue to perpetuate your own sense of loss, of separation and unlovability.

"Who is God to love me when I am so bad?" That is the belief, at essence, that carries you through an existence of isolation from yourselves as the aspect of your Creator that would come into form through this work that we are giving you now.

"I am not worthy." Do you understand this? This statement is a decree of truth. "I am not worthy." As you state this, you create scenarios of unworthiness. And this has been done for you by systems that have stated, again and again and again, that you cannot be worthy. That if you were in conjoining with your own knowledge as an aspect of the Creator, you were doing something to be vilified for.

Religion has created a structure, in many ways, that supports people in moving towards their own knowing with a caveat; and that caveat being, that when you move into knowledge, and with a capital "K," gnosis, Knowledge of what is true, you will be held back from the opening of the chamber where the majesty exists.

Imagine that you are in a bookstore or a library, with rows and rows of books of knowledge, and each one of them is fascinating and a great distraction for what lies beyond the secret door at the end of the hallway. What lies beyond the secret door at the end of the hallway is the vessel of the Christ in manifestation. And that is *you* in your knowing, *you* in your majesty, and *you* as the one who is working in your knowing as an aspect of God. Period.

All of the books on all of the shelves contain information, and they are helpful and they will support you, but they can also be a distraction and a way to deter you from accessing truth. It's like understanding that there is a book that will teach you how to spell when the words are there already and can be understood by you without accessing yourself through the intellect.

Now control as a system has its place. There are things that need to be controlled. We don't like it when you get a bug infestation. We don't like it when somebody pushes everybody over in a line to get to the front. Those are things that are not very healthy and are about other things than what we speak of today. We speak of control right now as limitation and adherence to rules that state that you cannot know, and if you know, you will be harmed.

The punishment that has been incurred throughout time by people who have accessed knowledge has been amazing, if you think of it. And if you look throughout the Bible at the amount of persecution, and then you look at the amount of persecution that was stated through the Bible and through people's perceptions of the Bible that have gone on ever since its writing, you will see that there are people, and there are systems at play, that would prevent you from accessing your own knowing.

Why? What happens if you know? What is so scary about your knowing that there would be entire systems created to support you in staying in your ignorance, or distractions entertaining enough to keep you asleep? So why would you want to wake up if you have everything you need? Because you have been told that there is nothing else to get. That is why. And you have also been told that if you were to get it, if it were to come, you would have to pay the price in retribution.

Now you understand already that you are seeking knowledge. You bought the book, you've read the book thus far, you've attempted the exercises. Now this is the chapter on constructs of control and the beliefs that you have that they are required for you. Now you all engage systematically in behaviors that state that there are certain rules that you must adhere to. And we're going to speak practically for a few moments.

There are certain paradigms that you accept as normal. There is behavior that you decide is eccentric, or sinful, or wrong, and the best way is to say it is these are all out-picturings of suppression of individual consciousness. If one man decides to live a life that is not in accordance with the vehicles and the dictates of his community, he has choices. He stands in his authority, or he leaves the community and finds others like him. And this is the way that you have created separation among your fellows.

Now if a woman believes that her love is in the arms of another woman, and that woman is penalized for that belief, that belief then becomes a structure that is oppressive, and she has choices. She can adhere to the obstruction of her consciousness that states, "I must listen to the voice of authority and change who I am," or she must arise in power and state her claim in freedom, "I am who I am, and my body is my own vehicle of my own expression. And who I share my body with in truth is in alignment with my own highest good and that is all there to say."

Now if that is the truth of her statement, and her body is being shared with those who are for her highest good, where is the argument, and whose business is it to dictate anything? But once you understand that every example you can think of someone separating from a community has been based on control, you will be shocked at the way that this can manifest itself.

You have a child that does not want to go into the family business. You have a church that wants to pray differently than the mother church allows. You have people that believe that monogamy is a rule and others that believe that it is a way of controlling. So everybody's operating in this crazy way, attempting to control, or suppress, or figure out how to operate within a landscape that has these kinds of dictates.

Now understand this: There is good control. Get the pesticide to get rid of the bugs. Ask the person who is running forward in line to wait his turn. But do not believe for a single moment that anything that has been created that suppresses the free will, the individual's will to express herself as an aspect of God, is anything but what it is: a way to keep you in your suppression and consequently to forget who you are.

You have all forgotten who you are on such a level that the cataclysms that you might create in order to wake yourselves up are such that we are interfering, and we are saying, "Guess what, everybody? You are all individual aspects of the same God. You are all manifested in perfect divinity and you have forgotten. And we beg you now, we beg you now, wake up to the truth of what, of who you are and are intended to be."

This is the mission not only of this book, but of the Christ coming again in man. This is the time of the new dawn of creation. Understand this, everyone. This is the dawn of the new Christ consciousness come to man, and the manifestation of this is required. It is required in order for this consciousness to come into form that you release any needs to control your brother. When you control your brother, you link into the larger systems of control and you go into agreement with them. And as you are in agreement with systems of control, you diminish your own aspect of the Christ and you align instead to a darkness.

Now we are saying a darkness, the darkness, whatever you want to call it. But understand this: Any system that perpetuates fear is created out of a need to control you. And as you are controlled, you are asleep. If you wake up now, now, now, to the possibility this will change and is changing, you are in your freedom as a Divine Being and all that comes to you is of God, you have chosen a new light, and that new light is the embodiment of Christ in man. Period. Period. Period.

We are rejoicing. We are rejoicing in the heralding of this new information to man. We are heralding the awakening of the masses through our choice to listen to the hearts of man who state:

"I am now willing to be in my awakening. I am now willing to stand in my truth. And I am choosing, choosing, choosing to listen to the Christ within me who will carry me to my appointed destiny. I am knowing myself as an aspect of the Divine. I am knowing myself as an aspect of the Christ embodied. And I am believing in my worth as a Divine Being."

Now we will tell you this. The descriptions of control we have given you are limited. As you walk about your day, make notes. Where am I being told to stop or go? Where am I being polite out of an expectation? What are the systems that surround me that are telling me who I am, and what I can and cannot do? Become aware of that which you have created, you individually, as a human being, and you have ascribed to culturally and on a planetary level. How is it out-pictured? Look around you. You will see more examples in a five-minute walk to the corner store than you can believe. It's always been there. It's always been present. It's so used to having its way that it does not even balk when you encounter it for what it is. And what we are speaking about are those structures that are in place today that live for the purpose of keeping you in your ignorance of yourself as the one in charge of your life.

The reasons we are spending time on awareness in this first part of this book is because you are asleep and you are waking up. We told you earlier to look at things as if they were permanent. The wall, the body of the friend, the trees. See them as permanent and then see them as what they are. See them as frequency, as vibrating energy. And even if your sight is not yet able to assume the ability of clairvoyance, understand at least that these things that you see before you have been in other form and will be again. That is the first step, see what is before you, and then see it as energy or see it as malleable and see it as available for transformation. Period.

If you understand now that the trajectory that this planet is on is one of diminished light, and the result of diminished light is death, you will choose today to awaken to the new paradigm. We are not threatening. We are giving you an accurate assessment of where you have taken yourselves out of your need to protect what you think you have. The boundaries and the territories and the borders that you think are so crucial, and the oil and the commerce and the food that is so essential. So much has been invested in protecting that which is already transitory in form, and the controls have been established that are put in place in order to keep these things where they are are now the things that can kill.

Understand this. What you believed would be your protection, the walls that you have built, the hoarding of your food and the gifts that could be shared that are locked away because someone will profit at the cost of somebody's hunger or cold, will be left aside. You are now listening to a new voice, your own Divine Self that says to you this:

"I am in choice. I am aligned. I am Word. I am now heralding the manifestation of the Divine Self within me. And as this is done in consciousness and in vibration by me, it will be shared by many. And as many awaken, the tide will change, the tide will change, the tide will change."

We are bringing you to awakening. And the awakening to what you have to create must be based on an understanding of what has already been created. That is the basis of this first part of this text. We are not going to tell you that mankind is going to have a party unless they get this right. That will not be the case. We are not speaking of doom. We will explain it very clearly. Mankind has created things. At this juncture the creations of man must be assessed and decided before destruction can ensue. Now ultimately this is all about choice. But we are telling you right now that ability for man to go into an awakening of resounding joy has been gifted to you.

We are not speaking about apocalypse. Be clear on this. The apocalypse is the apocalypse of the ego that can no longer run the show. And the apocalypse is the apocalypse of control that can no longer be allowed to exert itself in a way that will keep you from your own divine knowing. The apocalypse is the awareness of separation and how it is a lie.

When you understand now, today, that you are comprised of energy, and the man next to you, and the man next to you, and the man next to you are all comprised of the Creator in frequency, how can there be anything else but love? How can there be anything else but goodness manifested?

The controls that you have and that have been placed on man are responsible for individual distortions. Understand this, please. The child that has been raised in cruelty becomes cruel or becomes too afraid to operate in this world. And the reason the child was raised in cruelty had to do with someone else's perception of control, or their requirements for releasing their rage upon someone else. All of these distortions that you have experienced in your own life were born out of control. Someone else's fear. And fear is manifested through control, through action. And that has been what has distorted individual consciousness.

The teachings we are giving you in this text are large and small. We are speaking broadly about consciousness and we are speaking small about how to contend with your boyfriend. It doesn't really matter. The lesson is the same. You are in authority finally. You don't believe you are. You don't believe you are because you were told you were not. You were told you were not because if you knew who you were, you would be too powerful to be stopped in frequency.

You understand that Moses parted a sea. He knew who he was in consciousness. And conscious thought, "I am Word," is the creative force that changes, that transforms material form. That is what it is.

If you want to feel something now, state this intention:

"I am now choosing to know myself in my power, in my full realization of my divinity. Word I am Word through this intention. Word I am Word."

You are that thing. Somebody told you a long time ago that if you were, you would be in trouble, and you have diminished yourself accordingly. And you have done this through group agreement and through systems that remind you on a moment-by-moment basis that you are being controlled.

Now we will tell you this. The times are changing. The change is necessary, and this book is being written in accordance with the dictates of your own consciousness to become realized. That is the only reason this is happening now, and it's why you chose it. You know already on a real level who you are. It is in your DNA. It operates in your frequency. It is an aspect of you that is rising now to the surface to be claimed.

You each believed that having a spiritual life meant that you turned nice. That you got pretty. That you floated around and had floaty experiences. That is not what that time is. Empowerment is not nice. It is real, and it is active, and it requires you to act. Period.

Think again if you think that the reading of this book and the acquisition of this information means that you get to wear a crystal or do some volunteer work to prove to yourself that you are now on a spiritual path. Your spiritual path is a dictation by you on a level of consciousness from your own Christed Self, your own Higher Self in action.

The actions you take will be required by you at a soul level. Period. A soul level means your soul knows already what she is here for, and how she is to make a difference. Now this does not mean you quit your job or you become a healer. It means that you Know. Capital K. "I am in my Knowing." And as you operate from your knowing as an aspect of God in body interacting with material matter and individuals in frequency, you are knowing what you need to do.

Stop playing dumb. Stop feeling inferior. Stop feeling unworthy of your Creator. Every time you reinforce those things, those beliefs, you go into darkness, because you go into agreement with a level of control that seeks to retain its power over you. Do you understand this? This is so important.

Each way you find to diminish yourself promises you that you have gone into agreement with an aspect of the self that is in accordance with keeping the lid on the pot. The lid is off the pot; you are free the moment you realize you are.

"I am free in my Knowing. Word I am Word through this intention. Word I am Word. I am free in my understanding of myself as a powerful being. Word I am Word through this intention. Word I am Word."

As you do this, you wake up. As you are awakened, you see what is around you, and you act on what you see. And you make changes in your consciousness that will transform your world. As your world is transformed, the whole world changes into light.

That is the action of the time. The matrix of control that has been present since your incarnations began is having its last hurrah. The fight is almost over. We allow you now with your own permission to stand up and claim your own divinity. The matrix of fear will leave when enough of you say:

"I see you for what you are. It is a lie that I am not powerful. I am in my Knowing and I am free. And with the united will in consciousness of me and my brothers and my sisters across this globe, we will change the trajectory of our planet to one of manifestation of love. I am Word through this intention. Word I am Word."

The recognition of the times that you stand in is imperative. You do not see what is around you because you are asleep, and you remain asleep because it is the bidding of those who would control you in authority. You stay there, and docile in your experience, because the times are changing, and you are to be awakened when it is time again for you to act.

This is the time for you to act. This is the time; you are awakened. You have been given permission, and any authority that would tell you now that you are not empowered is not supporting you in your own awareness of your divinity. We are telling you now again: This is not about apocalypse, this is about freedom. And what has to be contended with is the ego and those creations that were born out of fear. Those creations that were created in fear, which is linked to control, have to be contended with now. And the way that this is contended with is a change in consciousness, first on an individual level, and then through a patterning and a heralding of the new frequency as it grows and grows and grows and comes into full manifestation.

So we said at the beginning of this chapter that this news was joyous. And we do not intend to shake anybody up by reminding you that man, in his fear, has created systems that can harm him. And that which is created in fear, in the name of protection, and we will say this, not on a level of psychic awareness but in a way of country and civilization seeking to inherit safety through walls and systems of protection, you can now see that what needs to change is you. You are the one in charge. Each and every one of you has a mission now, to serve your own awakening.

"I am now choosing to Word through all that I see before me. I am now choosing to become aware of all systems that have been put in place that have been controlling to me. And I am now choosing to release myself from any belief that I need to be saved by systems that were created out of fear, or out of a placement to keep me in my limitation. I am free. I am knowing myself as free. I am Word. So be it."

We thank you now for assisting us in bringing this message through. We have taken time today to teach you who you are in love and in creation. We are also taking the time to tell you what you are not, which is a being in limitation. The pot is off the lid, as it were. You are waking up. You are new to yourselves in this awakening. And we are gifting you now with this information.

Each one of you now will be asked to receive love, and the

frequency of love, through the energy field you stand in with this decree:

> "I am now choosing to acclimate myself fully to the frequency of Divine Love in a way I may experience in consciousness. I am now choosing to align my Divine Will to my own will in ways that are appropriate to my teaching. I am now choosing to listen to the voice of my Knowing in all things as I am moving into love. Word I am Word through this intention. Word I am Word."

We will call this chapter "Creation in Awareness."
I am Word. I am Word. I am Word. Thank you and stop.

Day Eight

We'll talk about love first and issues that have precluded you from claiming your ownership in dominion as a lover. Now we have given you examples thus far in awareness about those things that present themselves in consciousness that serve as obstacles to your ability to perceive yourself as lovable. But we have not yet addressed your own resistance to standing in your love as the lover, as the one who benefits others through the responsibility and through the action of acting as love.

This is important. When you are love, when you are love incarnate, when you have manifested the self to the degree that we now say you are capable of and align to love, what you bring forth is the manifestation of love. And those that are with you, that are in your presence, will be activated frequency-wise in their vibration through this interaction. It cannot be otherwise. You are magnifying the frequency of love as embodied. And that impacts structures and energy frequency. It cannot not be so.

Now the relinquishing of control of who you thought you were until this time is part of the passage that you are undergoing. The ego has an investment in running the show still, and your fear that you will not be taken care of by the light, by the Divine Self that you truly are, is what is keeping you at bay from full manifestation.

Now it's not a simple thing. It's not like you're opening up a wad of bubble gum and there, underneath the paper, is the solution. This is much more complex because the systems that the ego has created to define herself as the one in charge have surmounted those things that you can identify with as your Divine Self.

Quite simply, you cannot say, "I am in my Divine Self. I am operating as love," without believing on a certain level that you are lying. Actually, as we have stated, the lie has always been that you are not this thing, that you are not a creature created in the image and likeness of God. That is the truth in essence of who you are. But if you can already experience the level of resistance that you have to claiming this in fullness, you can understand the identity structure that has been built so high to preclude you from seeing over the top of the wall of separation from yourself and from your God Self, your Divine Self, the Christed Self, the Creative Self that you are in truth.

We are saying that the work of this text thus far has been to identify those things on a practical level that have been keeping you in unconsciousness of who you are. But we have not yet addressed completely your own desire to stay where you are and to stand in your unconsciousness and perpetuate the lie that you are not love, or not an aspect of God or a willing emissary of the divine.

Now understand this, please. Your choice, and we underline *choice*, is to stand firm in your own knowing. We will never tell you what to do firmly. We will suggest, we will ask, we will "possible-ize," if you would, scenarios that may come through if you don't take certain actions, but we will never, ever, ever override or tamper with your free will. We will talk about this now.

At any given moment in time you have two choices. You can honor your fear, or you can honor your Divine Knowing, which is never in fear. Fear does not exist at the level of Divine Knowing. You can be guided by a voice that will keep you from stepping into traffic, but that is not a frightened voice. That is a voice that says, "Look where you're going, friend, and look quickly." That is different from being told, "Watch out! Watch out! Something terrible will happen!"

We would never operate that way, really, because we honor you as a Divine Being. And while we roll the carpet out for you to walk towards your destiny, and we will happily escort you through that process, we are not going to push you, nor are we going to tell you that if you don't this, you will have something bad happen to you. That would be control.

Now we said in the last chapter that as a collective soul and a group consciousness you have already projected the means of destruction into your environment and now have to become responsible for un-creating those same things. And that is done through thought and through conscious awareness: conscious awareness, requiring you to stand in your knowing and then benefit from the information that you have received. But that is very different from our telling you that if you don't read this book, or you do read that book, or you listen to this man or that teacher, or that one, something will happen for better or for worse.

We are not in the market of controlling our students. To do that would make us a system of control, and we guarantee you that we do not work that way. So your choices, each moment, to operate in fear or to operate in knowing, which is your safety, can assist you in operating in new ways to the extent that you align to the choice to do so. If you stand in your choice in this very second and ask yourself, "Where am I operating from? Am I in my knowing? Am I in my fear? Am I responding out of cultural requirements for my behavior or not?" you get an understanding of who and what you are, and the choices that you will then make will be in accordance with your knowing.

Now we began this chapter by saying there was love to be talked about, and awareness. And we will say this. The embodiment of the self as love is the goal. It is the true goal. It is the blessed manifestation of God's gift to man, to be in accordance and congruence with that level of frequency. This is not a simple thing necessarily, but if it were not achievable, we would not give you this text in order to begin to get there. We would find some other way of manifesting a system for you that would help you along. But will we say it can't be done? Absolutely not. But you are the one doing it through active choice, and through choice in your conscious awareness.

Now you each have resistance to this on an ego level, which is defining you. It creates parameters and a structure that keeps you very safe. You don't see what's beyond you unless you have to, and you don't break out of the mold that you have been identified with unless you are forced to, and you are very happy in the small world that you have created, or you are miserable in the world you've created but you still don't see how you are going to transform it. The transformation of you will result in a change of your experience. It happens. And as it happens, you transform your knowing, and the knowing brings to you what you require to transform everything else.

Now there is latitude in how this occurs. You do not have to run out into the streets screaming, "I am Word, come with me!" That would be a funny way to go, and it might be interesting to see how people would respond, but we are really telling you that what you are doing is a private exercise of responsibility to your own soul's worth. By re-identifying the soul in its truth as an aspect of the Creator, you are giving permission for your soul to do the work it is intended, and through its own free will.

We discussed congruence earlier in the book at length. And we will remind you again that when the aspect of you that is the Christ, or the Creative Self, is working in congruence with your will, the Divine Will and the will of the individual unified in congruence, and what can be attained then is remarkable, and the manifestation that you are able to bring forth miraculously will astound you.

The journey of bringing the heart into its opening as a love issuance will be where we take you next in requirement. We will do this with you through the next section of the text, which we will call "Alignment to Love." That is Book Two of the three in this volume. And we are telling you now that the repercussions of the work that you have done thus far will change you, to the extent that you bring forth the work we ask of you.

To claim "I am Word" while you are brushing your teeth is more than fine. You are looking in the mirror and claiming yourself as an aspect of God, as an issuance of the divine operating through personality and through form. And that's a wonderful thing. To state "I am Word" when you are angry at somebody aligns you to a higher frequency, and it is of benefit to claim yourself as you are at any time. However, to state "I am Word" while you are rolling your eyes and doing the crossword puzzle may not be of much benefit.

So the work you put in, finally, is about your responsibility to the choices that you would make as an operative of this frequency. Aligning to it, which means becoming it, in congruence, in frequency, gifts you with the latitude you need to bring forth the response that is required of this work. And we do it with you.

We talked about resistance to this, in the self, and where that resistant is born out of is what we would like to address now. We can call it the ego, or we can call it the lower self, or we can call it that aspect of the self that believes itself to be in full separation from Source and has done the best it has known how to do without the information it required to bring itself to a higher state of knowing.

All of those aspects of you are in alignment with the frequency of fear. What is fear? Fear is an eminent action of a lower frequency. It is what it does, which is to maintain itself as the truth, as the ruler, as the systemized way of operating. Please understand that when we speak of a grid of light, or we talk about the planet transforming, what we are actually talking about is disassembling this matrix of lower frequency so that it cannot rule.

Now Paul is wondering if we are talking about Satan, or things like that, that he has no response to and would walk out the door if we started talking about. Cultural paradigms have been created throughout time to protect those things that could not be fully understood, or to explain things in ways that simple minds could understand and operate from. So no, Paul, we are not talking about Satan, we are not talking about anything like that. We would not. It is not part of the construct that we teach. What we tell you, though, is there is energy in lower frequency that seeks to dominate and seeks to hold, and this energy needs to be re-informed and brought to the light.

When you release an aspect of the self that has been held in darkness, opening a closet, as it were, as we spoke to you about in our prologue, you liberate that energy, you liberate that darkness, and it is transformed by the light it is exposed to. When you bring forth the Word in frequency, it informs structures much in the same manner. You are turning the light on, and that which has been held in darkness is suddenly revealed for what it is: a simple creation of fear that is time to move on.

Now these things that you have invested in greatly as who you are or where you live in terms of your consciousness may not be very mobile. They are happily entrenched. If you can imagine a behavior pattern, for lack of a better word, that sits back in a reclining chair with its feet up because it has been so comfortable for so long in terms of running the show, you can imagine that it takes a lot of light to bring that up and to clear it.

In fact, once you are able to identify it as what it is, it loses eighty percent of its power. You see it as the imposter. "Oh my gosh, this thing that I've been operating from all this is time is only a construct created by my beliefs that is operating with the sole purpose of sustaining itself and keeping me from my liberation. I can release this now, because I know who I am as a Divine Being."

> "I am Word through this thing I now see is my creation. And I
> am choosing to release it to the light with the assistance of my
> guides and my teachers, in the name of the Living Light. Word I
> am Word through this intention. Word I am Word."

As this is done, you bring frequency to the pattern, and the easy chair gets its ejector button ready and throws the thing off. Now we said to you earlier that when you have an investment in behavior so much so that you self-identify with that behavior, you have claimed it as you, you have the option of calling it back. And the issue that most of you contend with, believe it or not, is you are much more comfortable in your passivity and you are much more comfortable being ruled by the old behaviors. So you call them back. You like the company. It's nice to have that thing in the comfortable chair when you're feeling rotten to remind you why you do. So you call it back and you set up shop again.

Each time you set up shop again, which essentially means that you are re-issuing the pattern of behavior that you said you wanted to release, you must change patterning again. It's not that simple to say goodbye to somebody when you keep chasing them down the hall to make sure they're not really gone. And this is where faith comes in.

Faith, as we would describe it, is a belief in your knowing, that what you say is true in Divine Light. When you have a prayer and you have an affirmation, and you operate from it in truth, you bring it forth in faith. When you sort of believe it, you sort of bring it forth. And when you don't believe it, you've walked away before the emission in frequency was ever sent out into your field. Period.

So you are the one here who has to decide that when you say, "I am Word," when you say, "I am releasing this pattern in light, I am Word though this intention. Word I am Word," it can be so.

Now we would not fool you. We understand how hard it is at times to remember who you are and how much resistance you have had to face in knowing what you are, and how the years have treated you in remembering that you could not be so, you could not be this thing that you now claim you are. So we are unraveling the ball of yarn, if you would. And this first section was, again, about being aware and this is the beginning of the unraveling.

We have assignments for you now, which are to come, again and again, as this book continues.

We have asked you to identify those things in your life that are controlling you. Now we will change the pattern and ask you to see where you are controlling others, where you are operating from fear in such a way that you are creating requirements for others' behavior or for others to stand in the face of your will and do as you say.

This is actually important. We talked about relationships earlier in this chapter, and we talked about it at length earlier in this text. We will tell you again, as this book continues, and we will discuss healthier operations in discourse that you can bring to your companions. But as you self-identify as Word, you begin to come into your knowing, and you can be in charge in wonderful ways. But this also means that ways that you have controlled others through your fear, through your ego, trying to require others to conform to its will must be understood and dismantled. So each day, please ask yourself, "Where am I doing what I am doing? What do I know about myself today as I continue this road towards my conscious awareness of myself as a Divine Being?"

We are going to ask you now to respond to a question. We would ask you, what does it mean to you to embody yourself as your Divine Self? What does it mean?

We want to be very clear for each of you to know that this is not about abandoning the self that you are. It's about reclaiming the self that you are. And if any of you are operating on the presumption that at the end of this path *you* will not be there, you are very mistaken. Self-abnegation is the antithesis of the work that we are doing with you. This is about self-love and the understanding of the self as the one who stands in her dominion. So why you are doing this must become conscious as well.

We will give you an offering. We will state that our hope is that you are embarking on this journey to the benefit of your own self-worth, of your own ability to know yourself in fullness in dominion, and to serve the will of the Higher Source that you are an aspect of. For in that comes great gifts, great love and the promise of a new love embodying as you. And love, we will say, is the gift of the Creator to His creations.

We will stop today with this reflection:

We see each of you in your perfection as you stand today. We see each of you in the promise that you hold to be in manifestation as your Divine Self and we see each of you as an ally in the recreation of consciousness on this plane. So we extend our love to you and we extend our guarantee that you are not alone in this passage. We shelter you, we support you, and we offer you "I am Word." So be it.

Thank you both and stop.

Book Two

ALIGNMENT
TO LOVE

THE RIVER

Day Nine

We're ready to talk again about love, and the requirements of feeling and knowing and acting and being in love in alignment. "I am in love in my alignment with my own knowing of my worth." Let's start there.

We have discussed worth already and the belief that worthiness to the self as an aspect of God is primary to aligning yourself to the frequency of Word. As you have begun to work with this consciously, you have already activated yourself at a new level, and this is the level that you are now operating from in congruence, or alignment, with the light.

Now we will say light. Light is a frequency. And there are gradations of light that you can work with. And the frequency of Word, which is light in action, God in action, is the Source frequency of all creation. Now you can think of it this way: There is a vast ocean. And in this ocean there are inlets and there are rivers that connect to it. But all the waters spring forth from the vast ocean that we will call Source. You are working directly now with that aspect of the self that is incarnating as Source. You are this, in fact, as we have stated. You are being re-membered to this through this work and this instruction.

Now believing yourself to be out of love, or out of alignment, with the Creator has the immediate effect of moving your consciousness a step out of the way to the bank of the river, as it were. Now in fact that is only a false construct. You are always in frequency, you are always an aspect of the Creator, but your sense of flow and being in alignment with the frequency can shift and does shift depending on your availability to be in alignment with it. Now alignment, we will say again, is your congruence with it in frequency.

To decide today that you can be in this shape, in this body, that you stand in today and still retain your availability to become one with frequency has been a huge step for you. And what we are doing with you now, essentially, is taking you from the bank by the river's edge and throwing you in the river to go into alignment with the Great Source. That will be part of the teaching that comes forth in this next section of this work.

Now to be thrown implies no choice, so that is not the right word. But it's a wonderful illustration of someone who dives from the foundation that they have believed to be true into a new frequency that will carry them forward. So this is a blessing, as you perceive it as such. To decide, in this moment, that you are willing now to go into agreement with this next stage of this process will prepare you for the work that is to come. And there is work to come in this next section.

We spoke of awareness only to show you where you stand in your awareness in the life that you choose today. And now we are showing you what happens when you disembark from that structure and align to a new one. As you go there in journeying, in consciousness, you will be carried through your mission by those things that you decide are imperative for your soul's growth. If you can imagine that you know already on a very fundamental level that there are things that you came here to learn, you are going to begin to attract those to you in your consciousness in ways that you can work with constructively to transform you. So you stay in choice, but you are the one always emitting your frequency, and your frequency is emitted through your conscious thoughts. So the process of making you conscious through your awareness was a requirement to align you to this next stage of productive movement forward.

We like the river as a metaphor for where you are being taken. And we will show you what it is through visualization.

Imagine, right now, that you are standing on the bank of a river. And what you are tethered to on this riverbank are all of those structures that you have believed you required in order to stay safe, in order to self-identify as the one in their knowing in a landscape that was prepared for you by beliefs that were born out of being controlled. Imagine that you see all around on this riverbank a world that you have existed in that you have accepted and did not believe that you could move beyond in consciousness.

Now we are speaking dimensionally here, on one level. And we are also speaking about your experience of yourself, very practically, in your landscape, the landscape that you created in agreement with everyone else that is the landscape that could only be available to you at the level of consciousness that you had attained, with all of the limitations intact that were keeping you from your knowing.

So now you look around and you acknowledge it. And you decide in this moment to take responsibility for it.

"I am seeing what I have created. I understand that I chose these things. And I witness them as they are, as manifestations, out-picturings of my consciousness. And as I allow this knowing, I allow myself to release those things that I no longer require to tether me, to keep me on this riverbank of self-identity. I allow myself to release those things that require releasing in order to free me from my past creations. As I do this, I move out of fear in the knowing that my Higher Self, my Conscious Self, the Christ within me, will provide me with all that I need in order to make myself whole. I am now choosing to release the past in significant ways that will allow me to embark on this next stage of my journey."

As we say this with you, we see you moving into your awareness of your own freedom, of your own sense of releasing those ties, those attachments, those beliefs that have kept you tethered to a history of self-abnegation, of control, and of suppression by outside authority. All of these things now are to be witnessed and to be seen for what they are: systems of fear out-pictured. Systems of control accepted. And these are now being released in Word.

"I now set this intention: I am now choosing to release myself from all binding structures that are tethering me to systems of control and fear in consciousness. As I take responsibility for my creations I see that I am the one in charge, and have the ability and the freedom to release them in love. I am Word through this intention to release those things that bind me to fear and to control. Word I am Word through this intention. Word I am Word."

Now you are engaging in a process. And this next book, "The Alignment to Love," will create for you the showing of the way to carry you to this next stage of liberation. We are taking you to the riverbank and we are standing with you by the water's edge. You are now standing in the water beside us, and we are raising you high in love and in healing. And as we raise you high, we are lifting you in consciousness and we are showing you your magnificence as a free man, as a free woman, as a child of God embodying himself as Word. And as this is done, we release you in wonder. And we release you in love to your own experience of yourself as your worthy self. And we release you to the river to begin to flow.

We are now telling you this. You are in the river, you have always been, but now you are free to move. You are free to ride a current that is created in love and its intention is to carry you to the ocean, where you will become unified in your senses, in your consciousness, in your frequency with the love of your Creator.

We are carrying you, we are freeing you, and we are waving you well. This is the end of the end of the introduction to Book Two, which we will call "The River." Now we would like to move on to the next chapter.

SEVEN

FREEDOM

Day Ten

We're ready to talk. And "Freedom" is the chapter. And freedom is the news. And freedom is where we are taking you in this journey of congruence to your Divine Self. As you are operating from your Christed Self, from that spiritual aspect of the self that is unified with the Creator, there are no errors in consciousness. There is only truth. And in that truth comes alignment in your knowing in a new way where you are led to where you are meant to be every moment of your name, "I am Word."

Now we said "every moment of your name" intentionally because it's a way of saying, "As I am incarnating in my knowing, I am calling to me everything I need to bring forth my understanding of what is required of me." As you choose to stand in your knowing, in your Christed Self, what you stand on is your truth and, consequently, where you are at any given time is manifested from that place and cannot be otherwise.

Now the transition that you have to make in order to get here is where we have been taking you, in a way, one step at a time through one sense, through one body, through one piece of your knowing at a time. Now to understand, first, that your first requirement was to know where you were in order to know where you need to go, you can understand that where we are taking you is a place that has not been traveled by you yet.

Now we will tell you this: The map is a funny one. The map does not look like a map, because the map is your consciousness. And while you would prefer a cookbook and a bunch of recipes that will tell you what the cake will be, we cannot give you that in those practical terms, quite simply, because you are the recipe, you are the ingredients, and you are the cake come into form in your majesty. And this happens through you individually as you attend to your knowing in consciousness. As you create in your knowing, what you bring forth is truth. That is lesson number one. As you create in your knowing, what you bring forth is truth.

Now how do you know if you're in your knowing? Well, we've addressed this somewhat in the previous chapters, but we want to tell you now that it is through the activation of consciousness *in awareness* and *in congruence* with the Divine Self that one manifests from a place of knowing.

Now this is done very simply. "I am in my knowing" claims this for you in truth. It is a simple declaration, but as this is understood by you, you can begin to work with it consciously. It's not a lot different than saying, "I am walking." Now if you're not walking, you will not be walking. You can say it, you say can you're in Piscataway and not be there, and you will know the difference. But to state, "I am in my knowing," amplifies this aspect of this self in truth. "I am Word through my knowing" amplifies the Divine Self in this aspect of truth.

Now we want to talk about freedom and what this is. And this is exciting for us to tell you. To be in your freedom is to be in your majesty as a Created Being and to be without those tethers to requirements that you have believed were needed in order to bring you into alignment with cultural norms, or norms that you have believed were needed by you to adhere to systems of control.

"I am in my knowing of where I am *not* in my freedom" will actually give you the information that you will be requiring in order to move forward fully, in congruence with this intention.

"I am now choosing to stand in my freedom. And I am now aware that all that is before me is created in conscious choice in alignment with my Creator. Period. As I move forward, I change my knowing to align me into congruence with Divine Will and with my own requirements for my freedom. I am Word through this intention. Word I am Word."

"I am in my freedom." How does that feel when you state that intention, when you claim that as your truth? "I am in my freedom." How are you not in your freedom at this moment in time? Where are you right now? Where are you reading this text? Where in your life, in this very moment, are you not in your freedom in choice?

You are choosing to turn the page, or not. You are choosing to read the letters that are printed before you. You are choosing where you are sitting, or standing, or wherever you are, because you are there. Now in this simple moment you can declare your freedom. And if you start here in this simple moment, "I am in my freedom," you can begin to out-picture that in other places, in other systems, in other areas of your knowing as you operate about your days. Period.

Now we will tell you this. The structures that are limiting you in any way you can see are structures that you are in congruence with. And we will say this very, very clearly: You are in congruence with them individually *and* collectively in consciousness. When the individual chooses to move out of alignment with collective agreement, things happen, and they may not always be pleasant, and they can be ramifications of choice, but please understand that more than likely they are ramifications of states of consciousness.

If my belief is that I will be rejected by my family if they know that I love someone of the same gender, I will create that experience. If I know that I will be fired from my job if I speak my mind, you are sure to get it. Now we are not telling you that other people don't have their own limitations in consciousness and you are going to rub up against them and perhaps irritate them. But we will tell you this. As you manifest your truth, you go into a higher frequency and in this higher frequency what is created is changed.

Now your belief, in this moment, that the family will reject you, the boss will fire you, or whatever else you want to imagine that could possibly come from defying or releasing an expectation of the self to adhere to cultural norms are in fact a reflection of your own systematized belief in punishment.

We will tell you this again: You believe that if you are yourselves in your fullness, you will be punished. Now we will tell you where this comes from. This comes from a matrix that has been agreed upon by you all for thousands of years. It is the matrix of fear and it is the disassembling of this that we are working towards now.

Where does this come from? Why is there this thing?

The belief in limitation is a belief in control. And we will state this: There are frequencies and there have been frequencies that have an invested control over your freedom. If we would say what they are, we would move into language that would be silly to some of you, but we will tell you this: The frequencies that adhere to the frequency of control are running the show whenever you are frightened, whenever you are disempowered, and you are, in fact, party to the creation of them.

Now we talked about this a little bit in our last text. But there are, in fact, frequencies that are created by man through fear, and when these things are born they can operate independently from the energy structure of the being that has created them. We will give you an example, and we will call this an example of parasitic frequency.

When someone has a frightening intention for themselves—"Oh my God, something terrible will happen"—and they continue with that thought again and again and again, that thought is compounded and takes up residence in the energy frequency of a system. These things, in funny ways, can be seen as creations of the self, or low-level energies that attach and then work towards their mission, which is to continue to feed their need to exist. Now you have issues and you say, "Why doesn't this go away?" Well, the first question is, what is your attachment to them? Why do they stick around and what investment do you get in them?

Now Paul is wondering if we are sidestepping something. "Are you talking about parasites in frequency that can be attached or moved?" And in fact yes, we are. There are low-level energies that we will call astral frequencies that actually are available to the energy systems and can use them in their way.

We are not talking about demons. We are talking about frequency. And when we move into a higher range in our frequency, we are no longer led by them. You are no longer able to hold them because your frequency is operating at a high enough level that they cannot be there. You have risen above them, as it were. Someone yesterday asked Paul if rising above something was turning the other cheek, and in fact, that is the case. When you rise in frequency, the lower frequencies can miss you entirely.

When you are operating at a low energy in vibration, you attract that which is at lower energy. There is a reason that you have heard the expression "Water finds its own level." It is very, very true, and it's a perfect example or illustration of congruence, and that is this lesson. So your freedom, finally, is about moving up and above the lower level. "Like attracts like." "Water finds its own level." What level do you intend to express in your frequency?

We have given you a manifestation in consciousness through the claim, "I am in my knowing."

> "I am now choosing to live my life in accordance with my higher knowing. I am now choosing to liberate myself from any low-level frequencies that I may have attracted or I may have created through my fear, through my trauma, or through any interactions that I have had that may have brought this into manifestation. I am Word through this intention to stand in my freedom. Word I am Word."

We will not talk about frequency in terms of good or bad or good or evil. What that does, frankly, is compound a belief in separation, and it also compounds the systems that would strengthen a belief in the power of negativity. We are actually rising above it. And that is not engagement. When you engage with something in consciousness you are activating it, and then you move into congruence with it. And if it's a low-level frequency, guess what, everybody? That's where you're going to hang out.

Healing occurs in consciousness when one rises above the initial construct that was created so that it no longer has power. The child that was frightened of the dark now learns that it's safe to be in the dark, and that is a lifting in consciousness that renders the old belief powerless. It no longer exists. So the choice you have now is to raise your frequency and to align with it at a higher level so that your choices are in congruence with it. Do not go into thinking about good or bad, because what that does frankly is maintain the duality that you are moving beyond. When we say that there is lower and higher energy, we are not telling you anything scary.

You have all had very low frequency at different times in your life. And many of you have had interactions with low-level frequency that can actually manifest in many kinds of behavior and yes, we will say that will include much addictive or compulsive activity which then seeks to replicate itself through your energies. That is why when you let go of an attribute of the self that has been in manifestation that seeks to control, you can sometimes engage with a bit of a battle. But we are telling you that battling an addiction or a compulsive behavior has never healed it. Acclimating to it, accepting it, and then rising above it in consciousness to the place where your energy frequency can no longer contain it is the freedom you need.

Now are there ways to keep your frequency low? Absolutely. Greed. Fear. Envy. Sloth. Anger. Jealousy. All of those things that have a bad rap were given that bad rap for a very good reason, and this has little to do with conduct or moral worth. This has to do with how it appeals to lower frequency. When you are operating in your anger, you are calling in anger and you are moving into congruence with the sea of anger, or the matrix of anger, that is available to you. Everybody does. When you are moving into your envy, you are not hurting somebody. You are hurting yourself because you are, frankly, removing yourself from the freedom to create what you need by seeing instead a place of lack and asserting that you are not worthy of the good that you seek. When you present sloth, you are really presenting a fear of moving forward in higher frequency.

When you are operating in high frequency, you are free. And what you do when you are free is always in light. So if you are lying in bed and don't want to move and it's not because you are tired or processing something emotionally but it is because you are lazy or acting in that frequency, you can bet that your frequency is not high and you are not aligning yourself to Divine Will.

Now we don't want to talk anymore about lower energies. That is not the point of the book. But it is very important that you under-stand that your responsibility for your frequency includes becom-ing aware of where your energies are being controlled. And we are not talking, again, about demons; we are talking about creations, and things created in fear that have taken on their own energies. In our last text we described these as boulders. And this time we are opening it up to include frequency that is attacking itself in know-ing through lower forms.

We will tell you this: You are free at a moment's notice to give up an attachment to negative frequency in any day or night. You are the one in charge of your knowing regardless of what you think and regardless of the messages that you have inherited culturally or through mandates that you have accepted to be true because you were not able to see outside the box, as it were. So freedom for you, quite simply, means, "Am I outside of the box? What is the box? And where do I go with it?"

Now Paul is asking, "Isn't that more work in awareness?" And absolutely it is. More work in awareness is required. However, you cannot get out of a box until you know you are in one. So how about this? As you go about your day, identify in moment-by-moment understanding of where you are in your box. Where are you oper-ating out of ascribed behavior and not in your freedom? Now we tell you this again: You are *always* in your freedom. But we are say-ing, where have you believed that your freedom had a wall around it? Where have you believed that you would be punished if you overstepped a boundary?

Now we are not talking about breaking laws, and we are not talking about defying somebody, because that is actually not neces-sarily an expression of freedom. It might very easily simply be an expression of aggression. And robbing a bank is not about being in your freedom. It's about a belief in lack that you are not being supplied with what you need, so it is an action born out of fear and cannot be high frequency. But if you have created constructs throughout the day that are creating a box for you, see that they are there and then decide in that moment that you are no longer bound by their expression. Period.

"I am Word through my intention to self-identify as a free man, as a free woman, in all aspects of my life and my experience is now moving to reflect this in fullness. I am Word through this intention. Word I am Word."

Now freedom as we speak of it begins in consciousness. Can you believe for a moment what it would feel like not to be frightened of anything? Can you imagine that for a moment? How amazing would that be?

Now the fear structures that have contained you are all about control, and as you know already, control is born out of fear. So how you begin to identify the fears that are in fact keeping you from your freedom is an exercise that we would like to take you in. Now this is familiar to many people, but we will tell you this: Becoming aware is a process. And writing on a piece of paper everything that frightens you that you can imagine will be an exercise in order for you to see how much of your time and energy is invested in protecting yourself from fear or worrying about what could possibly happen. So make the list. Let it be a long list. Let it include the silly things, and the radical things, and the things that you might feel ashamed of. But then write it down and see it before you.

Now then, what you will do is you will look at it and see it for what it is: an out-picturing of your consciousness, a map of those things that are tethering you to fear. Now what we will do with this is as follows:

"I am now choosing to release myself from those fears that have kept me in limitation. I am now aware that I no longer am required to create from my fear in order to self-identify with who I thought I was. I am now free of those fears that have created my experience in ways that I am willing to let go of. And I am choosing now to relinquish the need to engage with them in my consciousness. I am free. I am free. I am free. I am Word through this intention. Word I am Word."

Freedom, we will tell you, is freedom from fear. Understand this, please. Freedom is freedom from fear. When you are operating from your fear, you are not free. And ninety percent of how you operate is unconscious and much of it is motivated by fear.

Now Paul is wondering, "Can it really be that easy? Can you make a list and then say a word and let it be banished?" Yes. We will say it is, to the extent that you align your frequency to the higher light. You understand this already because we explained it. But when you rise in frequency, you are rising above those things that have created fear. Those no longer have impact. Now that is very different than going down the ladder, as it were, with an axe and doing battle with your fears. What a mess.

Now we are not telling you that you may not confront these things in form. In fact, when you do you are being gifted with an opportunity to become free of them on an experiential level. Paul has had an experience: Every time he looks for an apartment all he sees in the street are people looking for apartments. It's very funny to him and he doesn't get why it happens. How can somebody run into five brokers in a two-block stretch on their cell phones describing apartments? The real reason is he has put into his frequency "I am looking for an apartment" and, consequently, what the Universe brings him are people who are sending apartments all over the place. And that is that experience.

When you are frightened of something, you call it to you. Now if you call it to you, you have the choice in how you deal with it in consciousness. You can work with it and realign yourself to the higher frequency in order to become free, which is to say, you recognize it for what it is, and then you move forward in your higher frequency, or you go into it, you do battle, and let the best man win.

But frankly, most of you when you are engaging in your fear are surrendering to the fear and letting fear have its way. There is really nothing there but an abnegation of self-worth and power in frequency.

"I am Word through my releasing of those fears that would keep me in low frequency. I am Word through this intention. Word I am Word."

Now you don't have to be frightened that if you claim these intentions you will call your fears to you in terms of creating them in order to work through them. That is not what we are saying is happening, and Paul is already bracing himself for an onslaught that is not required of him. Just because you are working on this does not mean that you have to create from it. And the reason we ask you to write a list is to see these things for what they are: simple creations in consciousness that have not come into manifestation. So again we tell you, yes, you can release things through intention and through bringing your frequency to a higher level where they will not be out-pictured.

You can remember things that scared you when you were a child. And you can remember that at a certain point your consciousness changed and they no longer became frightening. There wasn't somebody under the bed. Your mother did come from the trip all safe and sound. Whatever it might be. And those fears that were operating at that level of consciousness changed. They no lon-

ger operate in the adult self that has come into a new understanding.

So we will tell you this: That is exactly what we are saying here.
As you move into higher frequency, your experience changes. Your
consciousness is what is creating your life. And we will take you
now into the next exercise, which is an exercise in knowing the self
in your freedom.

"I am now choosing to experience myself as free."

Now we would like you to make a list of everything and anything you can think of that looks like that is not the case in your life.
"I am not free because . . ." List the things that you feel that are keeping you out of your freedom. And do this list now, please. And it can
be anything: a disability, a marriage that is not working, a place that
you are living that is problematic, a health issue. But write them all
down. Now once this is completed, we want you to look at them and
begin to decide that you are free in each of these areas. You are still
free to move. You are still free to change your consciousness in that
relationship, or withdraw from it. And your disability can be the
way that you move through this experience in wonderful expression
of who you are as a being. So those things that you have said that
are, in fact, not limitations will be allowed to be liberated.

Now understand this: If you believe yourself to be handicapped,
and we use that word in the broadest sense, you will be. But always,
always, always understand that conscious choice will choose the
higher way of self-identifying. And we say those things that you
perceive yourself to be out of your freedom in limitation with can
be transformed, first in consciousness, and then through the out-
picturing of your experience as a free man, woman, being of Christ,
of conscious intention: "I am Word through my knowing of myself
as free."

Now we want to finish this chapter with a description of you in your perfected state. And what this really means is who you are in truth outside of those things that you have believed yourself to be. You are emitting frequency always, and the frequency that you are emitting has different gradations of color and light depending on how you feel. So today, right now, we want to do an exercise in energy, and we want to activate you again in the Divine Light that you are. So we will take you once more into your hearts.

"I am now choosing to activate my Divine Self in fullness. I am now choosing to align myself to the frequency of light. And I am now choosing to become aware of myself as a being vibrating in frequency."

We will tell you this. How we see you is perfect. Perfect, perfect, perfect. You are perfect creations having an experience here on this plane that is teaching you and bringing you into an awareness of who and what you are in truth. So when we say, "See yourself as you truly are, hold a vision for who you are," you would like it if we were to tell you, "You look great, you have a lot of money, you're surrounded by loving friends and living in the home of your dreams in perfect health."

Well, guess what, everybody. That's your choice. That's part of your choice, at least, as you begin to manifest in consciousness. But holding the vision of who you are in perfection means something very, very different.

"I am now choosing to realize and to know myself in my freedom as an aspect of the Creator in form. I am now choosing to align my energy field in full activation of my divine worth, my divine accessibility to my own information and to my awareness of my remarkable splendor. I am now choosing to see myself as beautiful in the highest way possible, which is, of course, as an aspect of the Creator in form. I am Word through my being. Word I am Word."

Please do this with us now.

Go into your heart center and activate the light in the very center chamber of your heart between your breasts at the level of the heart chakra. And imagine turning that light on. This is indwelling Christ, the Creative Self, and the Inner Light. These are the aspects of the self that we call the God within. And activate that self now. Allow that light to be turned on in its beauty and let the light now begin to move now through your being, all the way up and all the way down until it enfolds you completely in physical form. And now the light begins to extend beyond the form you stand in and radiate all around you in bliss.

"I am now choosing to know myself as I am. I am an aspect of the Creator in form and I am in my freedom."

Your perfected self is the self you are. You are the gift. You are the light that you have been waiting for. It has always been with you. You have forgotten and you are now being re-membered.

Now the freedom we wish for you is a freedom of choice. You must always be in your will fully, and the highest way to be in your will is to align the will to the Divine Self so that the choices that are made are coming from a higher place. We will get to this in the next chapter. And we will close this chapter now by telling you a story.

There was once a woman who believed that she was not loved. And as she went through her experience, her choices manifested to prove that that was true. And one day, when she realized that all of her life had been without form in love, and that there had been no love, she chose, for a moment, to see herself as the God she knew was there somewhere might see her. And the reflection that came to her was one so beautiful that she realized once and for all that the only one who was not loving her was her. And she became free in that moment to embody as love.

The journey that we are taking you on, everybody, is the journey of embodiment as love. You are in the river and we are taking you to the sea.

God bless you each. Thank you and goodbye.

EIGHT

WILL AND
DIVINE WILL

Day Eleven

We'll talk in a minute about light. But first we want to contend with issues that are facing the channel and his friend as they move forward in dictation. The responsibility to be aware of one's own energy field includes monitoring the information that you access through the media. And it also requires you on a very basic level to see how you can be controlled through those outlets that would give you information.

Now we are not denying that terrible things happen in the name of God, and all of those things that are stated as acts by people who said that they were acting in the name of God were actually produced by psychosis or by lower frequencies informing behavior. The first thing you all have to understand is that Divine Light does not cause pain. And truth, at its essence, does not cause pain. It cannot.

Now when we say truth, we are not talking about a blunt offering or statement about someone's behavior. We are talking about a grand statement such as "I am in the Word." Now we say that is a grand statement because it bypasses structures of limitation, and therefore requires you to expand your consciousness to a new place of inherent worth. And by doing this you are defying a cultural norm that would state that who you are is a bunch of body parts and a brain walking about in this crazy existence where all these problems exist.

Please understand now that to keep your frequency at that level denies you your own experience of love. And understand, please, that when people create from a place of fear, the constructs that they create are distorted, and by distortion we mean that they are out of congruence with Divine Love.

Now we want to say something about will today, and the action of will. You have all been endowed with the ability to choose. And we spoke of this in our last chapter. Choice is an aspect and a by-product and an activity of the function of will, and will begins in consciousness. What you choose is what you choose is what you choose. Period.

Now the center of the will, as you expect it to be, is in operation as you go about your business and make choices. "I know what I am doing, I am in my will," and that is very, very true. And on that level we have already taught you that you must be accountable to the choices that you make and ask yourself bluntly, "Where are they coming from? Am I moving into my freedom? Am I aware of my choice as freedom, or am I acting on a basis of control or fear that I have inherited and acclimated to?" We have spent time on this and we have an expectation that this is understood by you at this juncture.

Now when we talk about will, we are also talking about higher will. And once you understand where you operate from on a day-to-day level in your choices, you can begin to shift the focus of your will to align it to the higher vibration and the higher frequency so that your will, which means *what you choose,* moves into congruence with the will of Source.

Now Paul is wondering, "Does this mean that Source has a will that we are expected to act from?" Not really. That would be an over-simplification and also discredit you as one who is capable of choosing your choices. But to be in congruence actually implies *alignment* and your will in congruence with higher frequency brings your will up into a handshake, as it were, with the higher levels of choice that are available to you.

Now the information that you have been gifted with thus far has been illustrative. We have told you what happens when you operate from one place or from another, and those choices that are made from a higher choice or frequency always bring about manifestation in a higher regard. That is understood. But we want you to know now that where you are being taken is into a new place of seeing the self as worthy of accessing that aspect of yourself that knows and corresponds to the requirements of your soul's choices for you. And by this we mean what the soul requires to move into higher frequency.

When you have a choice, in any moment, to go with the lower or the higher, you can choose the higher if you want to. And the results of your life, those things that respond to those choices, will become higher in accordance. Period. But the bondage that you have to your own self-will is something that we will discuss now.

To understand right now that the will that you correspond to most times is a lower-energy way of self-identifying, then you begin to move through it to access the higher information.

We will give you an example of what we mean: "I want to stay in bed all day. I don't want to go to work." Well, more than likely, you are operating from lower will, and you understand that the results of that will be calamitous. If you continue to do that day after day, things won't happen that are required to happen to get you where you need to go. Now while that is obvious, what we have not given you are the subtleties of the way the will manipulates. And it can be this simple: "I know that I don't need the pizza, but why not live it up?" "I know that my date's not available to me, so why am I pushing my agenda?" "I know what I am doing is based in fear, but I'm human, so what?" And you honor the choices through will that are not going to serve you, and you make excuses and you bypass opportunities for growth.

Paul is wondering, "How do I align my will with Divine Will? How is this done?" Now, Paul, we want to tell you that it is done through choice and through surrender to honoring the frequency of Word.

> "I am now choosing to Word through my own will to align my will into accordance with Divine Will. I am now aligning my will in alignment with the knowing of what I require to make this so. I am choosing now to offer myself at this frequency to the higher frequency that would accord my will into agreement and into congruence with Divine Will. I am Word through this intention. Word I am Word."

Now Paul is wondering, "Isn't this like a third step in a twelve-step program? Isn't that a simplification? I can just say to God, take my will and do with it what you want?" Yes and no. It is simple. Why do you require to make it more complicated? Simply saying, "I am willing to let my will be in alignment with the higher will" offers your will the opportunity to shift into the higher frequency. Why does it require more complication than that?

Now Paul, if you understand that the work that we have done so far is about manifestation and embodiment of higher frequency, you can already see that this is a somewhat different system of acclimation in frequency than you have been benefited from previously. And we will tell you why. The Word as a frequency, although it has been present and active since the beginning of time, is now available to you each to work with and through as frequency; however, the extent that you are in low frequency and not able to align with it makes it impossible for you to serve as a vehicle, or a channel, or an embodiment of this energy.

So the process of lifting you up, which, as we have explained, is about un-tethering you, aligns you to the lifting in vibration that you require in order to bring this through you. Now this is not different, in other ways, than systems that have been created that encourage you to surrender and to give yourself ways of identifying frequency in lower forms so that you can move past them. But there is a distinction here.

We are creating for you a system of embodiment of higher frequency. And the reason that this is happening now is the energy is available for this. And the requirement of this time is for man to access himself at this frequency in order to know who he is. This is quite different than embarking on a self-improvement ritual, or declaring that you are no longer going to engage in a compulsive behavior. Those things are wonderful and we are grateful for the systems that are in place that align to these needs in wonderful ways. But you understand now that the frequency of this planet is realigning itself and, consequently, the consciousness of all who inhabit this plane are being required to transform and realign because that is what is needed to disjoin from the frequency of fear that has been operative for too long.

As you create through your will in alignment with the Divine Will, you choose new things and those things that you choose will carry you up each step of the way. Imagine, for a moment, that you are walking around a path that wound around a mountain and there were signs pointing up and down at each turn. You always have the choice to go up the mountain or take it down a step. And each time you go up, you are creating a new opportunity to go up even higher, because that is where the path will take you.

So we are guaranteeing you now that as you align your will to the Divine Will, you will make the higher choices and you can, in fact, make this decision now:

"I am now choosing to align my will to the Higher Will in order to make those choices that will bring me into embodiment. I am Word through this intention. Word I am Word."

Now fear will prevent it, and fear waits to do its job at every turn. If you can imagine for a moment that you are Little Red Riding Hood walking on her path, the wolf is what would stop her and devour her. But it is not possible, truly, when you understand that the wolf is a creation of fear. And the moment you decide that you can be honest in knowing that, you can move through it and continue on your way. But we have never seen a case where someone has gone through their alignment to higher frequency without having to contend with the initiations that befall the initiate as he ascribes to a path of spiritual growth.

Now we will tell you what this means. Each time you are walking on that path up the mountain, you have the little choices: "Do I go up, or do I go down?" "Is this in a higher way, or is this gonna take me lower?" And that's very, very good and you honor those choices and you move up. But, apparently, once in a while you will come to a crossroads where you will have to decide that what you require is change. And those changes that are presented to you in consciousness through out-picturings in your physical reality may contain those things that would create fear.

Now we will give you an example. If you are in a job you do not like but you are frightened of moving forward, and suddenly you have an opportunity to do what you've always wanted to do but the security that has been offered you previously will not be there, what do you choose? Do you choose the security of the job that makes you unhappy, that will continue to keep your frequency at a low place and stagnate the creative energies that would like to move through you? Or do you take the risk and go to the higher place where you don't have the assurance that you have had previously?

Now you can always ask yourself practical questions, and we are not encouraging you to be silly here. But if you can understand that the new choice holds with it creative possibility and higher frequency, you can understand that making that choice will incur fear from one who has an investment in security. Now we will tell you, what you choose is your business, but we would encourage you to go into alignment with your own Divine Self and operate from your will in accordance with the highest will as you make this choice.

Now please understand something. We are not talking about being foolhardy. We are not talking about throwing away your money on a scheme or on an investment that may fail because it feels funny and exciting to do that. That is simply silly and unworthy of being called an action born out of your Divine Will. It's usually an act of self-destruction. But we will tell you this: When you deny yourself an opportunity for growth in whatever form it appears in, you are usually honoring your fear. And what we mean by this is you choose the lower at the cost of the higher. You choose to stay in the job because at least you can count on it and you don't align to the possibility that what might be before you is a higher opportunity that will lead to others.

Now one way Paul knows to discern these things is through his energy system. And we will give you the opportunity now to learn what this system is. Imagine that you are invited to a party that you really don't want to go to, and your energy feels low and draggy, and you really don't want to go. In all likelihood, you don't need to go. But if you were offered that same invitation and you feel fear and excitement but you don't want to go for whatever reasons—you are too shy, it means breaking out of your box, you might not fit in, it's too far away—you should still honor the fact that your system is sending you the vibration in response of anticipation. And anticipation is a very good signal that this is something that will benefit you in your knowledge, in your advancement, and in your way to honor yourself in alignment with Higher Will.

So know this, please. When your response is low—"I don't want to go to that job interview, it's going to be awful"—well, you can create awful, but if your system is saying "No," that is very different than if your system is saying "I'm scared to go on this job interview, I'm scared I might not get it, why would they want me?" etc., etc., etc. When you have no response to something or low frequency, that is very, very different than if your system moves upwards and you are responding in fear in a good way, in an anticipatory way. Then that is an opportunity to move through the fear and go up a notch.

Whenever you have a big choice to make, this is a way to begin to learn how to navigate through your own energy systems to make choices that will bring you forth in higher frequency.

Now today we want to listen to you for a little bit. And that means we want to start answering questions that may have come up through the reading of this text so far. Now Paul isn't expecting this, so we will tell you what we mean. We have prepared some ideas that we want to refine through this discussion with you and the reader, and we will do it as follows:

Who am I?

Who you are, in fact, is an aspect of the divine operating in frequency having an experience of himself or herself in form. Who you think you are is a material being that is tethered to the reality that you have known thus far and believe to be true. Where we are taking you on this journey is a refinement of your energy frequencies that will realign you to the frequency of Word, which is God in action, the true Source, to bring you into congruence with it.

Now Paul wants to know, "What are the questions we are going to ask?" Well, we will tell you what they are and we will afford you an answer as we can.

Why do I do this work?

You do this work for two different reasons. You do this, first of all, to honor yourself as a Divine Being and to realign yourself to the possibility that you can manifest in this way and for your own highest good. And you also do this to support a vast transition that is taking place in consciousness. And as you become party to this, you align to it and you bring forth the changes that will support others in an exchange of frequency that will realign the grid of knowing on this planet.

Now the grid of knowing, we will say, you can call a collective unconscious or a collective knowing that is available to you, which means, essentially, that when you dip the ladle into the well, you are drawing from a higher frequency in your knowing. You are accessing an aspect of yourself that moves beyond personality and into congruence with vast knowledge. You are no longer operating in limitation.

Now we want to explain something to you. The denial of the self that you have been experiencing thus far is born out of several things: the fear of being this thing, the fear of defying those mandates or structures that you have accepted as true, and also a fear that if you do this thing you will incur punishment. And that is a way that you are being controlled.

Now we will answer this question: *Who are we?*

We are knowledge, we are consciousness, we have embodied at times, and we exist now in form and out of form. But we are here to serve you fully as you shift and own your own possibilities of consciousness as an aspect of the Christ or as Source embodying. Now this is done not because we are nice guys, but because this is where this planet is in its evolution. And the requirements to accord the self as love are needed to bring forth the radical change that is required.

How can such things happen when there is so much pain in the world?

That is the big question of today and that is the elephant in the living room. How can there be God when there is suffering? How can there be God when there is pain? We will explain this to you as we can. And this is a book in itself, so you will have to be patient with the information because we will get there eventually.

Some of the resistance that this frequency has is the ability to work through the channel as clearly as we would because he will shut down if he doesn't like what he begins to hear and go walk the dog and think about something else. And the reason for that is the magnitude of the information that would come through would be a little too much for his consciousness to fully handle right now. But as we work with him in systems of teaching, he will get there.

Now we will tell you. God does not create pain, God does not align to pain, you do. And as you create through your fear, you create trouble. But the pain that is in the world now is the result of thousands of years of conscious restriction that has borne pain and suffering. Your choice now as a species is to become responsible to the self that thinks and creates and to the brother that stands beside you. How can you fear pain when you can truly understand that there is a Source that is made of love?

Now we will explain what we mean here. The evil that you see, and that is not a word we like to use, is an out-picturing of consciousness and it is controlled through an out-picturing and an agreement at a level of matrix that you have all engaged in. Now there are reasons that people have experiences in this life that you cannot understand or cannot accept as a good thing. And some of these, in fact, are chosen prior to incarnation by the soul in order to balance karma or to learn certain lessons that will be of benefit to others in later lifetimes. If you can imagine that it takes a form of humiliation for some to learn true humility, you will then understand that what is required of you is that lesson, so that you can learn it in order to be a vessel later on when that service is required of you.

We are teaching you the discipline that you need so that you no longer have to incur the kind of karma that you have created for yourselves. And by this we mean, when you are not operating out of fear, you are not making those choices that create pain. And consequently you don't have to rebalance it or un-create it. It is being stopped before it could occur. So the teaching of this book in consciousness is here to serve you from preventing yourselves more pain, more dissolution of light, more pain in action and experience.

You each are responsible for your experience. You don't get it yet, and that is why we are reinforcing this again and again and again. But if you can understand right now that as you un-create through light, through bringing light or the Word through situations that need to be realigned to bring them into accordance with Divine Will, you can understand that you can choose the higher. And as you choose the higher, you don't create situations that result in harm to the self or to others. Now you can look at this personally or you can look at this globally, but as a critical mass is received in consciousness, you will all change. It cannot be any other way.

You have all gone into agreement with many, many things that you now take for granted. If we were to tell you twenty-five years ago that everybody on the planet could be in a communication system without a telephone in a manner of seconds and access all of the literature and information in the world, you would have thought us crazy and that is how rapidly a paradigm can change. You are all in agreement now that this can happen. You are all going to be in agreement, eventually, that you are an aspect of the Creator, and this will be proved through science, believe it or not, that is finally catching up with the teachers of old who have always said, "You are one with the Father and you cannot be otherwise." We are not teaching you anything radical in that regard. We are simply reinterpreting that message to bring forth a new frequency as it can now be embodied.

Why do I suffer?

That is the next question. In most cases, we are going to have to tell you, you are choosing it, and you are choosing it for several reasons. It feels right, it's what you know, and it gives you what you want, which is reaffirmation of your own sense of limitedness and inability to change and also because you are actually linking into a matrix of suffering when you do this.

Now we want to talk about congruence again in this regard. We explained to you in our last chapter that when you are angry, you move into congruence with anger, and we used the example of an ocean and a river. Well, that is the high frequency. But if you want to stay in your anger and be creating from that anger, you will begin to operate in congruence with lower frequency. So anything, frankly, that you choose to be in accordance with is what you link to and call to you in consciousness, and you are in your own land-scape, as it were, in accordance with what you have chosen for yourself.

Now what do you do with your anger when your experience it? Well, there are several things you can do, and the first thing is to express it, to give it some form in order to release it. Now it is very important that when you do this, you be in your discernment and you also be in alignment with your own knowing. It is not fair nor is it wise to unleash your rage on someone who is not requiring it. It is not their business. But that is very, very different than acknowledging that it is there and giving it some form or some way to release.

Paul was wondering after our last session, "Isn't it true that sometimes anger can be about empowerment?" And yes, that is true, but frankly, that is not really anger, that is self-esteem that is being responded to. So the anger, yes, can lead you to self-esteem, but it is only one path. If you realize, for example, that everybody at your job is being paid more than you are for the same work, you are going to get angry, but it may empower you to make change. So the emotional response you are having is simply a vehicle for you to move to the next level of action to call to you what you require.

The other way to release anger—and get this, everybody—is to disengage with the source of it. If you are so angry at somebody because they stood you up for dinner, what are you going to do with that feeling and where is that feeling attached to? Now you can let go of the need to have people in your life that don't respect you and the anger that you feel will be in service to that change, but what you really may be dealing with are your own issues of self-worth that have not gone expressed. So does that answer the question? "Not really," Paul is saying. "If I have been stood up at a restaurant, I am going to be good and angry. What do I do with it?"

We will tell you the first thing to do is to release the anger in love.

"And I am doing this through this intention. I am now choosing to release the frequency of anger in Divine Love. I am now choosing to release this fear that this anger is born out of and any attachments I may be having to outcomes or expectations based on others' behavior. I am Word through this intention. Word I am Word."

Now we spoke of others, and expectations of others, and that's really what's going on here. So we are not telling you to dishonor yourself by not having your experience. But we are telling you that you are still the one responsible for your experience regardless of whether somebody shows up or not. And the experience that you choose will be the one you have. And if you want to get good and angry and link into that matrix of anger, which of course we have said, is usually based in fear, then you will have that experience. But you are not required to. You can be free of this in experience as you align to a higher frequency. As you go up a notch or two or three in frequency, you will see very quickly that what you call to you will change. And we will go back to the metaphor of climbing the mountain with the winding path.

There will be times where you will confront something, an obstacle in the path that will require you to change your notion of who and what you are and who and what you thought you were. And we will say always that these are opportunities to transform the self in consciousness.

Now we want to ask you a question. If you could do something with your life right now, for the first time, what it would be? Ask yourself this now. "Would I climb a tree?" "Would I make love to someone that I want to and am in love with?" "Would I want the job of my dreams handed to me?" Imagine for a moment that you could have what you wanted. And we want you to know what this feels like in your energy field. Imagine yourself getting what you want and then move into the frequency of that in your energy field. How does it feel when you claim what you want? See what it feels like, please.

Now we are going to tell you something. You have just chosen something that you said that you wanted. You did it automatically. You didn't ask yourself, your Divine Self or that aspect of you that knows what it wanted. And now we want to do this exercise again:

Go into your heart, please, and go into alignment with your own Divine Self. "I am in my knowing. Word I am Word." And now ask that aspect of yourself that knows everything what it is you need, truly. Listen to yourself and listen to the answer that you get. "I am in my knowing, Word I am Word."

If it is the same thing that you asked for, your will and your knowing are in alignment. If your Divine Will is in accordance with what you need in consciousness, you can call it forth radically in action in consciousness. It can happen very, very fast. But right now most of you will find that there is a dissociation between what your Divine Self wants for you and what your consciousness, in its existing form, says you need.

Now when we bring these two things into alignment, the heart and the mind as it were, what you will create can be wonderful. Now we are going take a little break and resume this session tomorrow. We will thank you both and we will say to you this:

"I am knowing myself as in alignment with the Divine Will. And my experience of myself in will is manifested in ways that I can know and experience. I am Word through this intention. Word I am Word."

Stop now, please.

Day Twelve

We're ready now and we're allowing this to happen as it's required. Resistance to channeling comes up when the body that stands in the channeling and the consciousness that receives that channeling has resistance to the information. The reader has resistance when the information that comes through does not adhere to past requirements of what something should look like or feel like or sound like. This is all about predisposition to existing norms. If this does not look like a meal, I will not put it in my mouth. If this does not look like a house I know, I will not abide in it. If this does not look like someone I should want to meet, I will not say hello. And these are all limitations you are placing on your current experience. We are still working with the chapter named "Will and Divine Will." And that is the name of the chapter, "Will and Divine Will," and we will continue on with it for some time and then we will tell you when we are ready to move to the next subject and teaching.

The requirement for you today as a reader is to begin to see that you are in charge and that you have a will that operates independently at times from your higher knowing. As you can begin to see where your will is operating in independence from the Higher Will, you can begin to move in frequency to bring them into alignment.

Now when you say something like "I am in my will," you are affirming your willfulness. When you affirm, "I am in my knowing," you affirm you are in your knowing. When you affirm that your will is in accordance with the Divine Will, you are moving the will into alignment. However, you can understand the concern that stating that "I am doing the will of God" can be an excuse for all kinds of terrible things. So we want to give you a system that can allow you to operate this truthfully. The barometer always is truth, and truth you can feel through your system in resonance. When you tell a lie out of your mouth, you do not resonate with the truth. You always know that it's not true. And you have heard things said such as, "This does not ring true." "Ringing true" implies resonance, clearly. The sound is off. The resonance is not there. It is not true and consequently it must be a lie.

The same thing can be said for how you operate in your will.

Now we will not tell you that you do not walk around wanting things and activating the will in order to bring them to you in any way you can. You are programmed, as it were, to do such things. And there is nothing terribly wrong with that, to the extent that you are operating from your knowing, which then implies that the Divine Will is in operation.

However, we will tell you this. When you are operating from your thinking and not your knowing you can begin to make errors, because your thinking is based in supposition and your knowing is based in truth. So we would recommend that whenever possible, you know prior to taking action and consequently lift the will to the center of acknowledgment of the Divine Self. It doesn't have to be more complicated than that, in truth.

When you are deciding that your will is in accordance with the Divine Will, you must be in resonance with that in order to act. And we will tell you something else that is imperative. That does not take away your responsibility. You are not giving your permission to act on some external force operating from outside of your energy system. You are not telling the world that God on the cloud told you to do this silly thing. We are not talking about things like that in this text. We are talking about accessing yourself in your divinity, empowered as the Christed truth you are. So we are saying "you, you, you" are the one in charge, but the little you that you have claimed power from in the past is being supplanted in some ways by the integrity and thought and consciousness of the will and the identity and the knowing of the Higher Self.

So you cannot blame anyone. And to say, "It is God's will," is actually usually an act of arrogance and ego or fear. To say that to someone else implies that you are in the knowing and this is the absolute. Guess what? You may be in your knowing and your truth may be in resonance, but that does not give you the right to create a totem out of it and align it to the will of others.

Now let us explain this: Will operates on an independent level through the individual's ownership of their own experience. And you can know very well on a level of Higher Will that your child requires something in order to be well. "My son needs a better school in order to realize his abilities fully." Now that is very true, and that is something that you can know, capital "K," Know. And that is very different than saying, "I think my son's algebra teacher isn't very bright, or up to the task of teaching him, because he is so advanced." That's a thought. The knowing is that your son needs more school of quality.

Now your son may have a very different idea of what is required for him. Since you are in governance of your son, you actually have the authority to move him to another school. However, if you have a friend and you know that that friend, capital "K," is engaging in behavior that is not healthy or "should" be someplace else, that is your issue. That is not your friend's issue. You cannot govern their will through your choices or through your knowing. You can give them information, but they must move into their own accordance with their knowing in order to operate from it. You can stand in your knowing, and then you are in your truth regardless of what somebody else says.

You all go into agreement about authority and what is around you. We all agree that this is the date that taxes are paid. We all go into agreement that somebody is a celebrity because we are told that, so we assume it must be the right thing to think. And you are all thinking about these things in agreement. When you move into the smaller things that you assume you have control over, you can begin to operate newly in the identification of Word.

"I am in my knowing through this truth. I am in my acknowledgment of my own awareness as a Divine Being. I am aligning now to my knowing and my will is operating in accordance with my Divine Will."

Then you can work.

Now we will work throughout this book on two different levels: the level of the individual will, which is what we are discussing here, and the group will, which is finally the big one, which is the thing that is allowing so much of your experience to unfold and regiment in prescribed ways. So when we start off talking about you and your friend and what you know your friend should do, actually, we are moving into a larger illustration of what you think, or know, or decide to be true versus the governance that you exist in to be true.

So we will say this: You Know, capital "K," that your friend is in a bad relationship and you can say that to your friend. But it is your friend's authority and her own knowing and her own Divine Will that may have to dictate her own acknowledgment for this to be resonant for it to ring true for her. You do not mandate, you do not prescribe, you do not change the will of another through your own authority.

However, if you are in your resonance in truth, and you are speaking a truth that others are in resistance to, you may just be confronting their resistance. Everyone has to go through their stuff, as it were, in order to come into their own prosperity as consciousness. And that means that once you have defied a construct and moved beyond it, you can allow others to as well through your resonance energetically and also through your example as a Divine Being demonstrating his, her ownership of her own abilities in truth. But you cannot make someone change their will. To do that brings their will into a defiant place.

We will say that there is a great reason why people are taught best through example. Other than owning your own experience in the best possible way, you give others permission to acclimate to your frequency and to the resonance that is you in a vibratory level in their way without propositioning them in your intentions to bring them to this place that you are now standing in in vibration.

Now to understand what this means might require you to imagine yourself as a frequency standing on a street corner. So think of this for a moment. You are on a street corner and you are vibrating in high frequency. Those who pass you who are in a lower frequency will see this in a certain way through co-resonance. And you are giving them the option to up-leap their own systems through showing them how possible it is. This is actually not done through passing out a pamphlet or holding up a sign that says, "Raise Your Vibration 10 Cents." It's not like that at all. It is a demonstration of *being*. And as you are active in your Divine Self, your authority becomes present in frequency and in action. And we will explain this. In your actions as a Divine Being resonating at a certain frequency, what you choose will be radically different than what you would choose when you are operating from past behavior or lower frequency.

The desires that you have had that would take to fulfill the requirements of the old identity—"I need to be this," "I have to look like that," "What if I don't get this?," "What will they think of me if I am not that?"—all go right out the window because they are seen for what they are: out-picturings of the requirements of the ego to remain in accordance with a system of outside, external approval. Period. "If I don't adhere to what they think, I may not be a good person. I may not be a success. And oh, what a terrible thing that would be. Woe is me."

Now we don't want to make fun. But we do want to show you how ludicrous it is to define the self through those structures that are completely intangible and not permanent.

Imagine that you were the one who built the tower and said, "Everyone, come look at the tower!" And then the next day, an earthquake comes and levels the tower. You were the one who built the tower. The tower is no longer there. Your ability is, and your ability is quite wonderful, and you can do it again. But to define yourself through outside achievement doesn't make sense as much as you think. Because all that is matter is transferable and will not be here in a hundred years. Understand this, please. Your achievements are created in consciousness. And what your consciousness creates then, in matter, at a high level, will be of benefit to all. And those are achievements to be celebrated. But they do not define the individual. You do not know who built the bridge, who built the dam. You do know that the bridge and the dam are creations that support the well-being of many people. But the individual who created it was doing what they needed to do through their talents, through their industry, and not for public approval. You can see it that way simply.

What you create in consciousness will be reflective of who you are. But what you create is not who you are. Don't get confused by this. What you create is an out-picturing of your consciousness. It may inform everything else around it, but it is not who you are. And people get very caught up in trying to define themselves through external evidence of their worth: their bank accounts, their positions, their relations to the esteem of their fellows. However, these things, finally, are very transitory.

You operate from an energy system that is creating twenty-four hours a day. And you don't see most of what you create because it is too present. You focus things through Divine Will or through lower will in order to bring them into manifestation. And you do this all the time through your intention, or through your thought on a moment-to-moment level. There is a real difference between working on manifesting something through focused thought and the thoughts that you carry with you throughout the day. And we will say what this means: You choose to manifest a house and you do all the work that you have been taught to do in all those books you have brought to bring that into being. And we congratulate you because you have learned that your consciousness then informs matter and brings things into being.

The other way we want to talk is that you are always doing this, and that what you feel about you and what you see around you is also a by-product of this kind of consciousness. Now the work that we do in this book does not dismiss any other teaching about manifesting. The only difference we want to bring to you is the idea of conscious alignment to your own Divine Self to be the one who creates with you through conscious intention. And that is very different than saying, "I want a Jaguar in my garage so that I can feel successful." You can create from that place. You can use energy to manifest at that level. But believe me, friend, what you are doing then is contributing to the matrix of fear through recognizing and acting on those requirements of ego that are about identifying the self through what you own and your material worth.

Do we tell you you should not be happy and successful and living where you want? Absolutely not. We are telling you you should have what you want. However, and this is the huge difference, we are telling you that what you want in accordance with the Divine Self you truly are may be remarkably different.

If anyone were to tell Paul at the age of twenty-one that at the age of forty-seven he would be doing this, he would have had a good laugh and probably never spoken to that person again. This has been a process of understanding and realignment with will in order to bring this to be. It was not chosen at a conscious level. It was realigned in congruence with his will working in operation with the Divine Will, and there is much, much more to go.

This does not mean that if any one of you aligns your will to the

Divine Will, you will end up a crackpot, or a healer, or a mystic, or however you want to define it. It is not about that at all. It's about being who you truly are. Manifesting the Divine Self as who you are is always about realizing the full potential of the individual, their gifts, their abilities, their wonder, and their truth. It is not about not having things. It's about having those things that are a reflection of the worth, the inherent worth, that you truly are. And if you are building a dynasty to prove to yourself that you are worthy because, in truth, you feel very small and unworthy, you may find that your happiness comes to you through very different avenues than you have prescribed for yourself to succeed.

What is success? How do we define success in our realm? We don't, actually, because success implies a balancing and a scale. You think of failure and you think of success and then you think of duality and the realm that exists between these two points. We will talk, though, about realization and demonstration as opportunities to see that your merit is here and now.

We say already that you are always demonstrating through your consciousness. You do this through every waking moment of the day so you already have evidence of your conscious awareness and your power all around you. And of course it is true that when you change your thinking in consciousness, what you will bring to you is vastly different. We have said this again and again.

However, here in this chapter on will, we are prescribing a system of going into relation with the Divine Self to find out what you really need so that you do not operate from the paradigm of fear that says, "you should." "I should have a boyfriend, everybody else does." "I want a partner because I believe I have much to share with someone special to me" is a very different way of looking at that issue. But "I want a refrigerator that looks good with my stove" is very different than saying, "I need a refrigerator. My food will spoil without one."

You are operating from a higher place when you think in terms of your soul's requirements. We are not telling you that you should not have a nice refrigerator or partner that you enjoy being with. We would celebrate both of those things to the extent that you put them in their proper perspective. And when you understand, finally, that your will in accordance with the higher will will bring forth the wonder that you seek, you will be creating from a higher place.

Is there a simple way to determine whether what you want is from a high place or not? Yes, there is, and a very simple system can be handed to you now. When you want something in your life, do you ask why you want it? That's the answer. "Why do I want the new refrigerator?" "Why do I want the boyfriend?" "Why do I want the fancy car?"

You can answer those questions.

Now we are not telling you, for the final time, that there is something wrong with having those things. But we are telling you, when you are working through manifestation, you must ask yourself why you are working on this in conscious creation. If you are looking to affirm the ego that requires certain things to make himself feel important or successful in relation to others, you are making a big error. If you just want a great car to drive around in because you love driving and you appreciate the beauty of a beautiful car, have a party with it, there is nothing wrong with that. But you can understand right then and there that you are creating from a different place.

"I love my wife because she is so beautiful" is very different than saying, "I love my wife *and* she is very beautiful." Do you understand the difference in that one sentence? "I love my wife *because* she is so beautiful" merits your wife's worth as the object of your love to her beauty. "I love my wife. Period. And she is beautiful" is the beginning of a list of attributes that you would describe your wife with. It is not to say that that is the delineating factor. If you choose a partner because she is the beautiful one, you really have to look at yourself and see what your consciousness is creating and why.

A system of identification with others based on their physical appearance, to us, is crazy.

But then again, you must understand that we see beauty as who you are, capital letters, "Who You Are," on a higher level, and the form that you walk around in is an out-picturing of frequency, but it is not Who You Are.

Who you are in truth is a Divine Being, a perfect creation operating in Divine Will in accordance with the will of your Creator. Who you are in truth is a perfect being, once and for all.

"I am Word through my knowing of myself as a perfect being. Word I am Word through this intention. Word I am Word."

Now we will stop and say, thank you both. This will be the end of this chapter. We would like to continue today after a very brief pause. We are going to ask you not to speak and to continue in three minutes. Thank you both now and stop.

Word I am Word.

NINE

IDENTITY AND KNOWING

Day Twelve (Continued)

Okay, let's go back and talk about knowing in a new way. We will talk about knowing right now as *what* you are. This is a little bit different. "I am knowing what I am. I am knowing myself as Word."

Now up until now, we have discussed knowing primarily in terms of what you think and then moving into knowing as a different frequency, or a different way of attuning to your information. What we will discuss right now is your knowing of yourself as who you are as Word.

Now this has to do with constructs and self-identification, and this is important to understand. You have been told who you were ever since you were born. And you have been told what you looked like compared to other people, how you ranked on a scale of success or worth through external things; you have chosen to abide by these things as if they were real because you have moved into accordance with them, indoctrinated into them, and gone into agreement with them.

"Of course I am this, I am told I am this." Well listen,

everybody, you've been listening to who you were as described by others since you were old enough to comprehend the idea that you were this thing that you were told. So why not rally around this?

"I am an aspect of God realizing herself in this body and through this experience. I know I am what I am. I know what I am. I am that I am. Word I am Word."

The self-description that you take on becomes who you are. It is about requiring yourself now to move out of that system of external decision-making based on others' constructs and begin to align to a higher frequency. "I am in my knowing of what I am." This still feels abstract to Paul, and we want to bring it to you each in a way that you can operate with. And the way that we would like to do this is with a mirror, a physical mirror, that you will now sit before.

We want you to see what you see when you stare at your face in the mirror: "I am seeing myself as reflected back in form. And the picture that I see is made up of images that I am viewing with my eyes." How do you see yourself in the mirror? "My hair is too this." "I have nice that." "My teeth are a little this." "My cheeks are a little that."

All of the "this and that" that you are now is based in someone else's ideal of who you are. You have not made your own decision about any of this. If you were living in a culture where everybody's nose was big and the nose was being celebrated, you would say, "My nose is great." But because you have been systematized to a certain aesthetic principle, you ascribe to what has been given to you.

So right now, accept the fact that what you see in the mirror is you, but how you perceive you, how you decide you, is very much based on external information that has absolutely not a thing to do with you. Nothing. Why would you believe it? Why would anyone?

And if you can see right now that this is the level of agreement that you have gone into with cultural approval and systematized beliefs, you would change it in a second if you could. Can you? Yes. You are. You are changing these beliefs right now as you begin to monitor them and see them for what they are.

Control. This is all about control. If you did not need a little nose, there would be a lot of plastic surgeons out of work. If your body didn't need to conform to a certain set of criteria, there would a lot of doctors out of work prescribing things to make you look slender. If you can understand right now that the group thought has created this, and you can separate from group thought, you will be blessed.

Now your physical attributes are a shallow way to bring you into this instruction about identity and knowing, which is the title of this chapter, "Identity and Knowing." However, your experience of yourselves is still shallow, so we will start on the surface and work our way in. We are in "alignment" still as a great subject, and what you are in alignment with now is group consciousness and collective thought. How one removes themselves from collective thought is done as follows:

> "I am now experiencing myself as sense of worth, a sense of well-being, and a sense of wholeness outside of the matrix of public approval and requirements for group experience. I am now moving myself beyond those limitations prescribed to me in identity by any and all external authorities that I may have accepted, gone into agreement with, and approved of or internalized. I am now removing myself from a matrix of group think that is prescribed in fear or in control."

Now we want to tell you something. That is a decree, and we will seal it by saying this:

"I am Word through this intention to be free of group consciousness that limits me and that is born out of the ego's need and
society's need to control me in my self-identification. Word I am
Word through this intention. Word I am Word."

There is a lot of deception around this issue of collective consciousness. And of course, what we are working towards through this text
is an experience of collective consciousness that will transition this
planet into higher frequency. So we are culprits only in that we
agree that the will of the group can command and create wondrous
change. However, what we are doing with you is moving you out of
a discipline based in adherence to public, cultural, and planetary
norms that seek to control you and to limit you. And when we say
deception, we want to talk about certain things and ways that
people adhere to things culturally that they think are for benefit,
and in fact are not.

Now we want to talk about prescribed behavior for a moment,
and what is appropriate and what is inappropriate. And this is a
simple example for you to know: If someone passes gas in a restaurant, that is not necessarily inappropriate. But the amount of shame
or discomfort that person might feel as opposed to celebrating the
fact that he has a wonderful body that is doing what it needs to do
is simple. And you can all understand through that silly example
that you all have behaviors that you ascribe to and that you adhere
to out of public agreement.

We will say this: The ideal of political correctness was born out of
a place of unity, but it has created division and it is being used again
as a tool of separation. And language, we want to say to you, is one of
your primary ways that you have the ability to transform. "If I am
not inclusive in my language, I must be doing something wrong," or
"If I am oppressing someone through my language, I must be terrible." Guess what, everyone? Choose your words well. When you are

in consciousness, believe it or not, much of what you believe to be separation disappears automatically and creating divisions based on political correctness that are about idealizing things can cause trouble. Paul will give you an example from his experience.

Yesterday he spoke to a friend who said, "I hated that someone said that this was not an inclusive panel, and everyone on the panel got very frightened that they were not being inclusive in their language or in their gender, and in that moment began to shift into fear."

Now we will tell you this: When you are propagating fear, one of the easiest ways to do it is to tell someone that they are wrong. "You are wrong" immediately puts someone on the defensive. But wrong and right are divisions, and wrong and right behaviors are always systemized culturally. It is not wrong to eat the explorer in the Amazonian jungle where that is practiced. It's very wrong to eat your neighbor in Manhattan. Do you understand the difference?

Now cannibalism is a bad example, but if you can look at cultural dictates and how they are prescribed from block to block, from neighborhood to neighborhood, from country to country, you can see that there are vast differences. "When in Rome, do as the Romans," are the examples. The Romans used to feed the Christians to the lions. That is a funny example too in how much change occurs culturally over time. And what is appropriate one week, or one century, is vastly different than what is appropriate today. So your prescriptions for behavior are all based upon principles that are vastly changing and will continue to change.

The extent that you do not perceive yourself to be at one with your brother or one with your sister is the extent that you are perceiving yourself in separation. And this is the extent that you have rules and parameters to shut you down from that knowing. "I am not allowed to smile at the woman on the bus; she might think I am doing something wrong." "I am not able to laugh too loud; they will think I am silly." "I am not willing to raise my hand because people might laugh at me if I say the wrong thing." "I am not willing to go to the dance; my clothes are not good enough, or someone might disapprove of the fact that I am clumsy on my feet." "I will not go to the store and look at what's in the window because I could never afford it and I would not be welcomed."

Do you see these things? They're all about control, they're all about fear, they're all about behavior, and they are all about prescriptions to cultural norms. You are free to be anywhere you want, you are free to laugh as loud as you need to, you are free to raise your hand and have an answer, "right" and "wrong" outside of math is always subjective, and you are allowed to be in your glory and in your magnificence as a Divine Being.

Self-identification as yourself at this level in your knowing is the job of the day. And we will be taking you there again when we commence with this recording tomorrow. We will stop now, and we will thank you both for your attentions and we will give this gift to the reader.

"I am now knowing myself as free of prescribed behavior that was born out of control. I am now choosing to become aware and to align myself to my knowing of myself as free. I am Word through this intention. Word I am Word."

Thank you and goodnight.

Day Thirteen

We're ready to go. And oblivion, the idea of oblivion, is something we will discuss today for a minute. What if there were nothing?

What if there were nothing to think? Nothing to see? And you existed as an aspect of this nothing? What would that be in your mind? How would you experience it?

Now the definitions that you give yourself through your experience of your reality is what creates form out of essence. And we will explain this to you. When there is essence, there is the substance of creation that can be created with and brought into form. So all that you see around you has been created through this frequency, through this essence that we are describing as an aspect of Source.

Each thing that is created has its frequency and everything is vibrating at a higher and lower frequency. As you move upwards in your own consciousness, you have to bring with you that which you are, which requires the body then to begin to transition to the new frequency as well. So what you're housing your frequency in must become aligned to this new frequency. And what this requires is that temple that you stand in gets refurbished in order to hold the essence that is you in this higher frequency.

What we are talking about now is a vibrational issue that you can see out-pictured, in that mirror that we spoke to you about earlier. Your form, the way you identify the self in the body, is what we are speaking of. And your announcement that "I am Word" actually contributes and motivates the systems that are intact and operational in your physical form to respond.

Now what we are saying is that when you claim this, you have to become this. And you cannot leave an aspect of the self behind. And those of you who believe that your consciousness is completely independent from the physical form have some waking up to do. Your physical consciousness, the experience of the self in the body, is indeed where you are having your experience of this plane. But as this plane is lifted in frequency, the physical form needs to adapt in order to honor it and still serve as an activation in the vessel that you stand in.

Now we want to talk about your bodies right now and what they really are. They are systems that are perfectly designed to give you an opportunity to stand, to feel, to see on this level of experience. The physical body has subtle bodies that are incorporated through it that work with you to access your frequency and your consciousness. Your emotional self, your mental self, are held here. They are not in the brain; they are in your auric field.

Now as you begin to understand that the work that is actually happening here is happening in a level of frequency, the physical body begins to shift in response to what you have created in your subtle bodies. So everything is going at once. Now you want to know how the body has to change and we will explain it to you as we can.

The physical body needs to become attuned to a system of vibration that will amplify it as higher frequency: "I am Word through my body." We have worked with this before; we will work with it again. "I am Word through my body" realigns the physical body in accordance with the Divine Self, the Perfected Self, to realize itself in manifestation. This does mean healing. This does mean change. Because the sickness that is held in a body is the result of lower thought and consciousness and can be claimed in Word and then moved into a higher frequency.

Now we are not telling you that if you mutter a few words, you will change a pattern that has been held for a long time that is now manifesting as a disability or an illness. But we will tell you that shifting your frequency to the higher level is where the healing will occur.

"I am Word through my knowing of myself as Word." This is the decree that realigns consciousness into remembrance, remembrance of the Divine Self as the truth of who you are. Now the resistance to this, as we have said again and again, is cultural, and as you move that past that, you begin to experience yourself in real ways in other dimensions. Now what this means is that as your vibration increases you lift, and as you lift, what you experience co-resonates with the frequency that you are now operating at. The reason Paul sees things in frequency is that he is aligned to them, and you are as well, the moment you do the work and acknowledge yourself as an aspect of the Divine and begin to realize that what you have to do is raise your frequency.

"I am Word through my frequency, Word I am Word. I am lifting my vibration. Word I am Word."

This will support you.

Now the body that you stand in resonates as well with its surroundings. And the body that you stand in, as it begins to shift, will require different things. And you have to begin to listen to the physical body that will tell you what it needs in prescription for itself to become whole and healed. And this is done through conscious intention. Now we will tell you, Paul, this is brand new for you, so sit back and receive.

As you begin to realign in consciousness to the value of what you are—"I am valuable because I am an aspect of the Divine"—how you treat yourself must change, and the body that you stand in, which is indeed the temple of God on this plane, in this incarnation, must be dealt with as well and honored. But honoring yourself through a set of systematized behavior, while it may benefit, may not be what you require. Now you can each begin to know your physical form through out-picturing it in your consciousness.

"I see myself in my perfect form. I am healthy and healed. I am Word through this intention. Word I am Word. And I am knowing myself as an aspect of the Divine."

As you do this, you will create change. However, if you continue to engage in behaviors that limit the body from its healing, you are denouncing this decree. Now it's not like going on a diet, or stopping smoking because you're supposed to be good and healthy. In a funny way, what you are really doing is creating a new body in this frequency, a new healed body. "I am Word through my body" brings the Christ consciousness, the Divine Self, into activation in the cells of the body to reformat them and to bring them into accordance with the Divine Self in healing, in vibration, and in manifestation.

So as that happens, engaging in behavior that resonates with your surroundings in lower frequency is contradictory. But if you engage in the will as the way to support this change, you will be embattling behavior. And what we would recommend instead is you do this:

> "I am Word through those things that lower my vibration and impede my ability to bring my form into conscious adherence with the divine blueprint. I am Word through this intention to heal. Word I am Word."

In this statement what you are saying is, "I am now choosing to realign myself to behavior that operates in congruence with who I am. The Divine Being that I am does not chew tobacco not because it's a bad habit but because it resonates at lower frequency."

Now we are not telling you all to run out and stop eating meat. But guess what? As you begin to coexist in higher frequency, what you choose changes. And the only thing that keeps you in past habit is habit and an attachment to past behavior. You think you still need what you need, but in fact that is an out-picturing of thought and it is not true.

So the physical body needs, now, to go through a process of realignment to this frequency in order to be able to self-identify as Word. Now we are not talking about perfection as if it is a magazine centerfold. We are talking about *your* perfect body, the healed body, that looks like you that is operating well. And this is a process.

Some of you have a great investment in abnegating control over your physical form, which means this: You don't identify with the body you stand in. You primarily identify with your consciousness. And now the body has to begin to realign to its requirements for its healing. But be very, very careful now that you do not take this instruction to mean that your body is supposed to look pretty in a conventional way, which once again has to do with adherence to standards. Your body needs to operate in frequency in a way that is congruent with your energy systems so that you be an operative of this issuance of frequency: "I am Word."

Now we want to talk a bit about healing in this chapter, and this will be rudimentary, and we will expand as we continue in our teachings. But the physical body can be healed of what ails it in frequency. It is always a matter of bringing higher frequency to the lower frequency to heal, and it may involve divesting the self of those issues that supported the creation of illness. Now we will tell you what we mean by this. We are not going into blaming people who have created physical illness in the body, and we say "created" to take you out of the thought that you have been victimized in any way by your body, and not to make you wrong. This is very important: Never use this work and this teaching as a way to harm the self.

But as you bring higher frequency to those aspects of the self that require healing, healing may commence. However, if what created the pattern of disease is still required to release, that will have to be contended with as well.

Now "I am Word through the broken arm I have" actually brings frequency to support that arm in its healing. "I am Word through my blood pressure" will balance and support the body in moving this issue: "I am Word through my knowing of myself as healed." What you are doing is you are bringing in the higher frequency through this decree, which actually brings frequency from your light body, from the Divine Self, to support you in this integration of material healing. This is process. We would not tell any of you at this time to eschew medical help. And Paul has always been the first one to say, "If I break my leg, take me to the hospital, we can lay the hands on later." So don't be silly, be wise. But do understand that your participation in the healing of your body through frequency will realign you and show you how powerful you can be.

This is not a setup for failure. This is actually a truth. There is nothing that cannot be healed, and God is greater than any distortion of frequency that could create illness. However, in order to bring that into manifestation, you must be able to be at a place of consciousness where, in fact, you know that this healing can occur. And we will say capital "K" Knowing.

When you understand mastery, which really has to do with commanding the elements or the material world with an awareness of who you are, you can understand how this can transpire. However, until you are there, you need to understand that you are in process and you are manifesting yourself as your Divine Self, and as this occurs, your world will begin to evolve in order to heal yourself and that which is around you.

Now you can talk about the laying on of hands and what, in fact, that truly is. And what that is is bringing forth frequency from a higher level through the system and the energy field of the body to integrate it and support another in her healing. It is not required nor recommended ever that you use your own system as the source of healing. We are working with Paul now as a channel. When you work in healing, you are a channel for the higher frequencies. You are not the healer; you are the one serving as the conduit for the healing. This will keep your ego out of the way. It will also align you to the frequency you require to begin to do the work. However, if you are ever in depletion after doing healing work, you will know that you utilized your own energies in passage, and that is not a healthy thing to do.

Now when we say this, "I am Word through the one before me," you are actually serving that aspect of the person before you that requires healing. "I am Word through my friend's liver." "I am Word through my friend's eyesight." "I am Word through my friend's heart, Word I am Word through this intention. Word I am Word" supports them in receiving frequency where it is needed. It does not require touch; it requires intention. And as this happens, the frequency in the body of your friend goes into receptivity and the energy is sent and dispersed by that person to where it is intended to go.

Now understand this. When you send the energy in healing through intention, "I am Word through the one before me," where the energy goes is the energy's business. You are not in charge of dictating the passage of this frequency. Allow the frequency to do what it needs to do in order to move and realign those aspects of those persons' self that require a higher vibration in order to heal them.

So this can be done always. But we would actually recommend that you begin with yourself. Think of a part of your body that needs some work. That left knee that gives you trouble, the pain in the back of the neck, or the feet, or the fingers. Now choose that part of the body: "I am Word through this part of my body. Word I am Word." Track what you feel. See what happens. Do you feel the energy move, and move to that center of the body in order to support it in vibration? This will be the task.

For those of you that are already empathic or have already

begun to feel energy, this will be significant, and what you will be experiencing is the frequency of the Word as a healing vehicle in action. For those of you who are new to this, it is a process of acclimation. And the first thing you have to understand is, don't have any presupposition of what it's supposed to feel like. Let it do what it is, which is heal. "I am Word through my body" sends the frequency of Word through the physical form that you stand in. "I am Word through my knowing of myself as Word" re-identifies the self as who it is in truth.

We want to discuss now a belief in loneliness, which is actually another way of saying separation. Now the first thing that you have to contend with in the belief that you are separate is the belief that you are inherently alone or lonely. And we want to make this an untruth for you now in an experiential way.

"I am Word through the one before me" brings frequency to the one before you. And as you do this, you experience your friend, or the one before you, as frequency in alignment with the frequency that you are. As you go out to a store, or out to the park, and you begin to Word through those you see before you—which is, in fact, a way of activating them into this frequency that requires no permission (again, their systems will decide how to work with the energy to retrieve it, to accept it, that is their job)—you will begin to see that you are part of them. That you are all made up of the same stuff. And what happens then is that sense of separation between you and your fellows begins to release, and you are no longer lonely.

Now we are not speaking of loneliness on the level of social interaction, but understand right now that when you do this with others, you are interacting with them, but at a very high level. "I am Word through those before me" brings you into congruence with the energy fields of others, and this changes things. You should do this every time you walk into a new room: "I am Word through those I see before me." What you do in this moment is you acknowledge in them their inherent divinity, their aspect of the divine that is incarnating as them regardless of what they present. And we will underline this: *regardless of what they present.*

You already know that it is much easier to see the divine perfection in the person that you know and adore than it is in the one you can't stand, or the one that doesn't look the way you think they should because they don't live the life that you think that they should live. However, the response is, regardless of your intention, to bring them into alignment with higher frequency; "I am Word through those I see before me," regardless of what they present, will shift the room and bless those people in frequency.

Never for a moment think that you can use this frequency to control somebody else. It is not allowed, it cannot happen, and it will not happen. So if you have your friend Joe who you think should be doing something very different with his life, "I am Word through the one I see before me" will allow his field to begin to move, it will not take him where you decided that he should go.

We will say, the same thing can be said for healing. When people manifest illness, they do it for different reasons, and you cannot be the one to decide on someone's behalf why they are doing what they are doing and how they should be fixed. In our last text we talked about "fixing," and this is not about fixing, this is about transformation.

When you understand that to move something forward in frequency requires that frequency to morph, to realign, and to change, you can understand that the process that the individual goes through who is changing may not necessarily be terribly graceful or look very pretty. However, it is not your job to know what they are supposed to do, how they are supposed to heal, or what they require to succeed in their mission as a soul embodying as their Divine Self.

We will say this again. Everyone's job at this time is to begin to access this information of what is available to them. However, how people choose to work with the information is individualized and is up to them. So once you understand that everybody here is in a process of integrating the higher frequencies that are available on this plane now, you can also understand that how somebody digests that, or processes that, will be up to them.

There are many, many, many ways that people process higher frequency. And much of what comes up in response to it can seem a little messy. And we've used this metaphor before, but we will restate it: If you are pouring clean water into a glass, the dirty water will rise to the top, and that is what is happening. And when you are aware already of what process you are engaged in through acclimation in conscious intention to divine frequency, you have a much easier time being able to identify the process. As we have said earlier in our other text, everybody is engaged in this process. Those of you who are reading this text are being given information and a vocabulary to support you through an experience that is happening anyway.

> "I am Word through my knowing of myself as standing in my knowing as a Divine Being. I am Word through this intention. Word I am Word."

Please understand, everyone. These are not just words. These are actually ways of calling in your own frequency and your own decision. "I am Word through all that I see before me. Word I am Word" states that you are seeing the frequency of Word out-pictured in all that you see before you. Once you get to the point when you are truly able to see that God is everything in material form, that it is all just stuff and it is all divine, you will have achieved a level of awareness that few can claim. It is there for you now. We are taking you on a journey so you can see that who you are is a manifestation of divine energy and consciousness.

We would like to gift you now with an awareness of yourself as unified, as one with Source.

"I am now in my action as a Divine Being. And I am doing as follows: As I sit in my chair, I become aware of my frequency and I allow my frequency to begin to lift an octave in each breath I take. I am Word through my being. Word I am Word. I am Word through my vibration. Word I am Word. I am Word through my knowing of myself as Word."

And now, as you lift in frequency, we want you to begin to align in your knowing to the truth that you are an aspect of the divine.

"I am knowing myself as an aspect of God incarnated in a body. Word I am Word through this intention. Word I am Word."

And as this happens, we want you to align to the frequency that is around you.

"I am Word through my oneness with my Creator. Word I am Word through this intention. Word I am Word."

And allow yourself to be received by Divine Light. Receive, receive, receive, receive, receive. Feel yourself as one with that which is around you. And become aware that you are not alone.

"I am Word through those I see before me." This is the decree that tells you that no one is alone; everyone is a part and an aspect of the Great Creator in experience and in form.

Thank you each. We will stop now for the day. Word I am Word.

TEN

LOVE AND REPRIMAND

Day Fourteen

We're ready to go, we're ready to go, we're ready to go. And we're going to talk about love and reprimand. And what this means is that we'll talk about how you love and how you withhold love from your brother.

Now these are two very distinct things and they operate in the same way. It's all about choice. You are always choosing. Every moment of the day you are standing in your choice. And as you choose, as we have said, you always have the choice to go higher in your consciousness by moving to the highest level available to you. As you choose this, you shift your energy frequency up and that makes opportunity for the next round of choices that would also lift you in frequency. As you choose love, as you operate from love, you move upwards.

Reprimand, we will say, is an opposite choice. "Reprimand." Think of how the word feels as it's spoken. It implies a cutoff. It implies a negative reaction. To be in reprimand is to stop the flow of love. Now we will say "reprimand" today and not "fear." Although reprimand in many ways can be looked at as a by-product of fear, we will say reprimand is not. And what we will say is that the opportunity you have of changing the word to "reprimand" will make you more accountable in your options. "Am I operating from love, or am I in reprimand?"

Now reprimand of the self is one way to say this. "Where am I reprimanding myself in any way as I go about my day?," which is essentially to say, "Where am I stopping the flow of love that would come through me in action? Where am I doing this?" As you understand how you do this, you can create a new pattern to release the reprimand. The image we give Paul is of a duct blocking water in a dam. And if you look at reprimand as that, as a block to a flow of energy—and we have said to you love is the ocean, you are in the river—you are simply releasing the duct that would block the flow of the water. You are releasing the dam to allow flow.

Now when you are in reprimand, you are in judgment. And we will say this to you once again: When you are in reprimand, you are in judgment. And when you are in judgment, you are stopping the action of the Creator from operating as you, because you have chosen his stead, as it were. You have decided to be the one who can judge.

Now we will not tell you that discernment is wrong. It's required. You have to discern many, many things as you operate through your day. However, judgment, which implies condemnation, is not yours to do. It is not your province, it is not your action, and to assume it is is to relinquish love and move into judgment and consequently, we will say, reprimand. Because, of course, when you judge, not only are you withholding energy, you are bringing forth an action of negative consciousness in the form of reprimand.

When one person holds any other person outside of love intentionally for any reason, that person stops themselves from acting as love in that moment. And that is tethering you to that person in a binding situation that does not relinquish until the water, the river, is allowed to flow again. So when you stand in reprimand of another, you harm the self as well.

"Unforgiveness," Paul is wondering. "Is this that again?" Yes, it is, in language that is much more appropriate to this time. "I can stand in reprimand of anything and assume myself to be in truth," and that is self-deceit. You all well know when you do not forgive, and while you can create reasons why you don't that might support you, you know full well what you do when you withhold forgiveness. You do not delude yourselves there. You know when you are angry. However, reprimand and judgment, which bring forth self-righteousness, do not feel like unforgiveness but consequently have the ability to keep you tethered and bound in similar ways that will block you from aligning to love.

Remember the riverbank we talked to you about at the beginning of this book? We said that the book would be a caution against withholding light. Well, we say the riverbank is where you go when you step out of the stream, or the flow, of love. Now when you want to get back in, which is always choice, you have to make decisions and you have to gain the insight as to what brought you to the bank again to begin with. When you need a rest for processing your experiences, you can pull over to the side. But when you are in unforgiveness, or you are tethered through your reprimanding of another, you climb out of the water and you sit happily and proudly on your riverbank while love flows right by you. And guess what, everybody? To the extent that you do this, you block your ability to be in love. And as you are not in love, you are out of the province and the jurisdiction of your Creator in terms of your frequency requiring a new alignment in order to move forward. You have the one ability to change this.

Now if you have an issue of reprimand and you have the self-righteousness that accompanies it, what do you do with it? The first thing you have to decide is that it is not required. It is not needed.

What do you get from it by being right? What do you get from it by being in judgment? To stand in judgment of your brother is to relinquish your own authority. It's an imbalance, finally, in frequency and in consciousness.

The ego would tell you that this is required. In order to stand firm in your knowing, there must be others that are wrong. But in fact, what you do when you stay in reprimand, in judgment, is stop the flow, and consequently the atmosphere that you are operating in no longer will be conducive to your own alignment to your own divine sense of being in love. And knowing, of course, comes with this. So first of all, we need to work on denial. How are you denying your own self through the judgment of others, and also where are you in denial of how you judge? Where do you see yourself as superior? Where do you see yourself as better? More knowledgeable? More appropriate? More beautiful? More esteemed? Make the list yourself.

As you do this, you will see that the investment in this and how you do this is all about adhering to the requirements of control that we have been speaking about since the beginning of this text. The belief that you need these things to grab onto as you navigate through your day are all about having mirrors to reinforce illusion and illusion of separateness from your brothers, which we tell you now makes you separate in consciousness from God, from Source, from the river that you flow in to join unity in the sea.

We tell you this so you can stop it. But like anything else, this will require your becoming aware and then realigning in frequency to this teaching. In this time, you have an opportunity to change your patterning and to do it rapidly.

Now the first way to do it, as we said, is to see where you stand in judgment or in reprimand. As you are operating from this, you can ask for a way, if you wish, to know. Ask your own knowing, that aspect of yourself that knows, to teach you. "Where am I in judgment? Where am I in reprimand? And where am I stopping

myself from the flow of the river? Where do I go now?" Ask yourself. We are going to teach you more as this book progresses about
how to operate from your knowing systematically as you hear your
own thoughts. But for the time being, whatever you get in terms of
response is appropriate to your learning.

So once you understand where you are doing this, operating
from reprimand and judgment, you can ask yourself: Why? Where
am I frightened? What am I protecting? Why do I need this? What
does this get me? You will see very fast that what it gets you is separation. And understand this: You can sit on the riverbank for a
long, long time before you realize that this is why you are there.
And understand this, please: The longer you sit on the side of the
river, the longer the illusion lasts that you are separate, the more the
river appears to recede from consciousness until the time you forget
that it was ever there. Understand this: This is always your choice.

So say, for example, you have not had somebody that you have
required to forgive for many years, but you stubbornly hold onto a
reprimand of the self, or a judgment of another, and you sit there in
your world and you have forgotten that you can go into flow, in
alignment, with the higher frequencies. How do you stop this? We
will tell you now.

The first thing is you become aware of what you do and where
you are unforgiving the self or another or standing in judgment or
in reprimand. The second thing is to ask yourself why. And then
the third thing is to allow it to be released through decision and
through relinquishing the control that you have invested in being
right. Even if it's about yourself—"I reprimand myself because I
always do this"—get over it and stop needing to punish yourself
because what it does is block the creative flow of frequency that
would serve to liberate you. How silly it would be to stand in punishment when there is no need.

The moment you understand that you are not the one in authority here in terms of judgment, you can begin to liberate the self. What this means, very simply, is humility. Are you in your humility? Who are you to judge your fellow man for their behavior? Do you know what they have come here to learn? Do you know what their choices are? What pain they have experienced? Or what light may be there for them at the end of their lesson? You do not know. How can you pretend to know at that level? If you are judging them, we promise you this: You do not know. You are in your illusion and in your self-congratulatory-ness, you have given yourself a nice dose of separation from your own knowing and from the flow of the love of the Creator that would work through you.

"Now it's impossible, I could never forgive that man who harmed me," "who took my child," "who stole my wallet," "who ruined my life"—whatever you want to say. How can you not if what is at stake is your own freedom? Would you rather be bound to this person, to this situation, to this past insult or pain for an eternity, or to release it now to the Creator to be absolved and to be released? It is your choice.

We cannot grab you by the feet and drag you into the river. You have to do it yourself. Now you can stay on the bank for as long as you like; you are not being judged for this by us. We honor completely your free will. And we will tell you this: We still love you, we still support you, we will still adhere to our promise to serve and to teach, but we can't throw you in the water. We can take your hands and we can gently lead you there. And we can raise our voice so that we can be heard above the din of your mind, but we cannot make you do something you are not willing to do. And that is a gift. It has to be your choice. It has to be or it is not truthful.

It is not truthful to drag a child to church and conform him to your beliefs and say to the child, "You have to do this, or..." because the child will resist, of course. His own will has not been honored. And that is not the same as teaching a child to learn what love is, what the Creator is, and what is available in frequency. So in this case we say to you, come to the river! Come, come, come! And leave what binds you. And that unforgiveness, that reprimand will stop you from entering. So release it now and come and join us in our love. We will gift it to you. It is there for you. But it is your choice.

Today we want you to do something. And that is to decide where you are in reprimand of your brother or yourself. Where you are unforgiving and why? What is it getting you and is it worth it? If you decide that you are better off on your riverbank in your unforgiveness, we will bless you and we will leave you there and happily move on in this teaching. You will be left until you are ready to release. That is not a threat. That is a gift. We are honoring your choice. However, if you decide today that you no longer require it, or you are willing to release, or at least are willing to learn where you are engaging in this behavior and reinforcing these constructs on a daily basis, you will be led and you will be taught and we will lead you to the river. We will, we will, we will.

Now we will tell you how we would like you to work. Take a piece of paper and write down a list of all of your unforgiveness, all of your rage, all of your judgment of people, places and things and why you are invested in keeping them. On each one make a decision.

"Am I willing to release this to the love of my Creator to handle? Am I willing to release this to Source to make right in His way? Am I willing to sacrifice my own soul's growth for this investment in reprimand and punishment of the self and another? Am I willing today to say, 'I am letting this go, and I am willing to learn how, and to be led to the freedom that will lead me to freedom?' Word I am Word."

Now we will teach you. You make your list and you write it down. And you read it, you itemize it, you decide, and then you say:

"Dear God, take this from me in this way: I am Word through my willingness to release the need to judge my fellow man. I am willing to release the need to be in reprimand, to stand in my knowing and in my forgiveness as a child of the Creator. I now choose to give this all over to the Great Source to make truthful, and I release the need to hold myself to separation in the need to claim my self-righteousness or my separation from my fellows. I am Word through this intention. Word I am Word."

Now we take you, and we take you by the hands. And we would like you to close your eyes when it is time. And you will do this with us. And these are the instructions:

As you sit, you imagine right now that you are on a riverbank. And on that riverbank surrounds you—all of those people, all of those situations, all of those constructs that represent your unforgiveness or your reprimand. You see them before you: the child, the brother, the husband, the co-worker, the parent, whatever is there that makes itself known. And as they appear, you bless them and you release them. And you bless them again and you thank them for what they have taught you and you allow them to go into the river and to be washed in love and carried to Source. And you do this individually until you have gone through your list. "I see them as free. They are un-tethered. We are unbound. And they are free in their love to ride the wave of the Creator and to be returned to their own sense of worth in love."

As you do this, you release them. And when you finally see yourself as sitting alone—the bank has been forgiven, the school has been forgiven, the lover, the child, the old friend who you departed from badly, all have been released to the river—you stand and you extend your hands. You see us before you. And who we are is Divine Love come to reach you. And if you wish to imagine an angel or a wise soul extending her hands, extending his hands, please reach for them. And we will carry you in our hands to the river and we will enter with you. And in this moment you become free as you allow yourself to ride the current of love.

"I am Word through my body. Word I am Word.
I am Word through my vibration. Word I am Word.
I am Word through my knowing of myself as Word.
And I am now free of all reprimand that I have inherited, that I have chosen, that I have carried, that has tethered me, that has bound me and has allowed me out of my alignment with my own knowing of myself as love. I am Word through this intention. Word I am Word."

We bless you each, and we say to you this. This is a process. This is not magic, but this is done when it is done. And when you say, "I am free," and you are in your truth, you are free. You may find that habit grabs you back and that the need to be right, or that the need to be in reprimand, still holds itself at times. But we have given you a system to understand what it is and to say to you: You can choose differently. You can choose differently. You can choose differently. Are you willing to? Do you wish to? Is this in your highest good and greatest worth to release that which binds you to your own sorrow or your own separation? If it is worth it to release it, we have given you the tools.

Now we will tell you this. To be in the current of love is to choose love. We said at the beginning of this chapter that it was both about choice. To be in reprimand is choice, to be in love is choice.

Now we will teach you something about who you are: You are an aspect of God. And as an aspect of God you have the ability to love as God. Now this is important for you to understand, and it may be a different way for you to realize yourself as we describe it. As an aspect of love, when you love you are choosing to love as the Creator.

This is a big deal, and it requires that you raise in consciousness to the place of love in order to see the love that is before you, inherent, in perfection, in everybody you pass. "I am seeing now with the eyes of the Creator. I am seeing now with the eyes of Christ. I am seeing now with the eyes of Love." Whatever the language is you wish to use, it will work if you attune to it as we suggest now.

At this moment in time, sit back in your chair and tell yourself that you are allowed to witness the world through wonder. You are willing to witness the world with eyes of wonder. This is the first step. The second step is as follows:

"I am now choosing to witness all that I see before me with the eyes of love. And as I do this, I raise my frequency to come into accordance and alignment with the frequency of love. And as I am in my love, the world greets me as love and we move into congruence in union in the frequency, in the vibration, and in this vision of love."

If you were to look at your neighbor today and see her as love, you would have this experience, but you are seeing with the eyes of God, and you are gifting yourself with the apparition that the Creator would see as he sees his creations in love. So we are benefiting you with this first as an exercise and second as an understanding and then third as a mission that you will undertake for the rest of your time on this planet. "I am now seeing those before me with the eyes of love."

Now don't imagine for a moment that seeing someone in love implies that they are cute, or adorable, or doing what you want, or adhering to a structure that you think love requires. Love is in everything. If you can imagine the Christ who loved all of mankind, you are choosing now to rise in alignment to see with those eyes.

"I see all before me with the eyes of love. Word I am Word through this intention. Word I am Word."

"Well, it's impossible. It will never happen. I can't stand the woman next door. I am having a fight with my boyfriend. I really don't want to love him right now, thank you very much." Okay, have fun on the riverbank and stay there until you choose differently. It is choice. It is choice. It is choice. Are we saying that this is easy? Not really. We say that it is change. And change is never easy when you are so invested in your old behavior and that behavior has been agreed upon by everybody as appropriate. "It's right to blow up my neighbor when they blow me up." "It's right to hurt somebody who hurts me." "It's right to be scary when I am scared," and "It is right to be in unforgiveness when I have been harmed." All of these things you have agreed upon, and all of these things keep you withering and outside of the light that would hold you and heal you and bring you to union with your soul's worth as an aspect of the Creator come into form.

> "I see all that I see before me with the eyes of the Christ. I see all that I see before me in love. I see all that I see before me in Divine Love and healing. Word I am Word through this intention. Word I am Word."

When you hold a vision for someone, you are healing them. When you see someone in love and you hold them in the frequency of love—"I am love through the one I see before me"—you are healing them. When you see someone as well who has been ill or is injured and you hold that vision for them—"I am love through the one before me"—you are benefiting them in their healing. When you see someone who is frightened—"I am love through the one before me"—you are bringing them love to heal the fear. You do not have to teach them through your language; you can be with them in this frequency and this frequency will do what it is required to do in order to heal. You will be welcomed by them in healing as this is done. It is done in congruence and an awakening in the auric field: "I am love through the one I see before me."

So yes, this is all choice. And we are teaching you now that the ability that you have to rise and be and inhabit this frequency is not something theoretical. It is not hard once you understand that it is why you are here and everything else is illusion and agreement to remain in illusion.

So you have said already, "I am willing to go on this journey." Now while much of the journey of this text has been informational, you are also being worked on in frequency. And the exercises we give you and the decrees that you are offered are there to sustain you, but also to be supportive of your ability to align to higher frequency. And indeed, yes, we are working with the reader to allow you to work through the issues that you require. We are servers, in this regard. We are not the Creator but we are of the Creator, and we operate in love. But we ask you now to state this intention for yourself:

"I am now choosing to acknowledge myself as an aspect of Source, an aspect of the Creator, and I am willing, now, to become one in my awareness with my knowing of this in truth. Word I am Word through this intention. Word I am Word."

When you operate from this knowing, you become empowered to make the kinds of changes that we are deciding with you will allow you to become Word embodied in form. And that is the job here. You have done it already in frequency. The acclimation to frequency, which comes through the decree, "I am Word through my body. Word I am Word. I am Word through my vibration. Word I am Word. I am Word through my knowing of myself as Word. Word I am Word" brings the energy field into accordance with the frequency of Word. It is there for you, you can work with the frequency. You have been attuned, as it were, or aligned.

However, the process of inhabiting this in your consciousness, which is the work of this book, is what is coming to you now. So as you hold the awareness, as you begin to operate from it, then you are free to make changes much more easily, because you are re-identifying yourself as who you are and not being bound by the personality self that is tethered to ego or the lower self seeking to control you.

Now there is "healthy ego," and we are not going to talk about those things in this way. But when we are talking about ego, we are talking about that aspect of the self that would keep you in your belief in separation so that it can feel that it is the Creator and that there is no other. Understand this, please: To be told that you are an aspect of the Creator means that it can come into your own dominion. Do not confuse this for a moment with our saying you are God and there is no other. You are an aspect of God, as is everyone else. And the moment you see yourself as this and you decide that someone else is not is when you stand on the riverbank again and you are without flow.

Now this is part of the teaching. When you are in flow, there will be these obstacles on the path. We have described them in different ways. We have talked about boulders and tree trunks and now we are saying there are things that pull you up to the riverbank. But they are all really the same thing: requirements of choice that will be out-pictured and seen in order for you to bypass them. If you've been engaging in behavior your entire life and you have been unconscious of it, believe me now, you will become conscious. You will see it for what it is in order for you to change. So these things are requirements.

So if you find yourself on the riverbank, do not be ashamed. Know that you are learning. And you have the choice again to release the unforgiveness or the reprimand and go back into flow. This is always choice, this is always choice, this is always choice.

We are forgiven the moment we forgive. We are choosing now to align ourselves to your frequency to bring you into this knowing as a readership.

At this moment in time please, allow yourself to become one with your energy field. Imagine that you are vibrating in frequency. "I am Word through my vibration, Word I am Word." And allow yourself to feel for a moment what it feels like not to be tethered to judgment of others. Not to be tethered to the unforgiveness of others. Not to be tethered to the reprimands of the self or your fellows or anyone or anything. Imagine, imagine, imagine.

Now allow us to work with you.

"I am receiving myself as healed of those attachments to anything and everything that have bound me to any unforgiveness of the self or others. I am Word through this intention. Word I am Word."

And we will work with you as we are permitted and as you align to us.

"I am now receiving myself as the beneficiary of healing. I am receiving the willingness to release that which has bound me. Word I am Word through this intention. Word I am Word."

We will teach you again in the morning. We are very pleased with this work today. We believe that you have taken an understanding step in your willingness and we believe that you will change. And we are grateful for your willingness and for your attentions as we move forward in this text.

I am Word through those before me. Word I am Word.

Thank you both and stop.

ELEVEN

I AM THE WELL

Day Fifteen

We'll talk about needing today and why you need others' love, and how you believe that your sense of self-worth is contingent upon the receipt of others' attentions. The first thing you need to understand is that everyone is a mirror for your own beliefs. And as you call people into you in your reality, you call to you the reflections of your own appearance, self-worth, identity, and frequency. You are calling to you on multiple levels different kinds of people to mirror back to you your own consciousness and your own reflection.

Now in order to understand *why* you need, you need to look at *what* you need. And what you need is the Divine Self embodying as you. That is in reality. And what you are looking for from others is that action within you. Now we will explain what we mean here. Your decision, on any level, that you are incomplete seeks you looking to find completion outside of yourself through an engagement with another, through esteem projected to you by others' awareness of your abilities, or from other things that come from outside that seek to stop you from feeling incomplete. So we will say that this need for others' love, in many ways, is simply the need for self-love out-pictured and called to you.

Now there is nothing wrong with being in love. And we want to talk about this again. To be in love requires you to be in the frequency of love and then that is the tenor, the level, the frequency of your engagements. But seeking love outside of the self requires you to denounce the self.

Now we are not talking about desiring affection, or physical attention, or things like that. We are very simply stating that when you believe yourself to be without love and you look outside of yourself to bring love to you in order to fill a space or a belief in your unlovability, you are doomed, as it were, to failure.

Now this does not sound terribly pleasant to Paul, who watches from the hallway and is wondering where this chapter will be taking him. It is not a bad thing to know a fact, and the fact of the matter is when you require somebody outside of yourself to redeem you in some way, to gift you with what can come from you, you are looking to someone else to be the Creator.

Now we will simplify this again. We are telling you very simply that the need for love as out-pictured and required from another is, in many ways, an affirmation of your own lack of love. So we want to work today very, very simply on anchoring your own love of self in the physical body, in the physical experience that you stand in. The reason for this is that it is impossible, in truth, to give love when you do not have it to give. And we want to offer you this: You have it, you do have it, it is present within you regardless of what your experience is, and we want you to help the self to understand how to receive it from you.

Say already that there is a well on a barren landscape. And you look at the landscape, which is dry and dusty, and there is no flora and nothing lives. We will say that that is the landscape that exists without an experience of love. Now we will say the river is there, but we're not going to access it by going to the riverbank. Because what you see before you is parched and gray and seems to go on forever.

Now underneath this ground there is a well, and it is a deep well, and it runs right to the river, which is Source, which is the love of God and the frequency of God. But for our purposes today, we will say yes, there is a well, and we have to find it and we have to break through to your own self-love.

Now the way we will do this with you is as follows:

"I am now choosing to realize that within me there is a well-spring of love. There is a wellspring of love that I am able to access and call to me and drink from. And as I become aware of this in my consciousness, my belief in my own lovability is exchanged for a deep knowing that I am in the well of love. I am Word through this intention. Word I am Word."

Now we want you to see the landscape before you. That gray area. The parched land that grows no love, that has no nourishment, and then we will tell you this. We are going to take a little axe, a little white axe, a light saber if you wish, and we are going to put it in the ground and we are going to say, "Yes, let it come."

Now what we will have to break through, in many ways, is just thought. But it is anchored to deep beliefs that many of you held that you are unlovable, and you are unlovable for any reason you can imagine. Now we will tell you that this is not true, but if that has not been your experience until this day, why should you believe us? We can agree with you, "All right, you're not lovable, let's get on with life in other ways," but when you do that, when you honor that aspect of the self that says you cannot be loved, you continue to create from it. And what is created without love will not flourish, will not grow. So how does one love a self that believes she cannot be loved?

The first way we want to work with you is to begin to recognize that what you are is a perfect creation regardless of what you think. And the self identifies at this level as a bright light in consciousness. It does not realize the self as a golden being having an experience. It does not recognize the self as a perfect body. It does not recognize the self as externally achieved. So we will go back to that light, which we say is that essence of you that is connected to Source, and we will operate from there.

Now the love that exists within you is indeed a well, and believe it or not, everybody, it is a deep well, and the love that is available to you in truth is powerful and wonderful and completely available to you to give to others. So if you can become this well—"I am the well, I am the well, I am the well"—what you can begin to gift others with is love.

Now we will tell you this: Imagine for a moment that those creations, those beliefs, those things that have kept you from love were all created in fear. Every single one of them. "I could never be forgiven." "I could never have what I want." "Nobody could ever love me because I once did a terrible thing." "They will find out I'm truly not healthy or good or loving and then I will not have what I want." The fears go on and on and on. But if you believe now, in this moment in time, that these are all structures that are not nearly as powerful as the light and as Divine Love, as Word incarnate, you can move them.

You understand very clearly that when you are digging for a well, sometimes you've got to move some dirt. Sometimes you hit some stones. But when the water is there, it will be addressed and it will rise as it is liberated and permeate and the land around it will be verdant and green and alive with what is grown in its love.

Now we will tell you, the pickaxe you are using to break through the soil is Word. And we are working with you this way:

"I am Word in order to release the granite, the blocks, the earth, all that has stood in the way of my accessing my own love of self. I am Word through the beliefs and the structures and the matrix that I have claimed to be true, consciously or unconsciously, that have kept me from my love. And I am standing now in my own knowing as a divine aspect of God who is worthy of his love, of her love, and I am claiming it now. Word I am Word through this intention to claim my love in fullness. Word I am Word."

And we bring the axe down and we allow it to penetrate and to clear those obstacles to realizing your love.

Now understand this, please. When you are the well, when you are love, you are nourished by love. You are that thing that is in nourishment. However, you will also call to you those who are thirsty and those who seek to know love as themselves.

So now we go back to this land, this gray and barren place. And you will see that it is beginning to sprout leaves and green and trees are growing. And as you stand there, you will see yourself as hold-ing a cup. And this is the cup; this is the Christ chalice, if you wish, that you will drink from. And you will say this with us:

"I am now allowing myself to go into union with my own Divine Self, and I affirm now, once and for all, that I am loved, and I am allowing love, and I am now in this moment in union with my Di-vine Self. I am Word through this intention. Word I am Word."

Now we will return to the well in time. And we want to talk right now a bit more about your needs from others, and how you project onto them what you are really needing for yourself. "I need him to desire me; I will feel so much better when he does." In that case, you need to desire you. "I need him to give me more money. If I don't have more money, what am I going to do?" Well, in this case, your need is to realize that Source, the Creator, the Universe, if you wish, is your source, and you are gifting yourself with what you need through adjusting your consciousness to that aspect of Source that will provide it. "He" is an emblem, "he" who you need the money from, for your lack. And as you expect the money from him, you have replaced him as Source. Do you understand this? When your boss, or your job, or whoever owes you money is Source, you have created a fake God. Your true source is the Great Creator, the Universe that supplies you, and he is merely a channel, and the channel will change. We will address this more in later chapters.

Now we will say, "I need you to love me," "I need you to stay with me," "I need you to comfort me." All of these needs, ultimately, are born out of separation. Now we are not condemning these needs. We are human in our hearts and we understand what you require what you call for love. But if you can understand, very simply, that the kind of love that you are asking for when you place the energy outward is not the river. It is emotional charge, it is based in fear, and you are confusing one thing for another. If you are in need, you are not in love. You are acting from fear.

Now you can ask yourself this: When was there a time in my life when I loved someone with no requirement for return? If you can remember this moment of truth, you will have something to anchor you to, you will have a sense of knowing of what true love is. But the manifestations of ego that disguise themselves as love are manifold and those fears that you have of being left, or not being lovable, or all of those requirements of the self that you mandate are needed in order to be allowed love are false constructs.

Now we will not tell you that having a love affair, a passionate and great one, is a bad thing. It can be a great thing and it can be an opening to true love. But please understand, everybody, that the truth in love is going way beyond biology, it goes way beyond hormones, and it goes way beyond physical attraction.

You may have all seen couples as when they age they begin to resemble the other, and it's a wonderful thing to see. And what has really happened is that their energy has become so congruent and so wonderfully adept at reading the other's that they are in co-resonance and equalized in loving frequency.

Now you understand already that physical attraction is transitory and standards of beauty seem to change with every decade that passes. But the idealized self, that which you truly are, is eternal and that is the beauty, finally, that you need to be working on in refinement. And we will tell you this: When you are in love with the self that you are, you will call to you love from elsewhere. But it will be a matter of co-resonance and it is very, very different to be in love in that frequency and meet others in that frequency than to approach them from a place of need, or lack. And those are both based in fear.

So you understand already this difference. However, you still act as if you must be what you think you are in order to get what you want from another. You are the source in this regard. Now we are not telling you to want things. But we are telling you that what you want you must first realize within the self. You must. It can come to you the moment you stop looking for it outside of yourself. And when you look to the self, you are also looking to the Divine Self as the source of your supply.

Your own inner knowing, which we are activating through this text, will support you in deciding how to realize what you need. But it is never, never, never a matter of going elsewhere. Now Paul is wondering, "Does that mean if I am not troubled, I should not go to a therapist? If I am not ill, should I not go to a doctor?" That is not what we are saying. We are specifically talking today about love and your belief that you do not receive it, so you go looking for it elsewhere. And you believe you do not receive it because on some level you have disguised your love with fear and you have believed the fear to be what you are, which are all those reasons you have decided love could not be you.

Now we will tell you again: The gray landscape that you saw is your frequency without love. That's really all it is. It's an out-picturing, an imagined design of an energy field that is not refined and in reception of love. And when we said to you that energy field was beginning to bloom because it had touched the water, we were simply saying that the frequency of love was beginning to permeate the energy field. And we will do this with you now:

"I am anchoring in the frequency of Divine Love through my choice and through my willingness to resonate with the frequency of love. I am now choosing this and I am giving permission to any and all resistance to love to be released from me and from my subtle bodies in perfect ways. I am Word through this intention. Word I am Word."

Your release of those obstacles to love will commence in consciousness as you decide that you are worthy of this love that you speak of.

If you can imagine one day that you've always had a job that you never liked, and you had a friend that always loved her work and would talk to you at the end of the day about how much she got out of it. And up till this day you had always said, "Well, she's lucky, she's got a great job. I wish I did, but I don't. But I should accept it, 'cause I must not be lucky." That is the paradigm that is set in place. But then imagine one day you get angry, and the way that you say, "Hey wait a minute, if she can have that, I can too, and why don't I have it? And what would make me stop myself from getting it?"

And then you begin to move forward in frequency to declare your own worth and to claim your own divine birthright.

Get this, everybody: Nothing is really handed to you in consciousness. It all requires a declaration or a claim of worthiness. If you are receptive to love, you will greet love. If you are not receptive to love, for whatever reasons, and love comes to the door, you may not let him in. Do you understand this? You may not let love in, because you have not claimed it or you have not allowed it for whatever reasons. And these are the reasons, we say, that have obstructed the well. You are the well, you are the well, you are the well.

And we are going now to show you what it would look like to be the well in full realization. Imagine now that you are standing on a grassy bed surrounded by trees and flowers and everything is alive and resonating in love. And you stand at the center with your arms open, and as people come to you they are nourished in frequency and they are reminded of their own love. And this is you, finally, as the well. You are drawing that well into you. You are the chalice, you are the expression of love, and you are being love incarnate.

Now this sounds magical. And, in fact, it's really not. It's all very, very simple. And we would not explain it to you if we did not believe this could happen through this work that we are describing to you.

We have told you first that you are not worthy because of beliefs that you have had in place. And because you don't believe you are worthy, you are operating from lack and you are seeking others to fill you up and to hold you, to give you what you need that you are not able to give yourself.

And then we are telling you that you must give this to yourself in order to be able to receive it from another in a true way. You can share, but you cannot use somebody else's frequency to build up a deficit in your own. That is more like an unhealthy need, an unhealthy relationship, and a dependent one, than one that is born, in fact, in love and in congruence.

And we have said to you that the bedrock, the obstacles that have been keeping you from your love can be accessed and broken through with the action of the divine, which is Word. "I am Word through those things that have impeded my ability to access myself as love."

And then we have told you that as you do this, you bring that love to you and you allow it to be you. "I am in my love." And as you are your love, you draw to you those people, those things that resonate with that love.

It is very, very simple. It is not impossible and only, if you wish, accessible to you through your own willingness to respond to this call. Are you willing now to believe that you can be loved by you? Yes? Yes? Yes?

That's it. Let it be so.

The self that is deprived of love holds itself down in frequency. Now we will tell you something that is really about hearing. And we want you to understand this: As your receptors begin to advance through the acclimation to higher frequency that you are being endowed with through the responses you are having to this text, your hearing of self will begin to improve. But understand this, please: Much like the well, which has obstacles to accessing it, and there needs to be some resistance in order to clear the stuff that has kept you from accessing it, the way your hearing works is somewhat similar. And as you begin to hear yourself in your knowing, you may have to contend with a little bit of rubble that has been standing in the way of this ability. Because understand this, please: As you begin to know yourself in truth and your accessing of your own information comes clear, you will begin to know yourself in many different ways.

Now we will not tell you today that you can go right to love without looking at the real reasons why you have not allowed yourself to be loved. And if you wish to make another list, you may: "I could never be loved because"—and then let the list continue. But then please, please, please see that that list is only an out-picturing of prior experience that was based in thought and can be changed in accessing "I am Word."

When you look at the fears for what they are, you can release them. But believe me, the fear that you have had has investment in sticking around. And you may be instructed by them at any time to put the book away, forget it ever worked, forget that you saw that aura, or had that experience, forget it all because it cannot be so. And that "it cannot be so" is the ego's resistance to taking you to this next step in conscious belief of your own self-worth.

The higher you rise in frequency, the stronger your energy field becomes and the less ability lower frequency has to hold you. And those things that have tethered you to low frequency are the things that are being addressed so far in this text, one at a time, so that you can begin to lose them. And much like a balloon, yes, you begin to rise as the sandbags are dropped. But sometime you will be told, "Hey, wait a minute, everybody, there is no balloon, there's nothing happening, and by the way, if you let go of me, you will not be safe and you might even fly away."

So understand, everybody, when you encounter resistance through this work, it is actually a blessing and a real indication that you are moving forward. Obstacles come up when it is time to overcome them, and fear will have its way when fear is about to be released.

So we will go back now to you as the well. What does your experience look like when you are in Divine Love and when you are becoming Divine Love? Well, the first thing we want to say is: When you are love, you are yourself as love and operating in frequency. It does not look like you become somebody else. You become truly you in frequency. And then what you call to you will be in that frequency, in resonance, and your experiences radically, radically change. But as you vibrate at this frequency, your abilities are aligning themselves in new ways as well. And how you will use your gifts in consciousness may be altered in order to reflect the new level you are living at.

Imagine always that you had a voice that could sing ten octaves, but that you thought you could maybe sing a few notes, or maybe an octave. And if you look at the music that you would sing, it would be at a very, very limited level. But if you can understand now that your voice can soar to the angels, the level of music you will be given to sing will be much, much wider in its range and in its scope. And with so many more notes available to you to play and to sing, what kind of wonderful music can come forth from you? That is what we are saying will be changing.

Your gifts already are known to you as gifts. "I am a talented singer," or teacher, or construction worker. It doesn't matter. "I am a talented giver," father, whatever you want to say. You can define what those are for yourselves. But they may be limited, and radically limited once you understand what you are capable of in frequency.

Most of you have settled, because most of you have operated with a very, very narrow set of parameters of what you thought you could be. And your achievement, for lack of a better word, has been held within those parameters. If you look throughout history at those people who have accelerated the growth of this planet, they have always been singing an eight-octave range. They have always been moving far past the limitations of their time and reaching forward to call the future to them. And that is how great art, and great music, and great science has been created throughout time.

We will tell you this: As we expand you in frequency, what you reach for will be higher. It may not look like what you thought you wanted. It may look very, very different. But you will be reaching at that level. And what you will be transforming is your own life and for the benefit of you and others.

This is not selfish work. When you are a well, you are in nourishment and you are in nourishment of others. Now you are not
filling a need in the way that we described earlier, someone is in
desperate need of love so you love them. In fact, when you are resonating as love, you are doing that but not from an ego level. You are
supporting others in rising to that frequency. When you resonate
as love, you are the gift of love to others. And as they resonate with
you, they begin to heal and become who they are as well.

This work that we do with you, in many ways, is systemic. We
will tell you this again. One person lights up and gives permission
to the next and to the next and to the next. And as consciousness
changes on the individual level, it can change on the mass level as
well. Now we are not magicians. We are working very hard here to
offer you what we can to support this change. But we are not
allowed to override your will. So we can give you the manual and
all the assistance that you ask for, but you have to stake your own
claim:

"I am the well of love incarnate. Word I am Word through this
intention. Word I am Word."

We will work with you and we will assist you in developing your
own abilities as you move forward.

The requirements of this time have to do with responsibility.
And we want to talk about your physical bodies right now and
where you are not being responsible to you. And this has to do with
operations and functions of behavior. And we want to talk about
sexuality and we want to talk about how you implode when your
systems are not being honored in health.

We are going to ask Paul to take a moment now to change the
CD and we will come back in a moment. Stop now, please. Don't
speak.

(Pause)

Okay, we'll talk about the body you stand in for a moment as a reflection of frequency. You all must start to take responsibility for the physical form that you stand in and only in order to assist that it be able to hold the level of frequency that is trying to establish itself in your form.

Your ability right now to magnify frequency is somewhat limited by the body you stand in. And please understand that as you realign your frequency to the higher levels, the physical form has to shift in order to be able to hold this. And consequently, the body will go through changes. This will manifest differently, but as you call in the higher frequency and acclimate to it, those things that are held in the body, in terms of fear, in terms of memory, in terms of dis-ease, will be revealed in order to be cleared.

Now in some cases, this will require an emotional release. In other cases, you will have a much more physical experience as you shift your frequency. This can mean you ache, you get light-headed, you're not quite sure what's going on. These are really all indications that your system is changing and you are beginning to acclimate to higher frequency.

We will recommend that as you are in this passage, you take time to ground each day. And by ground we mean reconnect with the earth and make sure that you are still in your body or not floating someplace out there. This can be achieved through a walk on the earth, bathing, eating, anything that you do in order to feel yourself connected to the body in present time on this planet. These are simple systems that will support you.

Now we want to talk about sexuality for a few minutes because Paul has been wondering about this, and also because it is not something that gets addressed too readily in this way in this kind of a text. Your sexuality also is an expression of your consciousness. And how you address your sexuality can come from a high place or a low place depending on where you sit in frequency. We will give you an example of this.

If you are operating from low sexuality, you are not connecting the physical act that you engage in with the partner you are with. You are not aware of their consciousness or their innate beauty. And we don't speak about physical beauty. We speak about true beauty. If you are going to conjoin with another in physical response, in order to do this well, you need to be at high frequency.

"I am Word through the one I see before me" is a reminder that your partner is also an aspect of the divine and your choice to merge frequency through the sexual act is then blessed in that awareness. But you cannot say this as a litany. It must be true awareness. If you are not aware of the divinity of your partner, you are operating at lower frequency and you are engaging in a physical act that is not a truly conscious one.

Now we will recommend that those of you that embark on this passage begin to monitor your own responses as they relate to desire, as they relate to behavior, and as they relate to the divine action of co-creation through sexual action and blessing the other in frequency.

To be in sexual relations, finally, is a blessed act, but it can only be done in the awareness of this in order to be what it is meant to be. No, we are not talking about procreation, which is the real reason that people do this in physical form, to create progeny. We are talking about expression of sexuality in love that is expressed through bodies in frequency.

We recommend that you each do this: As you go about your day and you have these experiences of desire, ask yourself first what aspect of the self is being addressed. Now we are not going to talk silly, and Paul is already saying, "I know what aspect is being addressed. What else is there?" We are really telling you this:

"Where am I in Divine Love, and where am I not? Where am I in an awareness of those I see before me, and where am I not?"

We will be honest with you. If you are objectifying someone as a sexual object, you are not in awareness of them as a Divine Being. You are focusing on the package. And the package might be nice, and in a hundred years it will be dust. And that is a fact. You are spending your time focusing your attention, frankly, on flesh. And the spirit, we will say, that holds the flesh together is the real person inside. So once you can see the person inside beyond the package, you have a much better chance of going into love.

Now we will not tell you that you need to be in a committed relationship in order to have this expression. We will not tell you that your partner needs to be a different gender. We will tell you this: Your partner needs to be in agreement with your frequency and with your intent in order for this to be holy.

To use another person as their body without recognition of the beauty that is within them is, frankly, a defilement of God. Now we do not say this in a negative way, we say this as a fact. And all we mean by defilement is to tell you this: When you are pretending that there is not God in the person you are with in order to get a need met, you are acting out of alignment with Source. It's that easy. We are not speaking of sin, we are simply telling you this: If your action is about something that precludes the divine in your partner from coming forth in agreement, you are working with lower frequency.

Now everybody has needs. You can all understand this. You can all agree with this. Nobody is perfect. People do all kinds of things for different reasons and in different ways. But what we are telling you now is that to remain unconscious in the physical body through this act is actually not healing you and it is also reconfirming the negativity that has been placed around sex for too, too long. There is shame attached, there is judgment, there is fear, and people are responding to these things all the time. It is really, really, really unfortunate that something as magnificent as the human body in conjoining with a partner in love, or in grace, or in conscious awareness could become pornographic, which is essentially to debase the frequency of love. Now understand this: We will tell you there is no shame in the body, there is no shame in the act, but that which you out-picture it with, that which you present to it. If it is not in truth, you know it already.

Now we are not telling you that there is anything here that you need to be frightened of, nor are we trying to create another moral dictate that will appease others in a certain way and make others angry. All we are telling you in this section is that your responsibility, when you are engaged in this behavior, is to please, please, please remember and see the divine within your partner. "I am Word through one before me."

You are an aspect of God. Your partner is an aspect of God. What you choose to do is your business, and you choose it in high frequency, you will be lifting your vibration. When you choose it in low vibration, you will be losing your frequency, and that's as simple as that. It is not about achieving perfection in behavior at this stage of the game; it is about achieving consciousness.

"I am Word through the one before me. I am Word through my sexual behavior. I am Word through my desires. I am Word through my love."

Now we will tell you something. Guilt, in all of its manifestations, is a puddle of mud that you roll in and that you walk around in. And you can choose not to crawl into it. Ninety percent of guilt is based in the frequency of fear, and self-condemnation is not a divine act. So if you ever go around debasing the self through that action of guilt, you can choose now once and for all to say, No. We give you permission. That does not heal. That maintains low frequency and we would recommend, at this juncture, that you let it go once and for all.

"I am Word through my knowing of myself as healed from all of those things in my life that have caused me guilt. Word I am Word through this intention. Word I am Word."

Now Paul is resisting this. He's still reeling that we addressed sexuality quite as directly as we did, and he understands that there is a correlation for many between sexual behavior and self-esteem, and guilt has been embedded in people since they were first told to be ashamed of their nakedness. So is there a correlation? Yes. Is this something to be feared? No. We will look at shame in a later chapter. But today we want to talk about freedom. And you are free of these things as you choose to be free.

Your investment in guilt is something you call to you as a way of self-punishment for behavior real or imagined. And you are doing this to yourself because in that moment you believe you should be punished. And punishment, we will say, always arrives when one seeks it. But we will tell you this: You are not the Creator in this aspect. And for you to be in self-punishment and blame of the self again means you have changed your frequency. You do not need to go there, you do not need to stay there, and we can release it with you.

"I am Word now through this choice to release myself from all guilt that is connected to issues of the body. I am now choosing to release all guilt that is connected to any behavior connected to other human beings. I am choosing now to release all guilt based on any assessment of myself based in cultural norms that I have not adhered to or held to myself in wise ways. I am now choosing to release the guilt that has bound me to fear. I am Word through this intention. Word I am Word."

The responsibility to each of you now is to remember always that you are free in your actions, but your actions must become in alignment with Source in order to resonate at a high level. And the choices that you make when you are acclimating to the frequency of the Word are in divine order and are recognized as such by your soul. So really, what you are doing, on a very simple level, is stepping out of the driver's seat and letting the Higher Self, the knowing self, that aspect of the self that is Word, to run the show.

We want to return to the well at the end of this chapter, and we are saying the name of the chapter is "I Am the Well." And we want to tell you one thing: Your ability to love yourself is recognized by you already. That aspect of the self that says that it cannot be so is merely a creation, and the releasing of that is what we are engaging you with today. And we are pleased for the progress we have made here.

"I give thanks to my own Higher Self for permitting me the ability to be in receipt of this divine information. And I am choosing now to learn, as I need to in order to acclimate to the new frequency. I am Word through this intention. Word I am Word."

Thank you both and stop.

TWELVE

TRAVELING

Day Sixteen

We'll talk for a few minutes first about freedom of creation, and how you are actually all able to create what you want, whenever you want it, through your choices and through your conscious actions based in thought. Now when you decide you want something, you must contain it first within the self in order to bring it forth in manifestation. You have to decide what it is you need; you have to work with it consciously in order to bring it into manifestation. And as you do this, you see what you are capable of and free to do in manifestation.

When you decide today that you can choose what you want from a different perspective of a soul's perspective, you can begin to believe that what you can call in to you by way of demonstration is beyond what you have expected of yourself.

Now we talk about freedom, in this regard, as a level of awareness. And freedom, frankly, is very little more than a level of awareness of the self as free. Any construct that could be created to withhold you from your good, frankly, has been agreed upon in consciousness by you all, and that is why it has remained in place. Now as you begin to accept the demonstration of yourself as a Divine Being, as one in manifestation, you begin to align to a new paradigm of what can be created and what you can choose.

Up until now, we have decided, very simply, to attend to the business at hand, which are those creations that you can already see or can imagine. And those things that you imagine, for the most part, still adhere to a central system of self-identification of one who is somewhat limited by the physical body that he stands in. We would tell you to go to the store and you imagine taking a walk and going to the store. But what we are really telling you right now is that you can go to the store without the body and you can have an experience of yourself without the body that will change your understanding of who you are, finally, and for once give you the self-identification of yourself in frequency that will command you begin to work at other levels of awareness than those that have been accessible to you until now.

You have taken a little class so far in *The Book of Love and Creation,* which has taught you that you create and that those things that limit you have been agreed upon by you. And those things that contain you, or take you out of flow in creation, need to be contended with in order for you to move forward in your self-identification and experience as a Divine Being.

Now to trust this means that you have to say today, "I have been on a course, I have been studying, I have learned some things, and all of these things that I have learned thus far have taken me to this place of self-identification." Now we want to move you past this place into a new understanding of frequency and the sense of identification with the self as frequency that transcends physical phenomenon and experience and moves into a higher alignment.

Now Paul is saying, "What are we going to do?" Well, we're going to lift you up, as it were, and as we lift you up we are going to take you somewhere new. And in newness, you will begin to self-identify as frequency in a different way. Our job today is to teach you to liberate the self from the physical body in a way that will align you to yourself as love.

Now when we tell you this, we are not telling you anything magical. The first thing you need to understand is that you leave your body a lot, and when you imagine things, or you daydream, or when you are sleeping, an aspect of you is, in fact, moving out of the body. "I am imagining I am talking to my friend Fred in his apartment." And guess what? An aspect of you is traveling to Fred's apartment and you are sticking around there in consciousness. When you imagine that you are going on a job interview, an aspect of yourself is already in the job interview. So a part of you, already, is used to drifting off.

What we would like to teach you today is what you can do when you're off on a little trip. Now imagine right now that you are a beam of light, and your frequency vibrates in accordance with the dictates of your consciousness. The first thing you need to do is raise consciousness, and we will do this with you as follows.

"I am now choosing to raise my frequency into a higher level of knowing. I am Word through this intention. Word I am Word."

And now we would like you to lift, in your intention, so that the frequency that you are is now manifesting itself in higher frequency.

"I am Word through my frequency with this intention. I am lifting my frequency one octave with each breath. Word I am Word through this intention. Word I am Word."

And we would like you to breathe in ten times. And with each breath, we want you to imagine that you are accelerating your frequency and bringing it up an octave in tone. Do this please. Now once you have completed this exercise, we want you to imagine that you are lifting and you are vibrating as you lift, and you are traveling in this light that you are to a place where you can conjoin completely in the frequency of love. Imagine, if you wish, that this light that you are in frequency is merging with another light, and this light that you merge with is beautiful and is love.

As you merge with this frequency of love, you are re-patterned in love, and that which has stood in the way, and that which has precluded you from your own experience of your love, is now being cleared in easy and perfect ways:

"I am Word through this perfect merging with Divine Love. Word I am Word."

As you vibrate in this frequency, you begin to accept yourself as what you are: an aspect of the Creator vibrating in the frequency of love.

And now we would like you to move in energy. And we would like you to go visit someone you know. Imagine that as this beam of light that you are, you are traveling to a new place in consciousness. And you are sitting beside your mother, or your friend, or someone you know and care for. And as you do this, we would like you to feel them in your frequency. What do you feel like when you tune in to your friend?

"I am Word through the one before me. Word I am Word."

You are a vessel, simply put, of energy, and you are responding to your friend, or your mother, or whoever you chose as frequency, and you are feeling them as frequency. "I am Word through those I see before me" sets the intention to call the frequency of the Word through all that you see before you:

"I am Word through this room. I am Word through this place. I am Word through my ability to transform frequency in this intention. I am Word through all that I see before me."

Now we would like you to understand something. When you do this work, in fact, you are moving inter-dimensionally. You are still present where you are and, in fact, you are traveling in consciousness, but your consciousness does not operate along physical lines. You do not have to travel to Detroit by car. You go there in a twinkling of an eye through intention. And as you are vibrating in this frequency, "I am in my love, I am Word," you can transform the frequency of that which you encounter.

Your self-identification, still, with physical form has precluded you, in many ways, from seeing what you are really made of. And what we are teaching you today is that you can bypass limitations that you have created or accepted as fact and go begin to have a new experience of yourself as energy. "I am Word through all that I see before me."

In your mind right now, we would wish you to select a place you have always wanted to go to. And we would like you to carry yourself there in frequency. We will simply suggest that you close your eyes, you vibrate at high frequency, you expand your energy field, if you wish, and you travel there as a beam of light. And as you are there, see what you see, feel what you feel, know what you know. Some of you may get images, some of you may get impressions, some of you may have no experience at all the first several times you work with this exercise.

We will tell you this: When you are traveling in frequency, you are traveling. And if you want a memento in consciousness from your trip, be clear that it is a good one and ask for it. And what we mean by this simply is: Ask your knowing to teach you and to show you what you need to know.

As you continue in this work, you become your own authority, because you have begun working in congruence with your own Divine Self, your own higher frequency, and these are your teachers. So as you choose to align the self to this level of knowing, you have the opportunity to ask yourself questions and to begin to trust the information that comes forth to you.

Now we will tell you this: As you manifest these abilities, you have to understand that you are responsible for your own frequency. This is for all of you and this is everyday maintenance. If you were a car, you would know to gas it up, you would know to wash it down when it was in the storm or in the mud, and you would know to get it checked once in a while. Your energy field also needs your attention. And you can clear it out with Divine Light through this intention:

"I am Word through this intention to call forth Divine Light to clear my energy field of anything and everything that is needing to clear. I am Word through this intention. Word I am Word."

You can visualize Divine Light if you wish, washing you down. You can do any number of things to clear your aura, and they are effective, but this is your responsibility. If you are not in the body and operating from that place of knowing, you need to be clear that your energy field is clear and safe. And you must do this daily through your own choice to maintain your own psychic hygiene, as it were.

Now once you begin to understand that you can begin to travel, you can also understand that you can begin to hear. Now this is a different process, and it has to do with telepathic hearing. And we will try to explain this to you. If you were to tune in to a friend of yours and ask them what they felt, and begin to feel what you feel, you might access information. And as you learn to listen to the way that information presents itself to you, you will begin to have an experience of hearing in a different way.

The belief, still, that accessing information at this level is something that you do not do already is one of the problems you are encountering. Eighty percent of the time you know what people feel about you, you feel it, and knowing and being in that feeling is a way of accessing information through frequency. When you are able, finally, to gift that frequency with language or, if you wish, image, if that is how you prefer to work, or how your energy system teaches you, that is acceptable too. But you must understand, now, that as you travel and as you think of people, you are actually tuning in to them. As you tune in to them, you can access information.

We would like you to choose a friend and to make an agreement with that friend by voice, or by telephone, or in person, or whatever way you communicate to make an appointment. And we would like you to tune in to that friend. And in doing this, what you do is very simple: "I am Word through so and so." And you begin to scan and feel them in frequency. Take mental notes of what you feel and then communicate it to them. If you wish, and they are a student of this book, have them do this with you as well. But as you begin to learn that you can transfer frequency this way, you become more adept at your own responses.

We have talked earlier in the book about clairsentience, we have talked about hearing, and all we are really doing now is lifting the stakes a little bit to show you that as you progress in your own frequency, as you begin to accept that you are beyond the physical body in terms of your abilities, you can change things, you can have a new experience of yourself in frequency.

Now we will tell you this: As you are changing your name to "I am Word," the self that is lower, the self that has self-identified as the one in power, will continue to object. And the easiest way to know when this is happening is when you get angry. You get angry at yourself, you get angry at the teaching. But understand, again, this is a sign of growth.

Now we would like you all to do something with us:

"I am now choosing to Word through my knowing of my own divinity. I am now choosing to claim the Word is amplifying and correcting any imbalance in my own awareness of myself as a Divine Being. I am now listening to myself in a higher frequency. And as I do this, I become aware of my ability to hear others in their frequency. I am Word through this intention. Word I am Word."

Now the ability to pick up information through the human energy field, as we have already told you, is something that you do naturally. People that put up a shingle and call themselves psychics simply have refined this ability to an extent where they can interpret information. They can read the landscape. And that is why they call it "reading." They are reading and interpreting the information that is given to them.

When you begin to hear telepathically, we want to explain something to you: It can work a little bit differently. When Paul works with someone and they say, "What is going on with my cousin Ruth?" Paul simply tunes in to cousin Ruth by the name and the name holds the frequency for him. So he steps into Ruth, as it were, and he feels what she feels like, or he may begin to resemble her in her features, or in her demeanor. The first thing he will feel is where she is at emotionally. That is the first thing that presents. And then once he feels that, he can begin to hear. And by "hearing" we mean he begins to interpret her with the information she offers him at a higher frequency.

This is not invasive work, and we will explain why. When Paul tunes in at this level of frequency, he is in connection with the Higher Self of the person being tuned in to and a conversation is ensuing. So it's always mutually agreed upon at a higher level and this is always for benefit. It is not uncommon for Paul to hear someone say, "I'm not talking about it," if there is a specific question, and then there stands their truth and it is honored.

However, if you tune in to someone in a general way—for example, "How is my cousin Ruth doing?"—and you feel depressed and you feel like your pores are blocked from too much cigarette smoke or that your mouth tastes bad, you may get a general sense of what cousin Ruth feels like, or how she is doing. But if you specify a question—"How is my cousin Ruth doing at her new job?"—and then you focus the request that way and you tune in, you may get something very, very different. She sits up straight, she beams, her shoulders are thrown back, and she pats her chest as if proud of herself. And there you go. Now you have information.

Now the way we just described this information was through physical response and tracking the emotional self that presents. Is it hearing? In a way it is, but it's not the same as hearing a voice. That can happen as well.

Now imagine this: We ask you to tune in to cousin Ruth again to find out what's been bugging her, and you hear the name "Arthur." Or she makes a face. Or you feel your own self make a face because you are tuned in to her and you get the name "Arthur." Or you get any other information. Listen to it, please. You may at first think that you are hearing it in your imagination, and in fact you are not. The way to find out, again, is to work with a friend so that you can begin to trust yourself when you begin to psychically open up.

Now when you are doing this work, always, always, always we require you to work with a protection of some sort, and it's only because you are going off into uncharted territory and you might as well have the sense that you are protected on your journey.

It is basic common sense at this level of training to be clear that when you go to a friend's house, you have remembered to put your clothes on. It's not a lot different than that.

Now we will tell you this: What you are doing when you are hearing is you are picking up frequency. And that frequency then is being translated into language for you by your own system. In a way, as you begin to open at this level, you will find that what you can do will surprise you because it is the benefit of a refined energy system. The work of the last book and the work of this book has been to work with you to refine your frequency to become aware of your own acceptance of your own frequency as a Divine Being. And the benefits of knowing this are as follows: You can begin to experience yourself operating in different dimensions of reality. The exercises that we have given you today have been about operating in other realities. Now always understand this: You are not going elsewhere. These other dimensions co-exist with yours, the one you are experiencing right now.

If you can imagine that there is a book and you are looking at a page, and you are reading that page, but you do not realize that if you turn the page beyond it is another page with new information, perhaps even talking about the same things from a different perspective, and then you turn the next page and more is revealed. That is how these dimensions operate.

You are systemizing yourself through this work to expand your consciousness to an awareness that there is more. Now we can tell you that there is more, and that will stretch the parameters of your experience. But, for example, to teach you something is very different than having you experience it. So part of the work of the book that we give you is allowing you to enter into the possibility of your own demonstration and your own experience.

We want to explain something. You have a mother and suddenly she knows that her child is sick. You are walking home and you suddenly have a bad feeling that something is wrong in the house. All that is happening in these instances is that you are accessing information through other dimensions. That's how these things occur. Why do you think you sometimes know who is on the phone when it's about to ring? You know this because the person who is calling you has taken a little trip in their mind and are imagining you in your home picking up the phone. You are feeling their frequency that is already present in your space.

So yes, we are teaching you, but we want to remind you now that these things that we teach you are what you are made of. They are part of your experience as you stand today, and they are changing, and they are amplifying as you continue forward on this journey in this work.

Now we will tell you something else. How you think about people impacts them in frequency. If you are angry with someone, you are sending anger. If you are fantasizing about someone sexually, you are sending that energy to them as well. When you see someone who is a public figure, those people are very, very protected in order to be able to support the kind of projections that are sent to them. They have to have that kind of armor to sustain that level of psychic visibility. If you are imagining someone as your lover, that person, believe it or not, is picking up on this in frequency, which is to say that an aspect of the person is already reframing their energetic system to counter that or to accept it.

We'll give you an example. Paul learned many years ago that when someone was angry with him he would feel it, a male at the right ear, a woman at the left, and this would come as a stinging at the ear, which usually meant that he was being discussed. Once you understand that your own energy system is also vulnerable in this way, it makes you much more responsible to the kind of energy you send out to others.

Now there is nothing "witchy" about this. We are not telling you anything that isn't already happening. But what we are telling you is that thoughts are creative and when you send out negative energy in consciousness and it is directed, it is impactful. And that is where you need to protect yourself or rise in frequency to the level that you will no longer be impacted by that frequency if it is sent your way.

Imagine this: You're operating at a low frequency, and you are standing in the middle of a field where there are people throwing rocks back and forth. You're gonna get hit. As you raise in frequency and as you go higher in vibration, your frequency no longer identifies with the rocks being thrown. You have risen above it, as it were, and it no longer impacts your system at all. When war is engaged in, it's a bunch of rocks being thrown back and forth. And as long as this planet is still in mutual agreement that that's a way to solve a problem, this planet will be existing in a dilemma of frequency.

On a personal level, you can begin to counter this. On an individual level now, practically, we will tell you that it is healthy for you at initial stages of development to honor the energy system that you are when you are working in light and honor yourself with protection. But we are not telling you that as you rise in frequency, the requirement of that changes because you are now aligned to a new level of self-identification where the problems or the dis-ease or the negativity cannot impact you. That is what ascension is about. And that is raising frequency. We expect you each to begin to learn and to begin to discipline the selves in these ways if you wish to continue forward in your study. As we said earlier, this is basic maintenance.

In our first book we spoke very directly about a paradigm shift that is occurring, and we told you that there is frequency available now on this dimensional plane that is lifting you, and that the kind of growth that is available to you now may have taken many lifetimes to achieve. So we are telling you this: If you wish to take advantage of this shift and participate in it consciously, we will recommend that you begin to work with the identity "I am Word," and as you do this, you lift your frequency.

"I am Word through my body. Word I am Word.

I am Word through my vibration. Word I am Word.

I am Word through my knowing of myself as Word. Word I am Word."

Your abilities will express themselves based on your level of consciousness. And understand this, please. If you are not demonstrating psychically yet, there is more work to be done in consciousness. And as we have said before, this is not psychic school. The reason for you to understand what you are capable of is so that you can re-identify the self as a spiritual being who has an obligation to support his or her brother in raising their frequency as well.

This is how the change occurs, and these are tools, very simply put, that will acclimate them as you lift to the new identity that is present for you now. We are each working with you as you request it, to support you in this ascension. If you can imagine, for a moment, that you are lifting your arms to the sky above your head, imagine that they are being met, as if from a trapeze artist who would lift you up to carry you to the next level of self-awareness. We are able to do this with you as you requested.

We are not God. We are an aspect of God, as are you. We have been doing this a while, and a good long time, if you wish to know, and we are pleased for this opportunity to support you in this lifting.

We would like to thank you each for your attentions now, and we will leave you with this:

"I am Word through those I see before me. I am Word through all I identify with. And I am now learning that I am much more than my physical form. I am Word through this intention. Word I am Word."

Thank you each and stop.

THIRTEEN

HELP

Day Sixteen (Continued)

"Help." This is the chapter. "Help." And we will tell you what we mean by this. When you require help, your first impulse is to go outside of the self to get a need met. Now we will tell you this again: When you are reaching outside of the self as a first impulse, you are usually requiring yourself to step aside and abnegate your own ability to get what you need. Now of course, if your house is on fire you call help, but you also douse the flame if it's one that can be doused. So we are telling you this: As you choose your journey we want you to get out of the habit of believing yourself to be in danger and requiring help. This is a paradigm that is serving to keep you in bondage to fear.

Everywhere you look, you are told that there is danger forthcoming. You have been told that you will be attacked, you have been told that the world will end, you have been told that your neighbor wants your money. Whatever it is you have been told, you have ascribed to on a level of acceptance because it's out there and it's doing its insidious work to keep you in place.

If you can imagine that every emblem of fear that you have ever been told was there to keep you in control, you would be astonished at how small your life has become in response to this. If you could understand that your life is expected to be open armed and welcoming and what you have instead is a defended existence, we would show you that the way out is through the action of love, and help then becomes an offering and not a cry of alarm. Do you understand the difference? Help as a frequency is meant to be a gift and a loving one. Help as a cry for support in danger is something very different, and we want to realign this word now for its truthful meaning:

"I am in help, I am being helped, and I am supporting others in help and I am safe."

The belief in safety is what we started this text with and we are returning to it now on a larger level. Your self-identification as a Divine Being, which has been commenced and is being engaged now in frequency, gives you a certain responsibility to the planet. And when we say the "planet," we simply mean existence, those who live here that are seeking to become awake.

The purpose of being awakened is to become a way-shower, and as you become aware of your own dominion of yourself as a Divine Being, your obligation is to teach others the same. Now you can teach through sharing this book with a friend, or you can simply teach through how you navigate yourself in your existence. As you demonstrate your own ability to stand in the light, to stay in knowing, to recreate those aspects of the self that have stood in fear into love, you become a living self-decision activated as Word, and as you do this you call to you others in frequency that you would help.

Now this design can happen on two different levels. You can do this with your brother and you can do this with your town, or your country, or your world.

"I am Word through all that I see before me." In your imagination, most likely, you are seeing a room of people. "Hello, everybody. I am Word through those I see before me."

Let's broaden it for a moment. In your mind's eye, imagine that you see a hundred people, a hundred people you have known or may never know. "I am Word through those I see before me." And allow the frequency to do what the frequency does, which is to realign the energy systems or seed them, if you wish, into the frequency of Word. "I am Word through those I see before me."

Now we would like you to imagine a thousand people. "I am Word through those I see before me." And a million. "I am Word through those I see before me." And a hundred million. "I am Word through those I see before me."

What you intend with this is that a hundred million will become activated into a frequency that will realign them into their own knowing of themselves as an aspect of the Creator. How their systems choose to operate with this must be in accordance with their own soul's will for them. You do not proselytize. You do not force. The energy does the work. "I am Word through all that I see before me."

And yes, this works across borders, across cultural lines and religions. We have spoken to you already in our first text that this is a work that is being functioned in different cultures, in different vocabularies, but the intent is the same. Each one walking on this earth is an aspect of the Creator whether or not they are conscious of it. Becoming conscious of it changes everything and those borders and those walls will begin to disintegrate, as this is truly understood. So, "I am Word through all that I see before me" does not turn someone Hindu or Christian or Muslim. It teaches them at a soul level that they are an aspect of the divine and this is shared by all men, by all women, by all theories of creation in religion. We are each born with the seed of God, and that seed is coming into its growth and its blooming. "I am Word through all that I see before me."

Now we told you in the last chapter that you could bypass physical form when you are working in frequency, and that is what you are doing here.

"I am choosing now to recognize myself as a Divine Being in full manifestation. And as I am activated in Word, I rise above this planet, I rise above the limitations of this physical world, and I claim this: I am Word through all those standing before me on this earth. I am Word through this intention. Word I am Word."

And as this is done, the earth is healed, it is helped, it is loved.

"I am now seeing all that I see before me in its wisdom, in its awakening, and in its manifestation. Word I am Word through this intention. Word I am Word."

We told you "Help" was the chapter and that the fear that tells you you require it and you are in danger needs to be dismantled, and we will explain this to you. It is the tool of control that keeps you in the belief that you are not safe. When someone says to you, "So and so is after you," you have been poisoned in the energy of that person and, believe it or not, not the person who may or may not be after you, but the one who told you the truth, or the lie, or whatever he was saying about his brother. "I know that someone is out to get you" prompts you immediately to put up a wall of fear. Now understanding this for what it is, frankly, which is a tactic and a mental construct, you can then contend with it and heal it.

Now we are not telling you that there are not situations when someone may be out to get someone, but believe it or not, the amount of fear that people operate in as if that were the truth far exceeds any realistic out-picturing of that kind of scenario. "You are all under attack," "The world is in danger," whatever you want to say, is there to prompt you to move into fear and, in this case, to ask an external authority, in most cases a government, to protect you: "You must protect me. You must protect me, I need help," and then you go into agreement about your own limitation and you give the authority to the one who is frightening you. What kind of sense does this make?

However, if you can understand that this is the agreement that you have all entered into and it is the way that you are being controlled, you can begin to change things. Everyone who has an investment in outcomes around ownership and control of property, of oil, has an investment in keeping others without. Do you understand this? These are the creations and these are the symbols of this time. There have been other symbols used to wage war historically, but this is what you have come to now.

Now understand this, please. In this moment in time, in this moment today, you are safe and you are sitting someplace and you are having an experience of a text. Now we will tell you this: You are always in this place in some dimension. How you understand time will change as you begin work in frequency. But you can as easily heal yourself when you were two as you can in this moment as you can in ten years once you understand that how you move through dimensions does not adhere to this timetable that you are working in agreement of. It is an artificial construct that you have created in order to organize experience.

Now understand this: If you imagine your safety is now, you can see your safety out-pictured and presented and claimed in future time because, as we have just told you, time is time is time is now is now is now. "I am Word through all that I see before me" is inclusive of what you would call the future. It happens now, it is accessed through the now, but it is a truth.

So we would like you now to take a moment and do this with us:

"I am now choosing to claim my power back from any systems of fear that have been created to keep me in limitation by any formalized structure, including government and including religion, that may be binding me to a sense of helplessness and fear. I am now choosing to become aware of myself in my power as a Divine Being. I am now knowing myself as free. I am Word through this intention. Word I am Word."

As you do this, you make a decision. You will see the artifice, you will see the control, and you will see the deceit in the structures of fear that are out-pictured on this plane. You are choosing this with an awareness to rise above it and to dismantle it through this intention:

"I am now choosing to dismantle all of the matrixes of fear that I have invested in in consciousness. As I withdraw my energy from them and lift to a higher sight, I know that I am free of external control and I am free in the knowing of my worth as a free man, as a free woman, as a divine aspect of the Creator. Word I am Word through this intention. Word I am Word."

As this is stated your reality will begin to shift, and it will happen this way: You will begin to notice very quickly where you are leading yourself in ways that you have been indoctrinated by: "I don't pick up a hitchhiker," "I don't open the door," "I have to unplug the phone; it might be somebody bad," "I have to change the lock," whatever the behavior is.

Now we are not telling you not to make sense in your choices.

You have been gifted with discernment and discernment means you understand what you are required to do. But once you understand that you do not have to make these choices based in fear, you will liberate the self to become inclusive and to be open armed, as it were, to those you see before you.

Every man and woman on this planet only wants to be loved. That is all they want, whether or not they will admit it. All they want is love. And what love truly is, is true acceptance regardless of who or what they think or they believe they may have been, done, seen, or anything else. So we offer you this:

"I am now choosing to see my neighbor, to see all those before me in love. And I know that love is unconditional acceptance."

As you work with this on a practical level, your life will transform. We guarantee you this. In our last text, we told you to sit in a bus station and see everybody before you as perfect. In this text, we are going to take it a little farther.

You are going to sit in a park, or in a café, or anyplace where there is transit. And we are going to imagine with you that as you sit, you become a beam of light. And if you wish to do it this way, you may: You may activate the light in the center of the heart and bring it all around you and radiate in your frequency. But sit in the park or that café and be a light.

Now as you sit there, we want you to do this. We want you to stand up and claim this silently:

"I am now knowing myself as an aspect of the Creator and all that I see before me will be reflected as such."

And then your job is to stay there. Sit if you wish, and hold this vision of all that you see before you. You are seeing them each unconditionally accepted and "I am claiming Word through all that I see before me." We want you to do this and we want you to be in practice with it.

Understand this, please. The work of this book, finally, is experiential. So as you stay there on your bench, in your café, and you witness the amazing creation that parades before you, you will choose to see them as God sees them, in their perfection, unconditionally loved and accepted. If you cannot imagine this, pretend you can. It is doable and it will gift you with the change that will carry you through the remainder of your experience on this plane.

The ability to hold others in Divine Love is, in many ways, the result of the work of this book. So if you wish, we would recommend the following:

> "I am seeing those before me with love. I am love through the ones I see before me. Word I am Word through this intention. Word I am Word."

When you claim yourself as love, you align your frequency to "I am in love," and that energy moves through you and that energy participates in this action that you are bringing forth to your brothers. "I am Word through those I see before me" brings the Word. "I am love through all I see before me" calls forth Divine Love to do that work as well.

Now you are serving others through this enterprise, but you are serving yourself as well. In order to do this effectively, you have to be operating at a high frequency. When you are operating at a high frequency, your life becomes magical. You are where you want to be, you are where you need to be, and you are calling to you those experiences you require to demonstrate your knowing of yourself as in alignment. So if you understand that by seeing the perfection in others, by being aware of their own inherent divinity, by claiming, "I am Word," you are blessed in return, there should be no hesitation in doing this.

Now if you have people in your life that you are still at war with, we have to work with that directly. Paul has been wondering about this. "What happens when I am angry and I am not in forgiveness?" If you are not in forgiveness, the first thing you have to understand is that you are frightened, usually of yourself or, perhaps, of the person that you still hold the anger at. So if you see that the anger is camouflaging fear, usually pride is the culprit, as has been said, we can tell you that you can dismantle it through Word.

"I am Word through this feeling of rage. I am now choosing to release it and to recreate it in Divine Love. Word I am Word through this intention."

As you begin to work with this actively, you will begin to realize that you are not passive to your experience as one healed; you are an active participant. And as you go forward in this work, you will choose, day after day, only to make those choices that will align you to higher frequency. It is habit to go to the old places of rage and fear, and you live in a culture where people go to the movies to watch other people get blown up. So you are being received with these kinds of messages day after day after day. And as you begin to realign yourself to this new identity, your experience changes.

Paul began to wonder about two months ago why he didn't want the television on. The real reason was that he was no longer able to comfortably resonate with the images of violence and the news that was propagating fear. He found it hard, although he did not know why. As you change your frequency, what you align to stops being what it used to be and you have to call to you a new set of experiences to demonstrate the level of resonance that you are now supporting.

This is very interesting to experience and it's not a lot different than finding out that one day, for no apparent reason, you had no desire to eat meat. Now the habit is to have the hamburger; however, the craving is for something lighter that vibrates at a higher frequency. And as you begin to honor those changes, your experience begins to change. And as we have said before, as you arrive at each new choice that is not based in fear, your vibration rises accordingly.

You are always choosing, every moment of the day. We are going to tell you now that your desire for help outside of the self is a valid one. But help as an alarm that is based in an understanding that you have been gifted with that is intended to keep you in fear or powerlessness is not. And we are choosing now to support you in beginning to operate in a new way.

We will stop this chapter for today and we will continue tomorrow. Thank you both. I am Word.

Day Seventeen

Freedom is the key to where you have to go next. Each and every man must now know himself as free in order to begin to engender the kind of transformation that is available. Everybody here on this plane is now ready to uplift whether they know it or not. If you can imagine right now that there is a tide that is rising and everyone is being lifted in this frequency regardless of whether they know it or not, you will begin to understand that what is actually happening here is a global phenomenon. And how this is out-pictured in each civilization as the civilization transforms will be the way this plays out.

Now we will tell you this: As you are all upwards in your frequency, you will know each other in a new way. And this transition,
this time of change on a global level, will be perceived at first as a
falling apart of old paradigms that no longer are able to support the
new vision and the new frequency.

We will use this image for you: Imagine that you are wearing
clothes that you have begun to outgrow and the body gets stronger
and bigger. The clothes break free from the body. There is an initial
kind of restraint and discomfort as the clothing becomes too tight,
but they eventually fall away. Now, of course, nobody wants to
stand there naked, so everybody's trying to cover themselves and
hold those pieces of cloth in place to stop the process. But the process is ongoing. You have outgrown the way you have lived, and the
way that you have lived on this plane has resulted in changes to the
planet that must now be rectified. You are the cause of the problems
on this plane and as you begin to counter that with truth, with the
resolution to move upwards in frequency, you can contend with
those things that have been your creations on a level of matrix and
foundation.

When you take down a house that is rickety, you will find the
foundation is there. When we work with the frequency of the Word,
we have poured a new foundation, for the house that is being built
will stand strong. You are the house, you are the frequency, and
you will stand strong.

We want to talk for a moment about requirements for change.
And what this actually means is that as you go on this path in your
ascension, you choose things anew. And as we have said to you earlier, what you choose in love will bring you to a higher frequency.
As you have requirements for anything you do that has a purpose-
ful result, you have requirements for your growth. And we want
to teach you a few things today to shift you into recreating the

self-identity that you operate from in a way that will hold you up as the tide comes, as the frequency lifts, and as you stand strong in your new foundation.

We have spoken to you already about fear and how you can be used by media, by others, to get amplified as fear and consequently self-abnegate your own power as you go into reaction. So we are going to suggest today that as you show yourself your truth, "I am Word," you begin to limit yourself in what you expect your responses to be to fear. Now we will show you what we mean.

"Oh my God, there is something terrible happening in the world." Well, you can go there and you can call it terrible, which is a way to label it, or you can move into a kind of accordance with truth and you can say:

"I am now choosing to see that which I see before me in Divine Love. I am Word through this intention. Word I am Word."

What you are essentially doing is agreeing with divinity and you are choosing not to go into alignment with a fear-based construct.

"Oh my God, something terrible happened." Well, it did or it didn't, but frankly, your response to the information and how it impacts your system is what is crucial here. When you go into agreement with negativity, you are lowering your frequency.

Now Paul is wondering, "Does that mean we go into denial?" No, we don't say that. We are telling you not to go into agreement about the merit, the good and the bad of the situation, and stay in holding your vision, instead, of divine worth and perfection.

If all that you see before you is of the divine, that must be inclusive of all that you see before you. And to decide today that that thing that you thought was terrible was outside of the Creator gives it merit and causes you to lower your own frequency. So of course, we can tell you when someone is presenting illness, you see them as healed. You don't deny their experience, but you hold them in a higher frequency of Divine Love and you are holding a picture and a vision for them of healing which then benefits their frequency.

You are realigning your own frequency to be in support of the divine action of the Word to do its job. "I am Word through the one I see before me." So if you hear of something you would decide is terrible or is frightening, how you react is your province. And remember always that your experience is manifested by you in accordance with your thoughts. If you can understand that you had a country that was paralyzed in fear by alerts of perceived danger for several years until people began to ignore the alerts, you can see what happens when people change consciousness.

Now if you are walking along a shore, it's a wise idea to know what time the tide comes in. You can be responsible for your well-being in that regard. No need to get swept out to sea. However, that is not an action based in fear; that is an action in wisdom and discernment. It's a simple thing. You do not cross the street when the light is red and the cars are passing you by; you wait for the signal. Now that is an opportunity, but it is very, very different than becoming frightened.

You don't become frightened when the tide comes in if you knew where you were standing was the right place to stand, nor are you frightened when the light changes and the cars begin to move again if you are standing securely at the roadway entrance. However, when we tell you that up until now you have been manipulated by what you were supposed to think in order to do what was expected of you, you can then begin to realign to new ideas about the information that you are presented with culturally through other sources. Now we will say these sources can be a close friend, it can be a newspaper, it can be anything. You are always responsible for your response. And to agree to go into fear will lower your frequency and allow yourself to become invested in the matrix of fear.

Now the job of fear, as we have stated, is to create more fear. That is what it does. And when you withdraw your attention from it, what in fact you do is you stop feeding it. And of course, when something is not fed, it withers away. It cannot sustain itself in your energy field and it will dismantle.

This is done first on a level of the individual but it is also done at a group level when a group decides not to be frightened. And we will explain this: There are always shared constructs when people go into agreement. Everybody decides to celebrate at the stroke of midnight even though they know that it is midnight at different times on the planet at the beginning of a New Year. You still go into agreement that this is the time to jump up and down and sing a song. So you can also go into agreement that there is nothing to be frightened of.

Now it has been said that the only thing to fear is fear itself, and it is actually a truism, but that still implies that one should fear fear. We will tell you this: When you withdraw your frequency, which is withdrawing your attention from those things that you have previously invested as fear, that will no longer be your experience. You will begin to live a life that does not approve of or resonate with the constructs of fear.

Now those things that you have invested in until now as your safety and your security that were originally born in fear, you must know, are not healthy structures. They are easily broken. When you have a wedding and the participants are both frightened of the infidelity of the other so they bond in a ceremony, that is a marriage that will not last. The ceremony was constructed based out of fear of losing the other and, consequently, it can be razed and mostly likely will be razed very, very quickly. However, a structure that is built in love or is built in grace, which is the support of the divine in your endeavors, will stand strong and will withstand the tide that comes.

So when you build in truth and you respond in truth, you are actually building the house that is you in your frequency. When you go into agreement with fear—"Help! Help! Help! Danger! Danger! Danger!"—you go to the other side, as it were, by going into agreement with limitation and you undo the work you have done.

Now we will tell you today that the reason we spend so much time on this text addressing the issue of fear is because it is time for you to start living without it. And as you learn to live without it and begin to experience yourself as free, you will have a new experience of your identity and "I am standing in my knowing" is the decree we will use to teach you to learn to live without fear.

When you are presented with something from an external source that would provoke you with fear: "I am in my knowing." As you respond with that, you can actually shift from a reaction into a response. And a response is chosen. And you can decide, in that moment, not to go into agreement with a system of fear. You are all frightened of aspects of the self still. And please understand this: Those things that you are frightened of within you you will see out-pictured in your experience. And those are the magnets, as it were, that call to you fears from the outside. So your first job, always, is to come into balance with the self in his knowing, in her knowing, of her own worth in the Word. And then the second thing is to stop buying the goods that you are being sold every day you pick up a newspaper that states that you should be frightened.

There is nothing to fear except that which you invest in fear. Do you understand this? We can give you lots of examples but we feel that this is apparent, and that you must each, as of today, learn to go into your knowing and respond to that information that is presented to you in order to stay strong in your foundation as the tide comes.

"What is the tide?" Paul asks. We will tell you this. The tide is great change. As consciousness changes at a vast scale, so does the landscape, and the resistance to the change is what is difficult for some. And all that is difficult is the amount of attachment that one has to the way one thinks that things should be. And those are the things, as we have said, that have tethered you to lower frequency.

As the tide rises, all is lifted. And as things lift, those things that are in lower frequency cannot rise and must be released in order to keep you afloat. So you're all in a process now of active engagement with transformation, which is here to support you in preparation for the changes that will come. And the changes, we will say, have wonderful opportunity attached to them

As consciousness changes on a planetary scale—which is, in fact, happening already—there is residual reaction and, as we said before, that is to try to hold onto the known and make sure that it stays. As people begin to loosen their grip on a status quo that was based in fear, they can be liberated to have a new experience of love. We teach the individual here in *The Book of Love and Creation*. We are teaching you to learn who and what you are, because you are already rising in frequency. And as you become conscious, your willingness to assist others and to offer help will become apparent to you.

At the beginning of this chapter, we said that help can be a cry for alarm or it can be an offering and a gift. Everybody at times requires support and we offer this to you as you will offer it to your brothers. We offer you love and we will stop for now and we will continue tomorrow.

I am Word through those before me. Word I am Word.

Stop now, please.

FOURTEEN

I AM WORTHY

Day Eighteen

The value you place on things is the value that it is given and that it holds. Once you change how you value things, your experience of your surroundings and those objects that you hold begins to change as well.

Now we are talking right now about value of things. But please understand that the idea of value extends far beyond things and finally becomes the system with which you navigate worth and the idea of worth. And understand that as you work with this idea, you extend it out even farther to commerce and to industry. So everything goes back, finally, to value. What kind of price do you accord something? How is it valued?

Now let's look at your own lives for a moment in terms of what you value. You value your security, you value your friends, you value those objects that you hold dear only because you have invested them with meaning. And everything that is valued outside of the self either is valued because it is invested with meaning, or because it's required to sustain you in some way. You value food.

You value shelter. You value those things you require that keep you warm in the cold and dry in the rain and cool in the summer. You value what you require and you value what you have invested in.

Now this is all fine. But let's open it up a little bit to include spirit. "I value my spirit." When you say this, you move into an acknowledgment of your own Divine Self as operative and as an aspect of you. Now once you understand that ninety percent of what you have valued, interestingly enough, you have only valued because you have been told to value it, you can start to change some thinking.

"I don't value the car because it gets me to work. I value the car because it's a great car, or because it's an expensive car." Now there is nothing wrong, as we have stated, about an expensive car. But please understand what we are doing right now is offering you a new way of looking at your surroundings to decide what you really need and what you have given value to because you have been told to. Fashions change. What is idealized in one culture varies to the next. Those things that are important one day become trivial the next in the face of something large.

If you were to understand today that everything that you own and that you cherish will not be here in a hundred years in the same form, or if, in fact, it is, it has no claim on you—you can begin to get un-invested in things. Things, things, things. That is what we are talking about right now, and what has value. The piece of rock that you wear on your finger is not valuable because of the worth prescribed at the store. It is valuable because it was gifted to you in love. If you need to exchange it for funds, it will have a monetary value and you can use it as you wish, but if you can accept the fact that the value that you have given it has been your own, or the value that the store has given it is market worth dependent on outside factors, you can get unattached.

Now Paul is wondering where this is going, and we will tell you. We are speaking today about knowing your worth, and what you are worth outside of anything else that you may have chosen to embellish the self with. We are taking you to the river now and we are going to wash away those things that are holding you down.

Now we are using that image symbolically to teach you something. If you were to ride a current and you had to carry with you your Mercedes, or that great handbag, or the cooking stove, you would have a hard time being light and you would not be able to flow. So we want to talk about un-attachment to objects, to commerce, and to those things that are weighing you down from this passage.

It has been said that it is difficult for a rich man to enter the kingdom of heaven. And what this really means is: Those things that you stand on to build your stairway to the light, if they are based in commerce, they will not sustain. We will tell it to you this way: If you have things that are tethering you, they will not carry you forward. And those beliefs you hold in the importance of things will stop you, finally, from moving forward.

Paul is wondering if we are asking you to divest yourself of things. Yes and no. We are not asking you to give up your car. We are trying to get you to see that if your car matters more to you than it should, it is an obstacle to your evolution. If what you require for yourself is a certain kind of house, or lifestyle, or thing that you believe will make you better, you are standing on that thing and trying to reach to light from it, and it does not work.

Now we are not telling you at all that you need to be poor and, in fact, this is going to be a chapter that addresses prosperity, but in the truest possible way. Your belief right now that you are required to own and to hold, or to hoard and to keep, are the things that banish you from freedom. They keep you in a tethered position. As you understand that your freedom in spirit requires you to release all of those things that you have put forward as a false God, as a totem, as a requirement for something external, then you can begin to allow yourself to become liberated from them. As you understand that your own divine worth is what calls to you what you require, you can become free to receive. But as you receive through the spirit, those gifts that can come in material form will be freeing for you.

Now please understand that in the past there has been a paradigm in place that you could not have money, or you could not have things, and progress spiritually. There have been vows of poverty taken by the religious in many cultures for thousands of years. We would like to explain this. On a fundamental level it is a sound theory because they were asked to practice a form of non-attachment to the physical realm in order to focus and refine their own spiritual lives. However, everybody here is still existing in the physical and is expected to have an experience of it. And of course we would like to say that this is an abundant universe and the belief in scarcity creates scarcity. So we would like to shift that a bit.

Now conversely, in the last twenty years or so, as people have begun to wake up to conscious manifestation, people have been looking at it from a place of greed. Now we want to explain something here. There is nothing wrong with manifesting what you want. You can have the car or the house or whatever you wish. However, as we have said earlier, why you want that thing is the question that must be asked. If you are just asking for things and requiring the law of attraction, as it were, to make them so from a place of hunger for materialism, you are embedding yourself in a false structure.

So we will say this: There is a pendulum swinging right now and our desire is that you understand, first and foremost, that anything that you require is available to you through conscious choice and manifestation, but you must not be tethered to it. What you put before your relationship to your own Divine Self or to Source becomes an obstacle in your flow and it brings you back to the side of the riverbank, as it were. So the gifts of the Father, as it were, are available to you each. But when you put those gifts before the

Father, you move into a form of idolatry. That is all you need to understand.

Now once you receive yourself as the one who is responsible for your creations, you can begin to decide their worth. What is really important? What can you release easily, and what are you overly attached to? What are those bindings that you still have that are standing in the way of your ascension in frequency? Yes, we are saying that you need to ask yourself this question.

"What stops me now on the physical plane in terms of my experience and of my values? What is standing in the way of my allowing myself to lift in frequency?" We will give you an example: "I could never live without blank." "I am so frightened of losing blank." "Where would I be without this?" All of those questions can be indicators of where you are holding on.

Now we want you to imagine something. Imagine that before you right now is an altar. Any kind of altar you wish. And it is a place of offering. And we are going to ask you right now to place on this altar your attachments to those things in your physical world that are keeping you stuck, or tethered. And these are the things we have spoken about. "Where am I bound by my physical experience through those things that I have placed too much value in or I have been told to place that value in? Where are these things? And now I will put them on my altar."

Now once you understand that what is placed on the altar is, in fact, released to Source, it is not your business what happens to them. Now this is an imagistic exercise, but it is also one that is palpable in its experience. What you choose to surrender to Source is no longer your own. And when you can truly release something as if it is not yours, you are free of it. When it sticks around, it's because it's still required or you have not truly released it.

So Paul is asking, "I put the car on the altar. What the heck does that mean?" That means your attachment to the car is no longer yours. And if the car is gone tomorrow, that's okay. If the car is in the garage, that's okay, too. But you are no longer operating from a place of attachment and binding to those things in your material world that would tether you and stop you from moving in flow.

The title of this chapter is going to be "I Am Worthy." And this is what we would like you to say:

> "I am now choosing to divest myself of those things that are without worth in my values. And I am choosing to call to me now, in my own knowing of my own divine worth, those things that I require to move me forward in consciousness. I am now choosing to realign my values to a higher level of perception, so that I may receive the gifts of the spirit and understand that they are in fact presents and not things that I own. As I am understanding my relationship to those things I have possessed and will release and will gain again, I am free of my attachments to those things that would keep me bound in this physical reality. I am Word through this intention. Word I am Word."

Now we want to explain something to you. You can be in your prosperity and, in fact, we recommend that you be, only because it's an opportunity for you to demonstrate that all is available through creation in consciousness. There should be no lack once you understand that the infinite source is the Creative Mind, is Divine Spirit, and that your aspect of this soul can be in receipt through conscious intention. You understand this. The only difference, we are saying, is that when you are manifesting from a place of fear, which is essentially to say, "I should have this thing because others have it," or "If I don't have this thing, I will not be worthy," then you are contributing to the matrix of fear. And again, we wish to say that anything that you receive in Spirit belongs to Spirit and please, please, please do not become attached.

Now Paul is wondering, "Does that mean if I manifest a great apartment, that's not really my apartment?" Yes and no. Here's an interesting thing to understand. Whatever you call forth to you in your consciousness has been created through vibration and, in fact, that which is called forth in this form of manifestation, which we will call conscious intent, tends to stay primarily because you are able to hold it in your energy field. You have gone into agreement with it, you resonate with it. So there is no reason for it to leave unless your frequency changes and you outgrow the form. Again, all we are saying is that the attachment to physical reality as you know it is going to be one of these things that trip you up on your path. As you go forward in consciousness and as you move beyond the physical body as a way of experiencing reality, your attachments to that which is around you must be lightened. You get light on your feet and you must practice un-attachment.

Now this sounds easier than it is. However, can you understand right now that when there was a world without televisions and big houses and lots of stuff, people were having a much higher frequency in their experience of the divine. There was a lot less standing in the way of the soul and that which created the soul. So all of these things that you have given so much value to, while they make your life easier, have been invested with value, that have no calling to be. Now we will give you an example:

Who is to say that the article of clothing that is there to protect the body, or perhaps to adorn the body, that costs a million dollars, is better than the one that cost five? You have all gone into agreement and said something must be so because somebody else told you it was. So please, please, please understand today that value is subjective and ninety percent of the time you are being told what you are supposed to value. Now please, please, please get with the program. If you value things because you have been told to, you are being controlled, and as you are controlled, you do not have your freedom. Your self, your knowing are your allies here.

And we want to switch the focus now to the value of the self:

"I am knowing myself as worthy of all that I require. I am knowing myself as succeeding in all that I do. I am knowing myself as having all that I need to grow and to learn and to prosper in the ways that will be in the highest alignment with my soul's purpose for me. I am Word through this intention. Word I am Word."

You can look at someone else and decide very easily that they are worthy of the life that they are living because it is perceived by you in a certain way. However, you have a much more difficult time with yourselves in this regard. And what we would like to teach you right now is to become aware of your own worth on a much deeper level than we have so far.

At a level of structure, you are all created in frequency, and it's an identical frequency to your Creator. You have been born and created in the image and likeness of God, and this is your frequency. The physical form that you stand in has been created *by you* to support your experience here on this plane to ascend in consciousness. It's the vehicle that takes you there.

Now we have told you so many times already in this text that you are a Divine Being and you get it intellectually. However, you do not know it and we want you to know it. And we want to give you a system now that will align you to Divine Love in your knowing so that you can accept that this is so.

"I am now choosing to go into alignment with my own knowing of my Divine Self as the truth of who I am. And I am in my value in my knowing of myself as an aspect of the Creator. Word I am Word through this intention. Word I am Word."

The habit that you have still is to negotiate your worth based on your physical experience. "She must be a better person than I am, or a more spiritual person, or a more wealthy person or a this or a that, because there she is and here I am." Or "I must be better because I have achieved this, or that." Now all of these things, as they are perceived by you, are lies and misperceptions. Period. Who you are at your essence is an aspect of the Divine.

Now we want to do something with you:

We imagine you right now standing naked in a small pool of water. You feel the water at your toes and it is a gentle water, cool and refreshing. And as you stand in the puddle of water, you look down, and water is beginning to glow gold, a beautiful golden white light that is at your feet.

You imagine now that this light is beginning to permeate your frequency until it is one with your feet, and you're standing in a puddle that is rising. And as the puddle rises, you begin to feel yourself as merging in frequency with this light that is you in your physical experience on this plane.

As you begin to imagine this, you feel your entire being beginning to go into a oneness with this golden white light.

"I am Word through my being. Word I am Word.
I am Word through my vibration. Word I am Word.
I am Word through my knowing of myself as Word."

Now allow yourself to begin to merge in totality with this light. And we want you to do this. As this light that you are, this golden white light, we want you to walk to the riverbank and we want you step in the water. And we want you step up to your knees. And then to your waist. And then we want you to go up to your shoulders. And as you stand in this river, you realize that you are filled with the frequency of Divine Love. And you allow your arms to open and you rest on your back and you allow yourself to be carried.

> "I am one with the God that has created me. I am knowing my worth as a Divine Being, and I am free of the limitations that I have placed upon myself in physical form. Word I am Word through this intention. Word I am Word."

You are in the river and we're taking you to the sea.

Now we would like to talk for a few minutes about the requirements of the next section of this book. And we are going to recede Paul as much as we can until we can get this through without interruption of his thoughts.

The next section of this book we will call "Frequency and Creation." And we are going to take you on a journey in consciousness to where you are allowed to go as a Divine Being in knowledge and in creation. There will be five chapters to this next section and then that will be the completion of the text. The removal of resistance to the reader has been commencing as this text has progressed and we are pleased with the work thus far.

The next section of the book is going be a triumph in frequency. And what we mean by this is, we are going to move beyond the intellect into an experience of frequency in a way that we have not attempted yet. Now Paul will be in resistance and we are going to stop it for the simple reason that the reason that this book is being written is to gift you with this vision of your own ability to vibrate as frequency in a way that you can know and experience. The channel's resistance is only about his own unknowing of where the work is going. And his job is to hear.

We will teach you, and we are teaching you clearly. Your choice, as it comes, will be to limit yourself in the way that you engage in your own understanding of who you have been in order to allow yourself the permission to evolve into what you are becoming. The majesty that you are, in fact, is the value we have spoken of already. The resistance to knowing yourself in your perfection has been the game that you have been playing since you were born. And the opportunity now to release this into the Word is present and is available for you.

We have spoken to you already about the Christ consciousness. The Christ consciousness is frequency and you align to it in your knowing and in your vibration. And as you go into congruence with it, it becomes where you operate from, and it resolves itself through your experience. As you continue to change, your authority is gifted to you in this knowing. And what we say this means is that as you know, your questions are answered. You become the one who is in your knowing and consequently can access the answers that you require.

This book is meant to give you this. Your own choices, your own sense of self-worth have been based so far in false constructs. And as we liberate you from them, we offer you the possibility that your love is as wonderful as the love of the Creator who has gifted you with life.

"I am Word through all that I know to be true. I am Word through my own ability to know. I am Word through all that I will know. And I am free of any restrictions of my knowing that have been placed on me by myself, by anyone else, or any systems or structures that may have been in place that I am no longer aligned to. I am Word through this intention. Word I am Word."

We are going to stop in a moment, but we want to tell you one more thing. How deeply you are loved is something that you may not know. However, we want you to know. And we want to gift you now with an experience of yourself as loved.

If you would just close your eyes when you finish this paragraph, we want you to receive love through the third eye and through the heart center and through all the seven chakras of your being. We would like you to begin to realize yourself in love, and let the frequency do its work.

"I am now calling to me the frequency of love. I am Word through this intention. Word I am Word."

Thank you and stop.

Day Nineteen

What we are writing today is hearing as you work. And so as we dictate, we are going to ask you, as channel, to relinquish authority in adhering to past performance. As these transcriptions evolve, the way they will evolve will have to alter depending on the kind of information we require to be heard. So understand this, please:

As you listen as you have, you have operated effectively. But where we are going with the reader now requires you to establish yourself as something other than this, which is the vessel of only vowels and consonants, and the concepts behind them must be relegated to our tenure and our teaching. As you understand that this job right now is to be the ambassador from another realm of frequency, you will see that you are the intermediary. You hold a hand to us, you hold a hand to them, and we run through you with our blessings and with our instruction.

Today we speak about triumph, and the triumph of love, and the triumph of God as a frequency. Today we want you to know that where you have been journeying to is a real place in consciousness.

It's real, it is effective, and it is a place of wonder. Today we teach you the mission of the book. And the mission of the book is to stand in your knowing at a high frequency and decide your worth as an aspect of the Creator and from that position respond to all that is around you as the frequency of love.

We have told you already, many times, that the work of the book is to align you to love. To love, to love, to love. Now the action of love, as we have said, is to be *in love,* in the frequency of love. And how you respond from that frequency is the mission, it is the decision, it is the wonder of this teaching. The love that you have so far self-identified as is a mission in possibility and now the possibility will become the reality. This is the next section of the book. It is where we are taking you, and it is the work that is to come.

What does it mean, finally, to stand in love and to express as love and to vibrate, to experience yourself in wonder as this thing? If you would take a moment now to decide *from your knowing,* from that aspect of the self that we have already identified as the Christed Self, the Divine Self, the Creative Spark of you come to this place, and ask yourself if you are willing to go now to the sea of love and express from there.

Now understand, please, that all of these things that we have asked you to divest the self of have been required in consciousness in order to carry you there. We cannot take you someplace wonderful when the trunks are too full, when the baggage is too heavy, and when your desire is truly to stay where you are.

As you stop and think about this decision—"Am I willing now? Am I willing now? Am I willing now to stop fighting the flow of the river? And am I willing to be taken to the sea?"—you can decide if you are willing to say yes. And if you say "Yes," we will love you and we will carry you to the water's edge and we will fly with you to the sea.

You have company on this journey. Everyone who reads the

book who has decided "Yes" will be there. Everyone in other cultures who is coming to this information in their way, yes, will be there. And we will promise you that one day all will be in the river and all will be in the sea. It is the mission of the time, the mission of the time, the mission of the time.

Our song today is a song of praise for the journeyer who is about to go on the road, who is about to sing along a new song of joy.

"As I go on my way, I stop and see all that I've seen and I recognize it for what it has been: a part of myself out-pictured in form. And I recognize the creations for what they have been. And I give thanks, I give humble thanks for my awareness now, and I will go forward and release them to the light. As I go, I know. As I go, I support myself in love. As I go, I accept the gifts of the spirit that are acclimating to my frequency so I may better serve the needs of others who I will carry to their next level of knowing. I am journeying now. I am in spirit, I am in frequency, and I am about to extend myself to the manifestation of love. I sing a song today of wonder. I sing a song today of love. And I am rejoicing in my choice to be free. I am Word through this intention. Word I am Word."

Our decision was to come here and to disseminate this talk in paper form for you to read and to take with you in study. The students of this book are many, and they are in frequency, and we would like you to take a moment now to recognize this. And the way we would ask you to do this is to sit still and acknowledge that you are part of a group, and a large, enlarging group of people in manifestation who are coming into their own consciousness as love. And as you do this, you extend your frequency to greet them. And you go into a unity and acknowledgment with your fellow travelers and allow yourself to be greeted as well.

Remember, always, you are not alone in this work. This work is passage work, and while it feels solitary at times, it is not. You have many friends and teachers who are standing beside you to usher you into this next phase of your evolution. You can think of this as a personal thing if it gives you support, but the net has been cast in a large way and there are many that are being gifted with their knowing as the times herald the new creation.

We speak today of manifestation, of what it means to call into being your own knowing. "I Am Worthy" is the title. "I Am Worthy" is my knowing. "I Am Worthy" is the song your lips must sing. "I am worthy of this journey. I am worthy of my God. I am worthy of all that I see before me."

We are telling you that this is the time of a new creation and the plane that you exist in is about to lift in a grand way. A light will come to illumine all that which is held in darkness and the darkness must be released. This is good news. It is wonderful news. But those of you that are already resonant with the light will already be lifting in frequency as this occurs.

It is happening already. The planetary changes that you have been witnessing are an aspect of shifting, and the consciousness that you are beginning to become aware of amongst the people on the planet, which calls for inclusiveness, is an awakening. The hands are reaching across the borders. The telephones are ringing across the seas. And as you begin to remember, to re-member that you are One Soul, one grand aspect of the Creator in many, many bodies, the songs that you can sing together will out-pass and bypass anything you could have imagined.

Now we sing to you in frequency. We sing to you in our knowing. We sing to you in the blessed action of God saying, "How about it, everyone? It's time to come home to yourselves as you are! It's time to remember what you came for! And it's time to remember why you stand in your body and see your fellows in love!"

We are working with you. We table the things that are not required to get to the real work at hand. The first two books of this text have been in preparation for what we are doing now, and that is the joy of consciousness inhabiting in form.

Now we will tell you that as we go forward, we will have to demonstrate to you the requirements of these changes. Of course we will teach you and we will lecture to you as we are required. There are things you still need to know about being in relation, about working in frequency, about conscious action and decision in knowing, and we will teach you. But we require you now to begin to have an experience of yourselves as frequency. The proof of all this work we have done is in you and is in your ability to stand in your light and say, "Yes, I am in my light. I express it and I know it."

Today we want to talk about the intellect, briefly, and the intellect's role as an organizing principle and as a computer that sorts through issues and assists you in coming to terms with those things that you require. Now we are praising the intellect, we are not diminishing it. However, we want you to understand that when you work in frequency you are bypassing the intellect and you are working with yourself as energy in consciousness. Which quite simply means that the language that you would give may be limiting to your experience. And as you decide, as you will decide to become open-minded—"open-minded" means the mind is open—you will see very quickly that you can expand in consciousness to adhere to the principles we will be speaking of.

You will be radiating light. You will be expressing your healing energies to others. You will be singing to them in frequency and you will be loving, you will be loving, and yes, yes, yes, you will be loved.

We will commence with this book in three days. We are doing the introduction in three days. As we teach you, we will require that you sing along with us.

Thank you both and stop. Word I am Word.

Book Three

FREQUENCY
AND CREATION

INTRODUCTION

Day Twenty

Time is coming to benefit the self with the news and the giving that is coming to you through the work you have done so far. The responsibility is yours now, and the template has been set. You have each been ingrained, as it were, with the manifestations you have called forth in your intentions. We will explain it to you:

As you have called forth the Word through your energy field in decree, you have set in motion the action of the Divine to transform you. These transformations have been in consciousness and those of you who are already feeling energy will be feeling what is coming as we speak to you in the remainder of this text. However, for those of you who are newer to the work and feeling energy for the first time, we will ask you simply to allow for the fact that the work that you have done to date has taken hold, and your energy field has been transformed by the dictation and by the decree and by the willingness to stand in your knowing as a Divine Being.

When you do these things, you call into form that which you have asked for. When one says, "I am a Divine Being," one is calling forth the truth, and the truth will will itself to be known. When one decides that one is empowered to manifest this way, one is free to resolve to become himself, herself, in full manifestation. And full manifestation, we would like to say, is the Christ consciousness come into form: "I am Word."

"I am Word" is the call of this time. It is the herald, it is the trumpet, it is the song that we are singing to you, and now you will join us in this resonance in this remaining section of this book. This will come about through a series of exercises and teachings that are designed to bring you out into the world as you are in Christ consciousness. This means that when you walk away from your living space, you are resounding in the bell ringing that you are. Your resonance will be heard in frequency, and as this happens you allow the self to be used as the vehicle for the transforming of others. This is how it happens.

Now the first day of the exercises will be commencing tomorrow. And today we would like to lay a little bit of groundwork about what you might expect from this part of the book. This challenge for you will be about remembering what you are at a higher frequency in a mindful way. And by "mindful" we mean you are aware, you are walking around, and you are having an experience that is mindful and conscious. As you do this, you begin to see things with new light. And as we mean this, we say you will begin to see things for what they truly are. The decision to do this, we would like to say, is always your own. However, the extent that you deal with this passively is the extent that you limit your experience.

If you were to run a race, you would have to get on the track and run. If you want to transform in frequency and have a new experience of the self in frequency, you have to be working directly with your system in this way. We are working with you, yes, but we do not do the work without your permission, nor do we do the work without your ability to hold the frequency. All of the work thus far has been about relinquishing patterns of control and expanding awareness in consciousness, which will allow you, then, to hold this new frequency. We have been leaving the past behind in one way or another to allow the new to come into form.

Now if you can imagine right now that you are a steamship disembarking from a pier, you will see that what you have been tethered to is receding into the background and you are going on to a new journey of the self as you are:

> "I am in my knowing. I am in my freedom. I am in my love. And I am choosing now to respond fully to that which comes to me in my Divine Knowing."

Now today we have a little talk to give you by way of introduction, which has to do with the history of your planet until this time.

Up until time was decided upon as a structure, mankind was in a process of evolving into consciousness. As this began, there was great support from the outside to shift the knowing of man into his awareness of his divinity. At one time there came a belief in differentials, as things being separate, and that manifested, once and for all, in the separation of man from his true self. And in separating from the true self he separated himself from the aspect of the self that was born into oneness with his God, whatever you wish to call it. The seed that has always been in man and primed to come into form was forgotten. That aspect of the self is now coming up to be re-membered. To be re-membered means to connect back to the Source from which it was born.

Now this time is choosing. This time is demanding, "I am knowing what I am." This time is recognition. This is all now, because what is to come is a new paradigm of awareness and your preparation for it is what will align you to it as it comes. There have been many gods worshipped on this plane and they have gone by many names, and they have differentiated themselves as aspects of one God. But finally, once again when the sense of separation from the self has healed, the separation from God heals and the multiple gods, we will say, will join force in their own unity. Frankly, we will say, there is one frequency. There is one Divine Love that holds all within it and that is the frequency we are attending to now. And that is where you are being chosen to mission to through this work.

We would not call ourselves Christians, as you would think. We are the Christ in manifestation because we have come into that knowing. And there is a belief among us that this is true for all of you, as we are all of one Source. So the emissaries of light from this plane that are coming into incarnation in their remembrance have a big job to do. And the big job, finally, is standing in the knowing and being in resonance in full term in order to align your frequency to the work that it would bring to it.

Now justification for this is required. Why now? Why is this happening now? And why do you need to do it? The changes that are coming to this plane of existence are radically different than you might expect. You cannot imagine change that is both visible and invisible. But the invisible change always becomes visible. As you move into your own frequency through the work of this text in a radical way, which means to say you are claiming your truth, you can call to you what you require. The changes are made first in the invisible, in the frequency, and then they are called into manifestation. "I am Word" will do this work with you. To speak the Word on behalf of another is to support them in their frequency and in their choice to resound with the frequency of the Word.

Now we will tell you a few things about the work to come. We will take you on a journey into an idyllic frequency, a frequency of true love that you will stand in. And as you stand in this frequency, you will have to become attuned to the possibilities that are inherent in it. It's as if you are going to be reading a text through experiencing it. Now we told you in the last chapter that part of the work to come had to do with bypassing the intellect, and this is crucial. That aspect of the self that would tell you no, or would decide for you that this cannot be so, is the aspect of the self that has to go for a nice walk while we do the work with you. And this will heal you. And this will allow you to expand knowing.

The trajectory of this work is about becoming whole. It is about becoming one with your self on multiple levels. And the segmentation and separation of the past will be cleaning up as we continue to work. The first challenge you will face is in being, just being, allowing yourself to be without the influence of external response through choice.

Now this is a big deal. If you were to walk down the street and have an experience fully of your own where you were the one decider, you would know yourself fully. But so much of your experience to date has been informed by what you have been told. So we tell you now, the choice to listen to yourself in a clean way, in a new way, will respond well with what we will be teaching you.

We would like to talk for a moment about the other things we have addressed so far in this work. We have talked about healing, and we have talked about your relationships, and we will continue to teach you in refinement as we go forward. So while we say this is experiential work, it is also a continuation of what has preceded it. We would like you to understand, though, that your decision, right now, to create yourself anew in wholeness is a decision only you can make. So we would like you to say this if you are willing to choose this, and we will say it with you:

"I am now choosing to relinquish all of my attachments to my identity as I previously knew it in order to allow myself my true experience of myself as manifested in Christ consciousness. I am choosing now to see with new eyes, to hear with new ears, and to feel with refined feeling in my knowing of my choice to realign my energy field in fullness with the octave that sings of the Christ consciousness come into form in man. I am Word through this intention. Word I am Word."

Our blessings are upon you and we will continue tomorrow with the first chapter of this part of our text. Word I am Word. So be it.

FIFTEEN

RE-MEMBERING

Day Twenty-One

Freedom is here and you are here, so let's work together to stand in freedom. The choice you have today is to relinquish the pattern of needing to know: "I don't need to know what's gonna happen next. I don't need to know what I was. I can be in my not knowing for this next stage of instruction." And the reason for this is it will keep you out of the picture long enough to respond to the frequencies we would like to invest you with. And what we mean by "invest you with" is to give you to appropriate and to use. You are the intention made manifest. "I am Word" claims you as this. And as this thing, as this aspect of the Creator in embodiment, you have to choose where you wish to use your frequency and how.

Now if you understand right now that you are this frequency always and it is your choice to turn up the volume, as it were, to "sound," as it were, to "sing," if you wish, then you will understand that the journey is on, the music is playing, and where you choose to sing and to whom becomes your choice. Our choice with you is to sing with you, and what this means for us in tutelage is that we will gift you with the words to the song and we will teach you the melody so that you can go about singing to others.

Now the choice that you have to make now, in this moment, is to give permission:

> "I am now choosing to realign my energy field in Christ consciousness. I am now choosing to realign my thinking to activate itself in higher knowing. I am now choosing to become myself in truth as what I am intended to be: an aspect of God in its creation as Word."

Here we go, everybody:

> "As I make this choice, I decree that I am now coming into my ownership as a Divine Being and the recognition of this will be in my own knowing and in my own experience of this existence. I am in my knowing as an activated aspect of the Creator. I am Word through this intention. Word I am Word."

As this is said, your frequency is lifted and you are moving patterns of change throughout the auric field to realign your knowing to the vibration of the Christ consciousness. This is manifested in you in choice on a moment-by-moment basis by saying this:

> "I am in my acceptance of my knowing, I am in my knowing. I know, I know, I know. As I am in my knowing I express myself in frequency as the Creator as part of an offering to the Almighty. I choose to gift myself to Source to be recreated in full manifestation as who I am in truth. I am knowing myself as Word. Word I am Word through this intention. Word I am Word."

Now in this resolve you have changed the trajectory of your

knowing. And as your knowing is transformed, your body will be reclaimed. Your physical senses will be shifting and your acknowledgment of yourself through your experience will be recognizing what this means. And what this means is this: Your choice to realign your knowing and your frequency in Christ consciousness manifests as a complete realignment of your frequency into a higher octave of understanding, and you will resonate in recognition with this and with others who are offering themselves to this recognition as well.

Now we will speak about this. As you have joined energies in consciousness with the Creator through intention, your field has been transforming. And with this intention today you have decided to climb the mountain to the top. The top is essentially the awareness of the self in his Son-ship, if you would, of complete manifestation.

Now we will tell you what this means. This means that you have to stand in truth and that your frequency will have to move in order to meet this new choice. You will be dropping veils, if you would, and you will be relinquishing self as you have identified self. The skins are falling away, the separation is releasing, and the divinity that you are is now being expressed in your resonance and in your safety of your consciousness.

Understand this now: "safety of your consciousness." If everything in your world is a creation and your consciousness expresses itself in its safety, there is nothing to fear. There is no longer a challenge to the reaction, "I am knowing I am safe," because you cannot be otherwise. The challenges that you have known up until today have all been about mirrors. They have all been about reflections of lower frequency as out-pictured by you, singularly you and collectively you. And the choice the individual makes to rise above that mirror so that it can no longer reflect fear permits others to do the same. Understand this now, that as you are rising in frequency, you can imagine your frequency as lifting you past those reflections. And we will say those reflections have been obstacles to awareness of truth. As you have risen, you will recognize others who are also in this passage and releasing the tethers:

"And I am knowing them as Word. I am knowing them as the light. And I am knowing them as my compatriots in the journey of ascension. As we gather together in one light, we herald the changes that are to come and we draw to us the resolve in our knowing to call to us the many, many, many who are ready to lift in their knowing as well. The collective frequency will change and I am now choosing to benefit myself through this conscious knowing that I am willing to become a knowing soul, for the work to come will be wonderful. I am Word through this knowing. I am Word through this intention. Word I am Word."

You are an individual cell in a wonderful organism. And as you vibrate in this new frequency, you will recognize those who are vibrating as well, and those who wish to be shifting, who wish to be realigning their consciousness on a soul level will be called to you as well. You become an activation, if you can understand this. You become the mechanism through which others are activated in consciousness. And the decision to do this has been made by you on a level of frequency.

The decision was made, in truth, prior to this incarnation. And you might as well understand that your decision to ascend and to come into form to do this work was created for you by your soul's knowing prior to birth. Everyone who comes here at this time has come with the recognition of the significance of this time. We have said before that this is a dance and this dance is in its perfection, and we will remind you that your partners in the dance are everyone, and everyone you will ever know, that you have ever known, and that you have seen. This is a truth. You are all in this dance as one frequency moving into its remembrance of itself.

Today we want to teach you something. And what we will teach you is love as embodying love. Now we have taught you before what love is, and today we want to give you an experience of it. And this teaching in love will give you an opportunity to recognize yourself as the loved one in creation.

"I am now choosing to remember myself as the loved one in creation. Word I am Word through this intention. Word I am Word."

The remembrance of love and of yourself as a loved one goes back to the memory of your soul's creation. It is in your DNA. It is part of what you come into existence with. And that is your kinship and your lineage with love as born in the Creator's love. Now we will ask you this: When is a time in your life when you loved perfectly? When were you in memory of love? We will ask you now to remind yourself that you are capable of great love. And the movement forward in this love is this action today.

Today we need you to stand up to yourself in all of the ways you can love and become love in all that you say and do. Now this is not abstract. This is about action and decision and nothing more. You all make it so difficult. You believe that you have to go through an obstacle course in order to be realized when, in fact, the realization is here already, and this is where the intellect seeks to complicate and obscure the most beautiful truth of the world. You are already loved and you are already an aspect of love. And the Creator's love for you in dimensional knowing is apparent here the moment you acknowledge it.

Now nobody, frankly, is without love although the experience can be of the self as being without. And that is always made in decision and consort with the personality self who has been taught, on some level, that he or she is not worthy, cannot be worthy of love. We have given you directives earlier in this text to heal this and we want to re-member you once again as free of fear and free of those knowings you have carried that were based in un-charity, un-love, and un-truth. We want to gift you with a clearing in frequency, and we want you to do this with us:

We intend now that the reader will now receive the creation of love through the seven chakras and the chakras above to realign her, to realign him, into an awareness of the frequency of love. And we gift you each with the response of love in your own knowing.

Now what this means for you is we are going to transmit frequency through the seventh chakra at the top of the head and down through the seven lower chakras to move frequency. As we do this with you, our intention for you is that you become aligned to love and those frequencies that have stood in the way of this understanding of the self, of this knowing of the self as love will be transmuted and released in recognition of your worth as the loved one.

"I am now choosing to receive Divine Love through my centers of energy. I am now choosing to align myself to my knowing of myself as the loved one. Word I am Word through this intention. Word I am Word."

Your knowing of yourself as loved will permit you to gift love to others. Today we would like you to see people, see those before you, in love, and we want to add an exercise to the one that you have done in the past. Previously we have instructed you to see the divinity in those before you: "I am Word through all that I see before me." Now we want you to radiate as love: "I am in my knowing of myself as love. I am Word through this intention. Word I am Word."

As you do this, you are aligning the auric field to vibrate in this frequency. "I am now choosing to see those before me with love" is an intention that will allow you to recognize them, those before you, in love as aspects of love. And as we have said, by doing this, you gift them in their frequency. But this new step is as follows:

"I am love through the ones I see before me. I am love through the ones I see before me."

As you state this intention, you become an ambassador of love and the frequency of love is transmitted from your frequency to those you see before you. This is a healing love. This is love that is held unconditionally and can only be offered as such. This is love in the truest sense. This is unconditional. There is no expectation of return on a personality level. "I am love through the ones I see before me" is a gift of God and you are the emissary of this gift as you do this work. Your recognition of this on an experiential level will begin to transform you.

You have an opportunity now to put the work of this text into practice. Earlier in this text we invited you to work with a partner and to see what you felt when you stated, "I am Word through the one I see before me." We asked you what you felt, what you heard, what you knew. "I am love through those I see before me" will benefit those before you and it will also support you in the refinement of your own empathic abilities. Your own knowing of those before you, and consequently your ability to heal, will be supported through this intention. "I am love through the one I see before me" calls love in frequency to the frequency of the one before you. And that love is transmitted where it is required. As this happens, you may begin to know where love has not been held. Where in the body there is pain. Where in the soul there has been a wound. And then you can work as follows:

> "I am now choosing to see the one before me as healed in love. I am seeing the one before me in his perfection, as a child of the Creator, in recognition of his worth and his healing. I am Word through the one I see before me. I am love through the one I see before me. Word I am Word."

You can create your own language if you wish, but the intention is clear. The healing happens through the action of the Creator as demonstrated in the frequency of love.

Now we want you to have an experience with this. We have told Paul in the past that the worth of this book is the work of the doing of it as expressed in your own reality and your own choice to do this and to bring this work into creative manifestation.

So when we ask you to go out, we mean it. This is not about turning to the next page and saying, "What an interesting idea," or "Oh, that's impossible," or "Oh, maybe some day." Why not go out today and have this experience? Now we will honor this with you. As you are working with us in this frequency, we are reminding you that there is an author level of implied response to all that you ask for. For example, if you are to question, "Why?" and you are to put that question out in your frequency, you might as well start expecting answers.

We are trying to tell you that we are here, we are working with you. We have a troupe, as it were, whose assignment is to support the learner. No one is alone, truthfully, but we want you to know that when you work with this energy, you are in accordance with our teachings and we do not abandon our students for a golf game. We have nothing better to do at this time than to dictate this manuscript and to ensure that the legacy of this work is carried out in truth. And what this means is, you have sponsorship. You have authorial support from the writers of this text in your endeavors to report and to work with this energy. Please, please, please do not keep this text in the province of the intellect. Then it becomes a crossword puzzle that is forgotten. You put the pieces together, you have a brain exercise, you congratulate yourself for finishing it, and you move on to the next teaching.

We are asking you to commit now, at least as much as you are willing to, to see the fruits of your labor come into manifestation. We have said earlier that this is not magical, but it is miraculous. And by saying that, what we are telling you is, your choice to do these decrees with intention in Word will realign you. That realignment first happens in the frequency of your being, in your auric field if you wish, and then is brought into manifestation in consciousness.

The higher you rise in frequency, the more rapidly you will manifest, and you will see the changes happen for you as you choose to. And this means you are in party to this. If you tell yourself today this might happen to John or to Bill but not to Paul or not to Mary, you are lying to yourself, you have an investment, then, in this not being truthful, or you have an investment in being left out of the light show that is now in progress.

Please, please, please, realign that belief to this one:

"I am now having my experience of this text in alignment with my own worth as a Divine Being. I am knowing this is true. Word I am Word through this intention. Word I am Word."

Your willingness is always key. We have devoted a chapter to will with the intention for you to understand that when your will is in congruence with the higher frequency, if you wish to say "Divine Will," that's fine. But when you are in alignment, your life becomes blessed in its trajectory because you are being carried by choice that is made from a high regard of the requirements of your needs. And that is, very simply put, "You are in your knowing." So what you choose is called forth in your knowing and then that becomes your experience here.

The claim of this book is to give you an experience of yourself in the mission of the text. And this is the mission:

> "I am in my knowing of myself as love, and I am inhabiting this choice through all of my knowing, doing, and being. I am Word through this intention. Word I am Word."

Our respect for you is great. It is not an easy task to realign an energy field and, in fact, it will involve your cleaning out the attic, as it were, because those things that are in the attic are impeding you from inhabiting the higher place. And we will say that the attic is the top floor. When you are ready to stand on the roof, you'll be there as well.

Now the release of these things that we have discussed in prior chapters will be an ongoing process. On Tuesday you don't just make a decision to relinquish all your fears and then on Thursday go dancing without them. In fact, it can happen that quickly. But to the extent that you still require fear, because you identify as it, is the situation that will then require you to go through process in order to release it. It's really very simple.

So the transit you are taking is an enormous one and we respect it. We also want to remind you that this is happening to everybody, regardless of whether or not they are reading this text. This is not about privilege. And understand this now, this is not about making you special or "better than." We are simply giving you a vocabulary and a means by which to navigate the changes that are here already and will be coming into manifestation regardless of whether or not you had ever heard of this book. This is all happening across the globe. This is the manifestation of the New Age. We will say it has come, and it is here, and it is in its knowing as you are acclimating to it.

Our tribute to you is this text, is the first text, and is the text that will follow. There will be more in time. But the journey text is where you are now. "I am learning how to put this into action through this mission." The realization of all this on a global level will be the work of our final book. It is in practice, and there are secrets to be revealed because the time has come to know them. But for the time being, we realign you to your own promise, to your own majesty, and to your own blessed self in the name "I am Word."

Our asking of you now is to give us permission to work with you to realign you in your knowing as a frequency, and we ask you this because we require permission. We do not go around un-bugging people unless they ask, and un-bugging simply means removing those things that are standing in the way of your system operating effectively. If there is a bug in the works, there is something that's not solved, not required, and needs to be released. So we do this with you, with your permission. We also remind you that, as a matter of course, when you are working in frequency, that you are required at this stage of development to work with a level of protection. This will calm you. It will also give you the reason to realign in your own amazement to what can come to you without concern. So we say this with you:

"I am now choosing to align my own energy field to the perfect protection for me that will hold me in Divine Light and Divine Love in order for me to do the work that is before me. I am knowing I am safe. I am safe. I am in my love. Word I am Word through this intention. Word I am Word."

And then, if you wish, you can always ask for support and you can trust that the support you will be receiving is of the Light. So ask yourself this: "Am I now willing to give permission for my energy field to be realigned in appropriate ways in accordance with my highest good?" Yes? If you say yes, we will come.

"I am Word through the one I see before me." This is our choice and we are here to serve.

Now blessings to all who come in choice. Blessed are all who stand in their love. And blessed are all who understand, once and for all, that they are loved. It's a wonderful place to be.

So we sent you out on the road:

"I am love through all that I see before me. I am love through the one I see before me. And I am seeing them as a manifestation of the Creator inhabiting their own experience of knowing."

As you see those before you in their knowing, you give them permission to acclimate to their knowing. As they are in their knowing, they will begin to be awakened. And this is the blessing of the time.

Paul wonders if this is a kind of pollination. And we say that is not the right metaphor because that would expect pollen would be carried to a place that needed it. In fact, all you are doing is resonating at a high frequency in such a way that allows the other frequency to remember what is already there in truth. You are not implanting anything. You are seeing what is there. There is no one here on this planet who is not in God's love. And anyone you would hold outside of that love requires your choice, today, to be released into that love.

When you hold another outside of love, you hold yourself outside of love and you are back on the riverbank. So, again, you are just telling people who they are.

"I am Word through the one before me" is an acknowledgment

of what has always been true. The only difference is you have become activated in this frequency in a way that is tangible for you. The initial decree, which we have spoken to you—

"I am Word through my body. Word I am Word.
I am Word through my vibration. Word I am Word.
I am Word through my knowing of myself as Word. Word I am Word."

—is what has established this in frequency. And once you are aligned to this, you can begin to work with it in active ways.

Now those of you who are already feeling frequency have an easier time. But we will promise you this: Everyone is already feeling frequency. It's only that some of you know it. Now if you would, put your hands together. Put the palms of your hands together for a moment and see what you feel. Feel your fingers press and your palms touch. And feel the energy between your hands.

Now withdraw your hands very slowly until there is a foot length between them. And feel the energy between your two hands. Feel the frequency that lives there. "I am Word through my hands. Word I am Word. I am Word through this frequency. Word I am Word."

Now we are reminding you that the frequency is always there. You can feel frequency between your hands. You do not need to change it with the frequency of the Word. However, the frequency of the Word is there as well when you are attuned to it.

"I am Word through my knowing of myself as knowing that I am one with my Creator" is a reminder and a truth, but it is not something new. We are remembering you. And that is the title of this chapter, "Remembering." Please put a hyphen in it: "Re-membering."

Now we want to talk for a few minutes about disillusion. Disillusion. "I am so disillusioned because this happened, or that happened, or this was taken from me." Please understand, everyone, that that is attachment, and the grieving you go through at times is about relinquishing what you have thought you knew to be true. Some of you may go through a process of disillusionment as you go forward on this journey, and this will happen for several reasons. You will begin to realize that what you thought was so may not be so, and you will believe for a period of time that you cannot trust what you know as a result of this. This is actually a good thing. It's actually a way of your releasing your attachment to the past and living in the empty space that will then be filled with truth. But it is not always an easy process.

Those people who have believed in God and then, for whatever reasons, found that they could not, have a very difficult time realigning to a possibility of a Creator that could love them fully, let alone a Creator that would like to inhabit as them in an aspect of His manifestation.

Now learning a new language can be helpful here. "I am Word" signifies a frequency in tone that can be experienced. You could call it a moose, we suppose, but if the intention was still Word, the frequency would still be the same. However, the symbol that we work with, and it is a symbol, is an ancient one and it creates and that is why we have chosen this as the language to serve through at this time.

Please do not get caught up in language; it is a diminishing of meaning. When people fight about the meaning of something, they are often losing the intent behind it for the sake of the debate. So please understand this: The meaning behind this is God, an aspect of God coming into form in man. If the word "God" does not work for you, release it. "The Universe" is fine. "Source" is fine. "All That Is" is fine. "Consciousness," if you wish, is fine. But please, please, please don't stand in the door to the party and think you cannot come in because you are wearing the wrong clothes. All are welcomed here. All are coming in one language or another, in one form or another, through one system or another to this same place.

> "I am in my knowing that I am one with a Creator, a frequency, whatever you wish to call it, that unifies me with all that I see before me, and I am one with my brother in love. I am Word through this knowing of myself as one with my brother in love. Word I am Word through this intention. Word I am Word."

We marvel at you, you know. You may not know this, but we are amazed by your beauty, and we are amazed by the gifts you bring and we celebrate you, each and every one of you, in your unique beauty. We are in love with you, and this is our testament to you. We gift you now with the understanding and the recognition of your own remembrance as the loved one.

> "I am Word through those I see before me. I am Word through the love I see before me. And I am blessed in my knowing. Word I am Word."

We would like to stop today and continue tomorrow. Thank you both. Word I am Word.

Day Twenty-Two

Hearing, again, will be the topic for this morning's discussion. And hearing in a clairaudient sense. We want to gift you with some answers about your abilities. As we have moved through this text, we have introduced a theme, we have elaborated, and in this final section we want to talk about those same issues in manifestation.

And in this case it means, "I am now hearing myself and I am now hearing my knowing and I am now hearing my brother."

Now when we speak of this in this chapter, we are going to tell you that we are implying, still, that you can hear now. You are already doing this. However, the next step is to begin to acknowledge it and to rely on it. And by this we mean take it out of the realm of expectation and into practice.

"I am now hearing myself as the one who knows. I am Word through this intention. Word I am Word."

Your remarkable self, that self that is already created in the image and likeness of God, is already hearing. And the issue, at times, is the difficulty you have in accessing your own ability. "Why didn't I know that?" "Why don't I need to know what I need to know?" etc., etc. Now we would like to explain it to you: If you are wearing a coat that precludes the elements from touching you, you do not feel the rain or the fire around you. You are protected. And in a funny way, the systems that you have protected yourself with against the unknown have actually created boundaries against your inhabiting what is open to you.

If you are standing behind a wall and there is someone singing to you on the other side of the wall, you may not hear them as clearly as you would if the boundary was not erected. Now the boundary was erected, as we have explained, through your own denial of your abilities and your own fear, and has been kept in place through systems that explain to you that you are not allowed to have these things, or they do not exist, or through systems that would frighten you of them. "If I start hearing things, I must be going mad." "This is the province of the madman or of the saint, but it cannot be available to me."

Now we would like you to know something today. The extent that you keep these beliefs alive through projecting into them their worth is the extent that you do not align to them as your own purview and your own province. So today we want to take the wrecking ball out and tear down the wall between you and your own ability to hear yourself and your fellow and your knowing in the most basic sense that you are the one who knows.

Now the attention we give to this process is of knowing what you need. This is the first emblem: "I am knowing what I need." As you begin to know what you need, you can begin to manifest it. When you don't know what you need, you're in your thinking and your thinking is what has created your problems because it is a beneficiary of that aspect of the self that would tell you you do not know.

So as we go through this process with you today, and it is a process, we are going to realign you to the belief that as you know what you need, you can call it into being. As you call it into being, you manifest it, you create with it. And we do this with you today as a tutelage, a teaching in hearing and manifestation.

Now the first thing we would like to tell you is that your ability to hear can be allowed through a clearing of those things that have prevented you from truly knowing your truth. And we need to work backward for a moment in your energy system.

"I am now choosing to release from my energy field any and all things that have precluded me from standing in my knowing and hearing with my own knowing what I need. I am now choosing to dismantle any and all structures, barriers, hindrances, obstacles that have stopped me from aligning to my own ability to hear myself in fullness and to know what I need in order to create. I am now choosing to stand in my knowing as the one in authority because I am in congruence with my own Divine Self, and I am knowing myself as a conduit for my own knowing of myself as a Divine Child of the Creator. I am Word through this intention. Word I am Word."

Now we would like to bring frequency to you. We will bring it through your auric field through the seven chakras in the lower system and through the chakras above the body and around you. And we would like you to begin to fill yourself with light.

"In the name I am Word I am now free of those obstacles to my own knowing and to my own ability to hear myself, my fellows, and my knowing at a higher frequency. I am Word through this intention. Word I am Word."

Now we celebrate this action with you, and we want to give you a promise. As you begin to work with this actively, you will have exercises with it. And as you begin to hear, you must learn to differentiate what you are from what you are hearing and learn what belongs to you and what belongs to someone else.

In the past we have asked you to sit with a partner and to know what you knew, to feel what you felt, and today we want you to do it again. You can do it with someone who is with you in presence or you can choose someone at a distance. But we want you to be in your active frequency and we want you to go into your own knowing of yourself as light.

As you are vibrating in the frequency of the Word:

"I am Word through my body. Word I am Word.
I am Word through my vibration. Word I am Word.
I am Word through my knowing of myself as Word. Word I am Word."

You are vibrating at a high level. And now you set this intention:

> "I am choosing to tune in to my sister, or my brother, or my fel-
> low by name, and I will feel and hear what I need to in order to
> know what I need to know."

Now you do this in consort with their own energy frequency.
You do not do this in an invasive way. It is not as if you are finding
a crack in an aura and going on a hunt. It is quite simply witnessing
and feeling and being in conversation. Do not look too hard.
Allow it to inform you. Allow the frequency of the person you
have chosen to inform you. What are you hearing? What is it like?
Again, what happens in the body and in the emotions? Please,
everyone, don't expect the voice right away. You may begin to hear
at this level soon, but frankly what you are hearing is frequency
translated to sound that you can access through inner hearing, not
outer.

Now this is done in mutual agreement. The person you are tuning in to is gifting you with the frequency and the acknowledgment
of what you are doing in order to work with him or her. And as you
work, you hear and you know.

Now the plausibility of using this in an active way, then, has to
do with what you know. "I am now knowing what my friend needs"
will be a way for you to affirm your knowing is supporting the
transmission of frequency in energy and clairaudience. As you are
working on this level, you begin to hear and you begin to refine
your ability to be the one who knows. Now we give you this example
and this exercise so that you can understand that there is a separation in the differentials between hearing yourself and hearing
someone else. "I am now choosing to listen to myself in higher frequency. I am Word through this intention. Word I am Word."

We would like you to understand that, as you always know

yourself in the physical self, you can always know the self in your frequency. But to do this, you need to bypass again the intellect that would shut down the sense that you can be larger in your experience. As you get in the habit of working this way, in fact, what happens is that you expand your consciousness and then the intellect accepts it. The intellect accepts that there is life on other planets the moment it is given evidence and the self accepts the paranormal, or the gifts of the Creator as manifested in spiritual knowing, the moment one has ability that can be shown and proven and accepted.

There is nothing in this text that we would recommend you go forward with until you have your own experience of it in a way that is truthful to you. It is a teaching, but it is an active and experiential one. So your own knowing is the key again. What would it be like, finally, to be able to be in response to yourself to the level that you could know what you need from a clean slate of truth?

Imagine, for a moment, that you are looking at a blackboard. And on that blackboard a word appears and floats to the top of the dark surface of the chalkboard, as it were. "What do I need?" And allow the answer to be summoned in a way that you can see, or know, or experience. It can actually be that simple.

Now when we said "a blank slate," it's because so often where you create from is a belief in a need that is born out of external requirements. "I need a better home" not because you need it but because your neighbors have them, or you were trained to believe that a home should look a certain way. So that is not something that should appear on that knowing level. However, what might appear is "I need to know my worth, and as I know my worth I can begin to create experiences that will show me my worth or perhaps show me where I am not honoring my worth so that I can transform that."

So if you wish to use the exercise of the words appearing on the screen, the blackboard, if you wish, that is a simple way to access knowing "What do I need?" You can also do this through your hearing—"What is it that I need?"—and begin to listen. And ask yourself this: "Am I now knowing what I need?"

As you know what you need, you experience the truth of it. Now don't worry about things at this stage of development. When you get wrong information it will not resonate, it will appeal to the ego, and it will make you feel special. "I need to go out and tell the world that I am the Second Coming." Guess what, everybody? That would not be an accurate message, unless you were to tell everybody that they were as well. Then you would be closer to the truth. But "I am knowing that I need to celebrate myself more," "I am knowing that I need to allow love," "I am knowing that I need to go buy groceries"— these can all be valid knowings, if you wish.

Now hearing on an experiential level will be something that you have to develop, but you can begin today on this level to hear. And we would like you to do this with us:

You are now sitting where you are sitting, and you are quieting your mind. And you are imagining for a moment that you are protected and you are vibrating in frequency as Word. As you do this, you imagine yourself as a receptor. You are a receiver and that which you receive is your own knowing and that which would be gifted to your knowing. As you receive this frequency, you align to it and you are allowing yourself to be the beneficiary of the information and the knowing that would be gifted to you:

"I am receiving this information in accordance with my highest good. I am Word through this intention. Word I am Word."

Now again, we would like you to understand that hearing is one of the ways you will begin to experience frequency. And the manifestation of this in your life has to do with several things: the extent to which you align to your own knowing, the belief that you can do this, and the awareness of others so that you know what is your information and what is somebody else's.

Now we will not talk about those people who run around the world saying God told them to do something crazy. We are talking here about frequency and your own knowing. And we have already given you a test in knowing what is truthful and what is ego, or based in fear and the need to be special. So once again we tell you your protection is your system of acknowledgment that you are safe. And the recognition of the divine in everybody else is what allows you to temper any needs the ego may have to keep you in separateness, because that will get you nowhere.

Now your experience today in frequency is going to be a different one. We want to realign you today to your remembrance of your soul's path. This is a little bit different. But if you can understand that this is an ongoing journey and everybody's journey, finally, is to reach the home base, to swim in the ocean, as it were, you can understand that that is the grand gesture. However, each lifetime presents opportunity to develop and to grow and to reach a new level of at-oneness with self and Source, and this is ascribed to you through choices made prior to incarnation.

Now we are not telling you all that you have a grand destiny that you are expected to fulfill here, and we will acknowledge again that you all have free will. But when you incarnate, you generally have a sense on a higher level of what you need to learn and what your path will be in this lifetime.

So we want you to do this with us:

"I am now going into my remembrance of my soul's path. I am now going into my knowing of what I came here for and why I have chosen as I have chosen in this lifetime. I am now receiving

the knowing that I require to accept my abilities in this lifetime
as they are called into service to realize my higher purpose."

Now we will give you some explanation. Imagine your whole
lifetime you were a worrier and you didn't know why you worried,
and you knew it wasn't terribly spiritual because of course we
accept that worry is a form of fear. But then one day you realize you
have been working towards a way of figuring out a puzzle, and that
as you have done this you have liberated yourself from the pattern
of worry. The fact that you have been able to achieve this, in one
way or another, gives you permission, then, to teach and to be a
way-shower for your brothers.

Imagine for a moment that you are somebody that for all of your
life needed to figure things out and you couldn't and it made you
crazy. And that set you on a path where you learn that the conscious mind was an aspect of the self and that the intellect that had
always been your God is fallible and is not the sum total of who you
are. That ability, for you to break through that system, might be
required for the work that you are here to do.

Now we will not teach you a concise method of learning that
you are here to be a developer of systems, or a painter, or a doctor.
That is not the issue here. Because if you can understand that all a
profession really is is a way to acknowledge and work with your
gifts, whatever they may be, and that the titles can be changed,
your gifts can be manifested in many, many different ways depending on what your interests might be and you must honor the path
always that lifts you higher.

The news tells you now that you should not leave your secure
selves. You should tether yourself to the bed, to the terrible job, to
whatever is there because there is so much uncertainty in the world.
And of course, if there is an earthquake, the first tendency is to
stand someplace safe until the ground stops shaking. But really, the

image here is of a dog shaking off her fleas and those things that are not healthy to the dog are being cleared.

You also, in a way, are in this system. So those things that you are holding onto for dear life that you are so frightened of losing, once liberated may give you the knowing of what you really desire. Do you understand this? If you're holding onto something so tightly out of a fear of losing it, you are not knowing what you need. You are paralyzing yourself in fear and you cannot be in the knowing that comes through alignment and congruence.

"I am knowing what I need. I am knowing what I need in order to bring it into manifestation."

We would like you to know that to create in consciousness is not a solitary act. Everybody is running around still manifesting those things that they believe that they need or they want. And they are doing this through active intention or just through conscious thought. As you know, where you put your attention is what you will create with and that becomes your truth.

However, the group knowing, which we will be addressing in a later chapter, is the big thing you will be contending with. And when you bring into manifestation what you know, you call to you wonder. And we promise you this: Your choices, once they have been resolved and they are operating in congruence with a higher system of knowing which is your own Divine Self incarnating as you, will call to you that which is wonderful. How could it not? It knows who you are in truth and that is the aspect of the self that you are now hearing on an experiential level.

So if you wish to take some time, and some simple time, to meditate, to simply be quiet and know "I am in my knowing, Word I am Word," and then you allow your frequency to lift in the frequency of Word and call to you that information you need, you will be gifted with it. Just don't expect it to sound like your uncle Harry or your aunt Martha out on the corner yelling at you to come back into the house. That is not how the voice sounds.

Your own knowing actually sounds like you and is always peaceful and is always wise and it may be you, in fact, without the intonations you are used to, or the vocabulary you are comfortable with, because the eternal you, the knowing you, has been here much, much longer and has great wisdom to impart. This is the aspect of the self that works in tandem with those beings who would help you who are your individual teachers and your guides. Your Higher Self is privy to this information and would like to gift you with it as well. So an exercise for you would be to know your guides, to know your teachers, would simply be to ask that aspect of the self, the Knowing Self if you wish, to create an introduction for you. And you can ask that this be gifted to you in your dreams, in your meditations, or in whatever way that is appropriate to your stage of development.

Now we are not telling each of you that you will be developing so rapidly that by the end of this text you will be having a tea party with your spirit guides in your kitchen. But believe me when we say, we tell you that this can be so. It is so, already, really, on a higher level. It's about your understanding evolving into your knowing and then your inhabiting and experiencing yourself as frequency so that this can become a party, as it were, with your Higher Self running the show.

Many of you really already have these abilities and have developed them in prior incarnation. And this book will be a reminder and you may find that you develop very quickly. Others of you simply have to be patient and attune to the knowing that this happens in perfect order.

"I am now knowing what I require to allow my development to excel and to move as quickly as is for my highest good. Word I am Word through this intention. Word I am Word."

We would like to remind you not to be so attached to outcomes that you develop an attachment to external realization of spiritual matters. Then that puts you back in the game of the ego that requires prominence: "I have to be the best clairaudient." "I need to see by tomorrow."

The chapter that we are still dictating is "Re-membrance" and re-membrance means that you are being re-membered, you are being called back to be reattached, as it were. The image that Paul sees are of many small rivers, many, many small streams growing in power as they propel themselves on their own current to the sea from which they all came from.

This is what is happening there. There is no rush because, as we have told you earlier, this is happening anyway. Everybody is being re-membered because the planet requires it, and by planet we mean the energy system that you are all inhabiting.

Now we talk about manifestation in several ways. You have all been taught already that thoughts are things and that thoughts are creative. And we have reminded you that what you create from your own knowing in a sacred way from your heart knowing or your Divine Knowing will be alignment with your good.

Now we want to talk about bringing things into form, and we will do this quickly. As you choose something to manifest, we would recommend that you try this:

"I am Word through this thing I am now calling into form. I am Word through this intention. Word I am Word."

Now this is the decree to call into being that which is in alignment for the good of all. This is not for selfish reasons. But understand, please, that if you need a computer to do your work to get
the message out, that would count and that should be called into
being. It's not about calling into being those things that the ego
requires to acknowledge her glory. But "I am Word through this
thing I call into being" is a practical way of bringing frequency into
matter.

Now understand, please, that this is not hocus-pocus. You are
still required to go into your knowing that it is so. If you manifest
something in your knowing, it comes into form. You are simply
charging the thought with frequency in order to bring it forth in
accordance with your highest good.

Yes, Paul is sitting here going, "Well, we've never done that." In
fact, we have. Now the book we wrote earlier this year was transmitted in two and a half weeks and then saw the publisher in a
pre-arranged frequency before the month was over that we told
you it would be. That is how these things occur when there is
manifestation occurring at a higher level. This was not your job to
move this forward, this was ours. This was one simple example. But
if any of you look into your own lives at those things that have
worked in a synchronistic way when things just happened in alignment, you can understand that there is an aspect of the divine
working.

We are reminding you, everyone, that this is not about effort.
This is not about demanding. This is not about saying, "I want
it now." "I am Word through this thing that I require" brings frequency. And as this happens, it calls itself into being and we will
support this. Again, this is not magic. It's another way of deciding.
And manifestation, in many ways, is a decision.

This is not a new teaching. "As a man thinketh in his heart, so shall he be," sayeth the Christ. And that is another way of saying that thought is consciousness. "Ask the Father anything in my name and it shall be given." Now this is not the name Jesus. This is the name "I Am." This is the frequency of the Christ. This is the Divine Self.

The Christ, as Jesus, was a manifestation in action of Source and knew this to be so. This is not a new teaching. This is the oldest teaching there is. You are hearing it in a different language and we are teaching you in accordance to your times. Your remembrance is key now. Your remembrance of this information is who you are. All prayer is is an acknowledgment and a decision that the Source is capable and will bring forth that which is required on a knowing level into manifestation.

Our choices with you in our teachings have been to gift you with decisions that you would make yourself in the name "I am Word." Now we have done the decrees for you to date, but we would recommend that you start creating your own. "I am Word through blank-blank-blank."

We will teach you some more about energy frequency in the next chapter, but in this one we want to be in remembrance and if you would allow us, we would like to show you what this means. If you would, when you finish this chapter, sit back and do what we are going to do with you now.

"As I know myself in my divinity, I begin to have an experience of myself as the one who knows. As I know who I am in truth, which is an aspect of the Creator come into form, I align my senses, my hearing, my knowing, my sight, my touch, my taste to all that I can know. And I am aligning my senses in higher frequency in order to be remembered. I align my frequency now to the remembrance of its source. I am Word through this intention. Word I am Word."

We would like you each to imagine for a moment that you are in a river. You are floating in a river gently being carried by a current. Gently being moved forward. And as you move forward, all of the obstacles in the path of the current are being cleared with Divine Light. The light is doing the work. If you find yourself needing to pause while this occurs, you allow this, and you Word through all that you see before you until the path is again clear. And you move on this current. You ride it, and you are carried in love as you move forward. As you move forward, you extend your arms and allow yourself to float as you are moved through this passage to the gateway to the great sea of love and creation.

"I am Word through this journey I am partaking in. Word I am Word through this intention. Word I am Word."

This is the end of this chapter. Thank you and stop.

SIXTEEN

HEALING AND CHRIST CONSCIOUSNESS

Day Twenty-Three

Today we'll talk about knowing in a different way, and your vibrational knowing, and what the energy field knows that it then transmits into consciousness. We are teaching you tools for your own ability to clarify frequency and understanding and what this means is, when you begin to interpret energy—that which you feel around you—how do you move through it? How do you work with it? How do you understand or know what you are feeling?

You have an energy system that is comprised of your physical self and subtle energy bodies that are encompassing your field in frequency. This is all you and this is all aspects of you. And as you begin to differentiate in frequency what you are experiencing in matter and knowing in this way, you can begin to attune in higher ways to know what is happening in your field.

We will give you an example. If you are walking down the street and you begin to feel fear in your energy field, the first thing we have to ask you is to know what you are feeling and where it is coming from, if it is your own fear, or if it is fear you are picking up on. As you begin to attune to yourself as an energy vehicle, as a being comprised in frequency, you know yourself. So then you are allowing yourself to differentiate between your energy field and its "feelings" and those energies that may be intruding on your field, as it were. By intruding we mean impacting, and nothing more.

Now when you are walking down the street and you feel fear, you can choose to allow it to release from your system by stating this intention:

"I am now choosing to allow any energies that are not mine and
are not for my highest good to release from me in perfect order.
I am Word through this intention. Word I am Word."

And then you will be releasing frequency. But the example was only to show you that as you become attuned to your own energy field, you can begin to learn what does not belong to you. As you understand that you are an energy being, you also understand that your experiences do not need to be contained in physical form as you have identified with up until this time. When you are imaging someone in a land far away, in consciousness you are joining them there. You are working inter-dimensionally to reach them.

When authors have moved into the future to summon imagery for their fictions, they have, in fact, in many cases intruded on the membrane and bypassed it that separates the dimensions of time as you articulate them. Which is why an author might predict a science fiction that then one day becomes true.

You are always traveling in frequency. We have talked about this already. And today we want to teach you that you are the vehicle of light that can support others in their healing.

When one makes a choice in this lifetime to stand in wholeness, one can do this. But you are all being impacted in consciousness in different ways, and manifestations of physical illness come in different forms and for different reasons.

When you serve to heal one another, you are choosing to take into account the soul requirements of another. One cannot assume immediately that one's illness, or one's disability, has not come to teach them a wonderful lesson. And your limited perspective based on what one "should" be, can be, in fact, the distortion, whereas the body that is moving out of its form and into refined frequency may be doing exactly what it needs to.

Now the desire to heal someone you love is a noble one and, yes, we will tell you that anything can be healed, everything has been healed, and the disability that you have is in the awareness of this. Now we are not eschewing medicine, and this is a very important thing to understand. Throughout time there have been remedies of the earth for illness. And everything that is of the earth is of the Creator and information about how maladies can be healed with other means than frequency have been gifted to many through inspiration. The desire to heal one another from that which ails them is a truthful one and has always been supported. So we do not tell you today to bypass medicine for frequency. Medicine is frequency in a different form.

However, you can understand that when there is an energy system that is impassive, or is in form in a way that is not operating swiftly or healing well, it can be dealt with through choice in clearing and moving energy. When one tunes in to someone in frequency who is not well, the first thing one has to understand is that malady was created in a way as a teacher. And to bypass the teaching to heal is not necessarily serving the one healed. Now we are not talking about the bad cold. We are talking about a dysfunction in body that has been created for whatever reasons that now needs to be understood in order to be cleared. To go about throwing out the garbage without knowing where that garbage came from is not necessarily going to serve anyone. But teaching you today to be in the manifestation of healing frequency for the highest good of another is what we would like to talk about.

"I am now choosing to serve as a vehicle for the healing of my brother." Say you tune in to someone in their frequency and you move through their body in consciousness as if you are an x-ray or a scanner and you move through the body and you begin to feel in your own where they are holding pain or dis-ease. You can move into conversation with your own knowing and with the knowing of the one you are with to learn what is required to move the frequency to bring it back into alignment.

"I am now choosing to know that which would support my brother in his healing. Word I am Word through this intention. Word I am Word."

Now we want to talk about realization for a moment. And your realization of your brother as healed and in his perfect state is, in truth, a way to support frequency. However, we don't mean this to bypass a reality. We do not tell you this in a way to deny a present symptom, but instead to see the organism as healed and capable of healing. This is done through intention. However, a simple way to work in frequency is as follows: You have tuned in to your partner, you have felt where the malady lives, and then you set this intention:

"I am Word through this part of my partner that needs to be re-aligned in healing. Word I am Word through the one before me."

There are many ways to operate this, but it's always really this simple. When you are tuning in to the Word, the Word operates in frequency. And what you are doing when you are sending the Word is aligning the Word to do the work that is required in your partner.

"I am Word through Arthur's shoulder." "I am Word through Mary's bladder." "I am Word through John's knees." "I am Word through Bill's arthritis." Whatever you wish to say is setting an intention to allow frequency to be in to the work of realigning. And the realization of this, that this is so, is all that is required of you.

You are not getting in there to fix something. And to be honest with you, it is not your job to fix anything. We have spoken about fixing earlier, and fixing and transforming are two very different things. To bring an organ back into its perfect sate of functioning is not necessarily fixing it. It has been damaged, and putting a patch on something that is damaged may make it work a little longer, but that is not the same as transforming and healing, which is bringing the higher frequency to do the work consciously to realign the energy field in the way that is required.

"I am Word through the heart of the one I see before me" sends energy to the heart. And the heart will take the energy and do what it is required to do. Now we will explain this to you quickly:

We would like you to know that you do not need to be in the physical presence of one that you heal. You can tune in to someone anywhere, at anytime, and do this same work. It's very simple, actually, when you decide that this is something that can be done. You quite simply state this intention:

> "I am now choosing to heal through my frequency that which is required in so and so. Word I am Word through this intention. Word I am Word."

Now again, these are not a litany of words. You are simply asking the frequency of the Word that you are attuned to to work with the frequency of the others. And you are bypassing physical systems to work at a higher frequency. And you can do this for someone in China as effectively as you can someone in the next room. It's all there now. All, everything is in the Great Now, and actually on a dimensional level it's as easy to travel to China as it is to travel into the next room. If you are traveling by foot to the next room, you could be in China more quickly if you just tuned in.

Now we have given you a knowing already of your own energy frequency. And the reason it's so important to know this is so you can begin to teach yourself when you are working in energy what you are feeling. When you are moving through somebody's body, and you feel a pebble in the system, what is that pebble? Is it a cyst? Is it something else? Now we are not telling you at all to become diagnosticians. That is not appropriate for this text. But we will tell you that if you are tuning in to someone and your fingers hurt, you might learn to ask the person, "What's going on in your fingers?" and you get the answer and you get the affirmation: "I have tendonitis." "I have arthritis." "I have been typing too much." But you will learn. You have to have your own knowing in order to be effective.

Now if you understand that prayer is a form of healing, and when you are praying for someone you are teaching the field of frequency that requires healing through application to bring forth the frequency that is needed, you can understand that that does not require that you move into your own energy field in order to "track." It does mean that your intention is to see them healed, and that is lovely. However, to know that someone is being healed is not always in alignment to their soul's purpose, and you must always defer to that knowing.

If you ask someone at a higher level what they need, they may actually teach you something very different. You may learn that the person needs to move on. You can assume that a child needs to do well in school, but if you ask the same child on a higher level what he needs, that self may inform you that he needs to be believed in, not achieved, and that the achievement may be born out of the belief in his lovability. So do not confuse things. You can get the information that you require at a higher frequency *through your knowing.* However, what we are teaching you now is learning who you are as frequency so that you can support others in their healing.

All disease begins in frequency before it manifests into the physical body. So all healing, of course, must begin in the auric field as well.

"I am now choosing to see my partner in his health, in his wellness, and in his divine perfection. Word I am Word through this intention for my partner. Word I am Word."

This sends the frequency to the one you know and puts them in the position to work with the energies to bring them forth into healing manifestation. However, there is always free will, and you cannot dictate how this energy is used. You are simply sending frequency and allowing the frequency to do what it is required to do. Your job always is to be the Word. To be the Word means you are not worrying, you are not demanding, nor are you even deciding what is truthful for this other person. You are simply a conduit for the Divine Love that would move through you.

When we talk about love today, we want to talk about it a little bit differently. And we want to talk about emotions for a small time, and what emotions really are. We have spoken about them before and we have told you that emotions are ways you know who you are. You know how you feel through what you are experiencing emotionally. And we want to talk about the transformation of emotion. Now this is important. People believe, still, that if they suppress an emotion that they don't feel is a healthy one, they are doing something spiritual. "I am not angry because I am not allowed to be angry because that is not spiritual," or "I should not be grieving because I know there is a heaven, so I should just be happy that my friend has moved on," or whatever you would like to say.

Now denial of the emotions creates dis-ease. That's very, very simply put. And moving through the emotions to allow them to be transformed is a vehicle for healing. But you cannot identify what you have suppressed unless you are willing to go there. Now we do not want to spend a great deal of time going back through your histories in order to identify trauma. That is not our work here. All healing happens in this present moment. All healing happens in this present moment *now*. And that includes trauma that you may have incurred when you were two years old. The healing of that still happens in the now.

When we work with frequency, we are bypassing time, as you understand it. So if you were traumatized at the age of two, you can go back to that time and state this intention:

"I am Word through the knowing of myself as safe and perfect and I am healed in this moment of that which occurred. I am Word through this knowing of myself as healed. Word I am Word through this intention. Word I am Word."

And you are actually activating the self at cell memory to release that which has been held at that time. That which was created then that still exists in frequency today can be accessed and transformed. But back to the present:

Today you are walking around and you are angry or you are worried or you are ashamed. What do you do with these feelings as they emerge, and how do you contend with them in this system that we have been offering you? We would like to tell you that the quickest way to work is to move into acceptance of what you feel.

Do not suppress. Allow the emotion to arise and to become what it wants to be in its expression, but then understand, please, what is motivating you emotionally. What are you attached to? Why are you feeling this? Become aware. At that level you can begin to work on discordances that have manifested in these emotional responses.

For example: You are walking down the street and you trip and you fall and people look at you and you feel ashamed. What is the response of shame? What is shameful about falling down? Everyone's done it. Why do you need it?

"I am now choosing to Word through this need to experience shame. Word I am Word through this intention. Word I am Word."

You don't have to recall what prompted your first experience of shame. That would likely be impossible, but to determine that that is the feeling you are having and then to release the need for it would support you in clearing the attachment to this emotional response that you have been triggered to experience in response to certain things. It supports you in realigning your knowing to the fact that there is nothing wrong and perhaps what is wrong is that nobody has extended their hand to support you back to your feet. So there is an example of moving through an emotion.

"I am now choosing to release the need to feel shame. Word I am Word through this intention."

Now we would like to talk about the need for shame and why you each hold onto it so dearly. It's its own mechanism of self-punishment and it has been taught to you culturally, parentally, through this lifetime and through others. Those moments in your life that still prompt a memory of shame, that make you shudder when you remember them, would be ideally contended with through this decree:

> "I am now choosing to remember my own divinity in this moment and in this situation. And I see myself in perfect love at this time. I am Word through this intention. Word I am Word."

And you are supporting yourself in the frequency of love at the moment that pattern, or that memory, was cemented. And we will un-cement it, we will say, through the frequency of Divine Love. "I am love through the one I see before me" pertains to yourself as well as your brother.

Now your love, on an emotional level, is something we would like to talk about briefly. We have told you already that love is a frequency. But when you become "in love" in an emotional way that requires attachment, you bring to this situation your history of love, and that which you have experienced up until this moment. And that includes any history that has not been loving or supportive of the self in relations.

Imagine that you are a pipe and you are looking to hook your pipe up to another pipe. But what runs through your pipe is a lot of negativity based in previous experience. You have to clear the pipe out, as it were, so you don't pollute the new relationship with your old experience. This is the example you always use: You have someone who is in love with someone else, but they have a terrible history of relationships and they bring all of that history to them, to the new relationship, which then does not support the healing and the support of the evolution of the new relationship in a healthy way.

So what we have to do right now is understand that there is a way to heal emotional history. And emotional history, we will say, can be seen as a tree that runs through your body and your energy field. All of these things that you have attached yourself to we can say are like apples hanging on this tree. And we would like you to use this visualization to begin to clear them:

> "I am now choosing to release all of the creations that I hold that are impacting my ability to have a loving relationship with another. I am now choosing to release established patterns that are containing me in historical pain, in fear, or in ways that do not align my demonstrating a healthy and loving relationship. I am now choosing to do this in accordance with my own highest good, and I am living my life in my love. I am Word through this intention. Word I am Word."

Now if you would imagine, all of the apples are coming off the tree. Now if you don't want to use apples, you can use any image you like. But the demonstration we are trying to teach you is, those are things that have been created that you hold that are obstructing your ability to be *in love* in a healthy and healing way. And we will tell you this: As you see what these things are, you can begin to work with them in frequency.

We have given you the image of a river and we have talked to you about boulders and tree trunks and things that stop you on your path. This is more of the same. And we tell you this: If you are walking along a path at night, sometimes you stumble across something and it stops you and you don't know what it is. And your flashlight might not illumine the object to the degree that you require to see it fully for what it is. But if you wait a few hours, the sun will shine, you can see it in its wholeness, and you can clear it through this intention.

> "I am now choosing to release that obstacle on my path to a healthy and loving relationship. I am Word through this intention. Word I am Word."

We have talked about emotions as ways that you identify the self as who you are. You feel a certain way, so you decide that this must be a certain thing that you have an attraction to, or are repelled by, or whatever you like. But you systematize yourself based on your emotional responses. But you still don't always know how much of your emotional response is authentic to you and how much of it is inherited intellectual information.

"If I see someone like that do something like that, I should feel like that." That is taught behavior. That is what you have gained by being in collective agreement. So you might as well begin now to learn what you truly feel and not what you think you should feel. And then you can work with your emotions more effectively.

But how do you work with them on a day-to-day level to support the self in maintaining high frequency? We have already told you that your consciousness is your frequency. And it is your obligation, finally, to keep your frequency high. So claiming "I am Word" through what you feel will support you in realigning your feelings to the higher frequency. "I am Word through this feeling of rage," "I am Word through this worry," "I am Word through this sadness," believe it or not, will incur frequency response into the energetic bodies that correlate to the emotions and to the mind. That is how it works.

When you are Wording through your kneecaps, you are sending the frequency to your knees. When you are Word through your worry, you are sending the frequency of the Word to support you in aligning that energy field that would hold the worry to the higher frequency. It's really that simple.

Now once again, please understand that you are the one in charge here, and your emotions, regardless of what you think, are things that you have a big say about. You are not controlled by them. That's a way to keep yourself small. But that is not to say that you should not have your feelings. We want you to have your feelings. They're an aspect of you. We simply want you to know that you can work with them. If you suppress your emotions, if you deny them, you can manifest dis-ease. That is one of the primary ways that problems occur in the physical form. That is not to blame anybody, it's simply talking about what happens when frequency is not allowed to flow and things get blocked.

We are trying to move you into alignment again through this work. And our mission is to see you as healed of that which ails you. So we will do this work with you now:

> "I am now choosing to align myself to my own healing of body, mind, and spirit. I am now choosing to activate frequency to bring all of my energy bodies into perfect alignment and healing. And I am affirming that my body is healed as well. I am Word through this intention. Word I am Word. I am now choosing to believe that I am worthy of my healing and I am aligning myself to that which I require to make this so. Word I am Word."

Now we would like to talk very briefly about Christ consciousness and what this is. When you see someone else in their perfection, you are seeing them in Christ. When you see a situation that appears to be in distortion and you see it in its perfection, you are in the Christ. When you see yourself as an aspect of the Creator and you see your fellows as the same, you are in the Christ.

When we speak of healing today, either physical or emotional healing, you are operating at Christ consciousness when you see the one as healed before you. You are seeing them in the spiritual perfection. If the body does not take the energy to work with, the energy field will, and we will tell you each, everyone is loved and everyone will be held in love at the end of this journey. The existence in the body in corporeal form is a system of experience and one chapter, as has been said, in a grand book. So you are living a life today. You will always be alive someplace, and we are working with you here, today, in your consciousness to support you in your growth and healing.

We honor you each and we will stop for today. The title for this chapter is "Healing and Christ Consciousness."

I am Word. I am Word. I am Word.

Stop now, please.

Day Twenty-Four

We'll talk about knowing for one more minute before we move on to the next lecture. The amount of time spent on knowing in this text is a prerequisite for the work that is to follow. When you are told something that is not your own experience, it remains in the realm of conjecture or opinion and that is not how we wish you to incorporate the work of this text.

The work of this text is to benefit you on multiple levels of consciousness in order to bring about a transition in how you self-identify as an energy being, as an aspect of the Creator, and as the one who is in dominion of his experience on this material plane. As you believe this through those demonstrations you bring forth through the action of this work, you can have your own knowing, and your own knowing will bring to you the requirements in your experience to prove this for yourself.

Your manifestations, finally, are what matter. Your belief, as it is grounded in your knowing, will be the rock that you stand on, and that is the rock of truth. You must stay in your truth. And we do not wish you to bypass your own knowing for ours. We simply instruct, and we teach the methods that we are allowed to bring forth to you at this time and at this stage of planetary evolution.

Much has been said in this text about the transition that is coming forth. And what is happening, really, is the dimensions are shifting or, in fact, you are shifting in your own dimensional experience. And what this means is that your life on this plane will become malleable to another set of experiences that will be made available to you as this shift transforms your plane.

Now it is not as if a door opens and you walk through it into another realm. In fact, the other realm has always been coexisting with you, and all that is really happening here is that those bindings that have kept you tethered to lower frequency and those beliefs that have held you on this level of experience are being transformed to permit you to see, as it were, to experience, what we now speak of in consciousness. To expand consciousness is, in fact, to move dimensionally and as your consciousness is expanded what becomes available to you on informational levels is transformed. You no longer look to physical matter to give you the proof of a question. You actually access the information in the higher frequencies and bring them to you.

If you can remember, prior to the Internet the amount of time it took to look something up, you can see that the Internet, in many ways, was a precursor to the idea that people could exist out of body and in consciousness. When you are on a telephone, you are still very much anchored into physical reality. But the advent of the telephone transformed people as well.

So what we are telling you now is that this next shift in conscious awareness is the next level and the next stage of your evolution as a planet. You have relied on the physical form to do much of your work for you in terms of conference, in terms of action, in terms of what is expected of you. And of course we are not telling you that you are abandoning physical form, you are expanding form. And as you bypass the requirements of the physical, your experience is transformed and your beliefs will begin to change.

Once you understand that matter is frequency and that everything can be transformed in consciousness, you begin to realign the requirements for your daily life. And the choices that you make are chosen anew in this new awareness.

Now we delight in our teachings with you, and we have things to discuss with you today about romance and about fear and about the bodies you stand in. And this is a little talk about self-justification and adherence to paradigms that have pre-existed this lifetime.

Each one of you in this lifetime has made engagements with other people that you have mutually agreed upon that were actually made prior to incarnation. This book, in fact, was contracted prior to Paul's inhabiting this form. He knew it, but he didn't know it for real until it started coming through; then it was a memory of understanding and the pieces of the puzzle made sense. You each have things in your life like this, and you also have engagements with others that you have brokered on a higher level. Some of these have been in business, some of them have been in love, and some of them have been the most painful experiences that you have undertaken. If you understand, first of all, that when you come here you come here to learn, and when you come here you have unfinished business from previous incarnations, you can quite simply begin to understand that as you move through this life, you will have recurrent patterns and relationships that are provocative and are meant, really simply, to move you out of your comfort zone and into a new level of awareness.

Now the love that you have for others is always present. But if you can also imagine that those who have been your hardest teachers have also been in love and are choosing now to bypass former fears by moving into your system to create a new structure to move you forward, you can understand how certain occurrences establish themselves in your lives as difficulties or as challenges that will change you or propel you in a new direction.

Now those people that you know from your previous lives may not be your family members. They may be people that you recognize on a level in familiarity, or perhaps not. But please understand that the primary relationships in your life, the ones that sustain or the ones that provoke great change, tend to require an understanding and an acceptance and love in order to understand them and accept what they bring you.

If one is still blaming a partner for an injury of the heart, one never heals the heart. Now if one understands that a partner can harm based on whatever reasons and that the heart can then be changed and transformed through that exchange to open to a higher level of love, you will also understand that this pain has been your teacher.

In the past chapter we told you that much healing requires an examination of the emotions and that suppressed emotion can be creative in harming the systems that could then manifest in disease. However, the heart that has been broken can be healed, and the one that you would blame for the heartbreak has, in fact, been your teacher in love.

We all have choices we make. And the first thing you always need to remember is that you can elect to have an emotional response that is in accordance with your higher knowing. If you bypass lower frequency, that does not mean you are in denial of it. Not at all. If you elect a new response, you are actually choosing how you want to contend with an emotional situation. People believe that certain responses are required of them. They are expected. And not only do they go into them, they perpetuate them, because those patterns which can be based in fear will seek often to self-perpetuate. This is the downward spiral that some people experience, or the grief that does not release.

You can easily become attached to pain and the comfort of it, and it's not required. We are speaking with you today about transforming patterns in manifestation so that your life can then begin to reflect the choices that you would make from the higher frequency you have been attuned to.

Now we would like you to listen for a little bit about the requirements of this chapter.

We are going to teach you that your body is a joy. Regardless of what you feel about the physical form that you stand in, your body is a joy and it is a significant one. It is what allows you to have your experience on this physical plane. And if it doesn't look like you wish it did, if it doesn't perform the way you thought it should, it's still a wonderful joy. And the physical body needs to become attuned to this. It needs to vibrate as joy, in an awareness of its worth, in order to be healed.

When you are condemning the physical form that you stand in, you cannot expect it to change in a healthy way. A dog that gets yelled at becomes frightened. And if it changes and responds in behavior, it is never a happy dog. And if you abuse your body by calling it names or by criticizing it for not doing what you think it should, you are actually harming your frequency. So our requirement for you right now is to be in joy in the physical form that you stand in, regardless of what you would like to feel.

Now your choice is always made by you. And as you live your life, you dictate how you want things to be and how they are to be experienced by you. And this is always in choice and it happens whether or not you are acting consciously or not. Your mind is always operative and the thoughts that you send out create your experience here. So when you decide right now that your body is in joy, your body can begin to receive the benefits of that knowing. And by the way, that can include a transformation of the form that you stand in. But the body that had been criticized responds poorly and expects to be condemned.

Now we want to talk about what you put into your body and

how you elect to inhabit this behavior. It's really your call how you wish to eat. But how you eat and when you eat and what you eat for what reasons is something that requires a little bit of discussion.

Your choices, when they are made from emotion, are not necessarily conscious choices. So we want to differentiate how you care for your body from how you feel for a little bit and try to become practical.

When you walk around all day, your body needs hydration and you know it and you care for it accordingly. However, when you are in a rush and you grab something off a shelf without an awareness of what you are feeding yourself, you are acting unconsciously. When you poison the body with chemicals, with alcohol, with drugs, you are actually lowering your frequency. And we want to give you a requirement now that you become aware in your physical reality of your own responsibility to yourself.

Now this love that we have for you cannot occupy you in the way it would like to, to the extent that you do not allow it for yourselves. And the ways that you harm yourselves are very, very unconscious at this stage of development. You are all in party to it. You are breathing in gasses, you are taking pills, you are feeding yourselves junk without thought, and you have gone into agreement that this is okay.

It's okay to the extent that it keeps you tethered, that it keeps you unconscious and, on that level, out of the responsibility you actually have for your own well-being. The choice to become the caretaker of the self at this level is an important one. And Paul is wondering why we are bringing it up at this stage of this text. We are trying to teach you right now that your authorship of your life is inclusive of every area of your life. And in speaking of frequency and in speaking of consciousness, we have actually bypassed the basic step of reminding you that while you are having these experiences you are still here on a planet and having encounters in the flesh, and the flesh might as well be well kept.

Your body is in frequency. In the old days, spiritualists would attempt to bypass physical form and they actually found the body to be a dense frequency that they would seek to abandon. The movement that we are in right now in ascension is about elevating frequency. And as the frequency is elevated, the body needs to allow itself to transform, to accommodate the new level of frequency that would inhabit it.

If you can imagine a light bulb that can only contain so many watts without blowing out, you can actually think of your physical body this way as well. As the body amplifies in frequency, the body needs to readjust itself to transform to be able to hold the new frequency that is where it needs to be.

"I am now choosing to bring my physical body to the next level of its incarnation and become aware of all ways in which I still the hold the physical form in abeyance of the higher frequency. I am now realigning my knowing to become newly aware of my responsibility to heal my body as is required by my choices to feed myself, care for myself, and inhabit my surroundings in wellness. I am now coming to know that my body is a joyful vehicle and I am celebrating it in Divine Love and thanking it for being with me on this remarkable journey in consciousness. I am now choosing to accept the awareness and the actions that are required to support me in realigning my form to hold and vibrate at this new frequency. I am Word."

"I am Word through my body" requires the body to begin to realign itself into the frequency of the Word. And it is a big step because the body, up until now, has been expressed in consciousness without its own awareness of its divinity. But of course, as you are divine, the form that you stand in is divine as well. Now we would like to re-member you to your own health and well-being.

And to re-member is to bring you forth in an awareness of your own divine perfection and Christ consciousness.

> "I am now choosing to know myself in my perfect health and perfect body. I am experiencing myself as who I am in truth. And I am realigning the cells of my body to vibrant well-being and to a knowledge of themselves as manifestations of the Christ consciousness. I am Word through this intention. Word I am Word."

Our choices with you are always to lead you forward. And if you can imagine that our hands are taking yours to pull you forward, with your agreement we will do so. When you call this intention forth, the first thing you may become aware of is where you are not honoring the body. Where you are complaining about your back, or your weight, or a gesture that makes you uncomfortable, or the pigment of your skin.

You must understand right away that much of this is habituated behavior and can be transformed through the work that we have done so far. But as you realign to this understanding of your own perfection, the mirror that you stand before will be transformed. And not to make you resemble something you think you should be, but to show you the manifestation of who you are in truth.

We would like to remind you that the energy that you are is of God, and what is out-pictured in that mirror finally is the aspect of God that you are in form having an experience here on this plane. Your justification for how you have treated yourself in the past is not a claim to the future behavior that you can incur through the choice to live in joy in the physical form that you stand in.

Now our requirements for you in this chapter are about choice and form and understanding your lives as your responsibility. The work of this book has not been about healing as much as it has been about transformation of consciousness. And as we have explained to you, as your consciousness is transformed, the healing occurs as a default response to the new awareness you have come to. This is what happens when you lay claim to your own divinity.

Now romance. Let's talk about this for a moment. It's an ideal. And we want you to understand the benefit of it if you can understand that love, as a frequency, holds romance, but that romance itself is an idealization that is primarily based in desire and the ideal of longing. We are not bypassing true love as it has been expressed in the storybooks, we are simply reminding you that you detail things in accordance with prescribed patterns that may or may not serve you. So we would ask you each, at this time, to elevate your consciousness to a broad sense of true love to incorporate all and everyone that you see before you.

There are such things, of course, as soul mates and there are those people that you have gone into agreement with to learn and to share from. But please understand, everyone, that your dictate that something should last forever is primarily a construct born out of fear of losing something. What is true in love is everlasting and that will always be the case.

You all have choices. You all have responsibilities and the requirements of this time, very, very simply, are that you become conscious of them.

Respond now to this next section tomorrow. We are going to finish this today with this new ideal:

"I am now choosing to realign my physical body and my experience of myself on this plane of existence to encompass the higher frequency so that I may know myself in form as an aspect of the Creator. I am Word through this intention. Word I am Word."

Thank you and stop.

SEVENTEEN

MANIFESTATION

Day Twenty-Five

The realization that you are who you are is where we have taken you. And the binding that you hold still in the physical form that you stand in has to do with what you recognize as yourself based in previous performance, ways that you have self-identified through your knowing.

Now when we tell you this today, we want you to understand that we are not requiring you to forget who you have been; we are asking you to remember who you are. And these are two very different things.

Up until this stage of your development, you have believed yourself to be your name and your occupation and all of those things that have contained your history in this lifetime up until this moment. "I am the boy that became the adolescent that became the man." That is how you would self-identify. "I attended this university. I worked in that job. I married that person. I had this child." These are all ways of saying, "Yes, I had an experience here on this plane. I existed. And these are the material manifestations of what I have known."

Now we would like you to know that, as you already know, your history is eternal, behind you, before you. It is all one eternal stream and this is the stream of creation. So if you can imagine, right now, that the identity that you hold is ready to be relinquished once and for all to this new self-identity, "I am Word," you will understand the action of this next section.

We are teaching you today the art of forgetting, the art of forgetting what you have known so that you can truly incarnate as your Divine Self. When you remember who you were from this vantage point, you will remember everything in love because you will see now that everything you have experienced has brought you to this station, and the train that arrives in this station is taking you to your joyous destiny. Everything that you have carried with you awaits beside you and you choose now, today, to say to all of these things that you have held dear, all of these things that have held you down, and all of these things that you have dragged behind you painfully will now be leaving you to realign you to your next stage of personal knowing, "I am the Word. I am the Word. I am the Word."

Now we will teach you this. You can do this now and you will do this in progress as you proceed through your life. We are not going to hit you with a thunderbolt and we are not going to make a wave in this life stream to propel you too fast into the vast ocean of love. But we are going to show you what it involves and how you are now to inhabit yourself as your Christed Self.

Please understand, everyone, that this is not an intellectual exercise to be dismissed as impossible. What we are teaching you is who you are already. But we have to bring the physical self and the mind that has taught itself certain things into a place of receptivity so that it can truly hold this manifestation of the divine.

So, yes, you are divine, but the light bulb that we spoke of yesterday is only dim compared to how it will shine when you have achieved, when you have received and aligned to the Divine Light that will illumine you.

"I am now knowing on a cellular level that I am one with my Creator. And I am now accepting the Christ Self, the True Self, inhabiting as me in fullness, and I give permission to the conscious mind to begin to receive itself in its completeness as understanding that I am this thing incarnating in new knowing. I accept myself as this thing and I reacquaint my name, I am Word, to the truth of who I am."

Those things that have, up until this time, been theoretical for you will now become experiential. Your choice to walk down the street, to be in love, to stand in your knowing, and to say, "I see all that I see before me in the frequency of love," will now be so.

We are choosing you as an emissary of this work. We have chosen you as a speechwriter, as a teacher, as a liver of this teaching. We are now allowing each of you to reclaim yourselves in this knowing so that you can do your work here, on this level of existence and above. It has been said, "As above, so below," and that is this truth. You carry with you the frequency of the divine. The seed has always been present, it has always been there, and it had been forgotten by so many of you that there had to be a reawakening. And as the seed grows into its beauty and full form, it carries with it the remembrance of who it is and it recognizes all things in love because it cannot do other.

You are these beings. You have elected this; you chose it before you came. Everyone will wake up. But those of you who are awakened first become the teachers of this text. You become the masters of the classroom. And that does not mean you open a school; that means you show others the truth of who you are through your knowing and through the actions that you take. Your lives will now change. This is a promise to you. And the residual effects of the manifestations that we will work with you on will be felt for some time to come.

"I am now accepting myself as in congruence with my own Divine Self. And I accept through my seven charkas, above me and below, that which is required to align myself once more to this truth: I am Word. I am Word. I am Word."

Now we bring to you each the Creator. Now we bring to you each your knowing of yourself as at one with All That Is. Now we accept you as you truly are: as an ambitious perfect expression of the Divine Knowing come into form. I am Word. I am Word. I am Word.

Accept, everyone, if you would, through the bodies you stand in. Open your arms if you wish, but accept yourself as at one with the love of your God. Call the God whatever you like, but God is love and that is the truth. As you express this love in your life, you stand in the river. You stand to your knees. You stand to your hips and your chest. And then you are embraced in wholeness as you are carried to the sea. We are with you now and we are carrying you there.

"I am now accepting myself as being carried forth in unity through my life knowing and being into this sea of love. And I express myself in my knowing of this as so. And I now say this is so because I am in my knowing, I am letting myself become what I am: a frequency of the Divine Love that wants to say, 'I am Word.'"

Accept, accept, accept. We are working on your systems and we are radiating you as you truly are. You are each an aspect of the Christ come into form and we have been gifting you with this alignment from the moment you even imagined you would read this text. We are now accepting you as you are in frequency, and we are blessing you each in our tutelage and in our knowing of yourselves as Word.

Now we reach you. Now we hold you. Now we embrace you and we gift you with this:

"Each one who knows will know themselves as truth.
Each one who stands will know themselves as healing.
Each one who breathes will know themselves as breath.
And each one who loves will know themselves as love.

"Each one who gives will know themself as the Well of All
   Giving.
And each one who believes will be the Rock of Faith.
Each one who expresses will express the Divine.
And each one who sings will sing a song that will reach the
   millions.
Each one who is in free will untie their fellows.
And each one who laughs will sing with this in joy.
Each one who praises will be praised in knowing.
And each one who says, 'I am Word,' will be in themselves
   as love.

"I am Word through this intention. Word I am Word."

Today's talk for the remainder of this session will need to be about your responsibilities to yourselves and to this transition as the one who knows. We teach you this, and we express it to you with an understanding that you each imagine your trajectory to be somewhat different than it might truly be.

Your answers will come to you, now, in your own knowing as you accept it. And your freedom will come to each of you the moment you know fully that you have always been free. Your love will sing when you give your heart permission, and your faith will be your rock the moment you lay claim to it. You will sing this light in your frequency as you move forward in your work as a teacher, as a being who has come into form.

Now you each ask, "Will my life be changed, and how?" And of course it will be changed. But you are the changer, and your metamorphosis under your own control will become in alignment with the higher will that we spoke to you about once you accept that you are now working in congruence with it.

"Now I give myself over to this realization of my new name, I am Word. I give myself over to this new expression of myself. I give myself over to the willingness to believe that I am in my Christed Self as one with my love, as one with my being, as one with the Christ who indwells in me in expression as full realization. I accept myself as what I am and I go forward in my knowing."

Your jobs now are to say, "I am." "I am this. I am this. I am this." And as you claim it, you receive it. Nothing in your life until this time has been claimed by you without your approval, and that includes your sorrow, that includes your pain, and that includes your fears. And today we have said to you, you are leaving these aspects of the self at the railway station. You are leaving them on the riverbank. You are leaving them. You are leaving them. You are leaving them. And as you express yourself in this knowing of yourself as fully realized, you claim it. As you claim it, you call it into being, you give it the name it has come for: "I am Word."

Now your resistance to this, if it should arise, can be expressed and released. Much of what you fear, quite simply, is being out of control. And your beliefs—if you do this work you will be out of control, you will not be able to prevent disaster, you will not be able to stop something from changing if it does not suit the picture you hold for the way your lives are supposed to look—are quite simply those things that can be released through Word.

"I am now choosing to release any resistance that may occur to this work as I choose to. And I remember always that the illusion of fear is only that, a temporary picture that would like to become a truth when it is only a lie. I am now accepting myself as worthy of this journey in the knowing that I am safe. I am Word through this intention. Word I am Word."

The life that you have lived until today has been a full one. It has been full of experiences. You have learned many things. You have loved and been loved. You have known yourself through your achievements. You have feared yourself in your failures. You have believed yourself to be who you were told and you imagine you should be. And today we teach you that you are who you say you are in this moment in time. You are who you say you are. And your significance as a Divine Being is an eternal significance.

The body that you stand in may one day be dust, but what you stand in in your knowing will be with you for an eternity. The fears that you have carried until this date have been ideas and beliefs and they are not in truth. So let them go to the sea that you now stand in and be washed from you.

Our love for you holds you in knowing. Our love for you keeps you in your truth. And our love for you responds to your cries of worry or of pain. So we sing to you our song. We sing to you our love. And we bless you in this incarnation of self that you are now manifesting in form.

> "I am now realigning my physical form, my DNA, the structure of my very being to accept itself in its majesty. I now bless my body as the vehicle of the divine and I now express myself in all my subtle bodies in radiant light. I give the express approval to my guides and teachers of the Divine Light to hold me and replenish me and reform me in accordance with the Divine Plan for my evolution as a soul. And I express myself in wonder. And I express myself in thanks. And I say, 'Yes, I give permission to be myself. I am made new in Divine Love. I am made new in this journey and I am accepting myself as, yes, Word. I am Word through this intention. Word I am Word.'"

The beliefs that you have held until today have served their purposes. They have kept you alive. They have kept you fed and clothed. They have kept you in partnerships. And please understand now that divesting yourself of the knowing that you were does not require that all of these things go into the trash can. They do not. But you are no longer bound by them because, as you become yourself in this frequency, you express yourself in this frequency, because that becomes your language in frequency. It is your song. It is what your energy frequency does. It cannot stop itself.

When you sing in your light, your light is a wondrous song. So those beings, those situations, those objects that are no longer in co-resonance with you may not stay. They may not withstand this, and please, please, please accept the fact that if something moves from you, it is because it is time for it to move. If it returns, it is in love and it will be in accordance with your frequency.

But if you have always lived on the second floor of your building and your neighbors on the second floor greet you, and the view from the second-floor window has always been what you have seen, imagine what your life will be like now on the twenty-fifth floor, or the hundredth, or the millionth floor. When you see those people in their own rising, they will come to you; you can be a believer in their worth. But understand that the view out the window will be different and your neighbors may be a bit different, too.

You leave no one behind in truth, because you are all one frequency and you are all knowing this on a base level even if the consciousness of your brothers has not fully caught up yet. They do know. There is a reason that people feel badly when they injure others. It's not just the injury to the fellow. It is the injury that is done to the soul of the one who harms, because in knowing his own unity he knows that he cannot harm another without harming himself. Whether or not his mind is able to fully comprehend that fact, it is still known.

So we will wish you well on this next leg of the journey. Our work will be coming to a close soon in this text and our forgiveness of ourselves for anything we may have omitted will come clear. But we intend to get everything in, so we will ask you to bear with us for a bit longer.

The trajectory that you have chosen will require you now to reexamine every aspect of your life to see if it's feeling in congruence. But we will remind you that this is not an intellectual exercise and no lists are required. As something is not in congruence with you, you will know it and it will make itself known. It will feel uncomfortable, or not right, but in some way you will feel it.

We do not ask you today to leave a relationship or pursue a new career on a whim unless you are compelled to in your own truth and knowing. How your life out-pictures will become clear. How your life chooses to be lived will be in accordance with your Divine

Self. So we ask you to give yourselves permission to align to your own path as if in knowing that it is all for the highest good. That will support you in moving forward.

Our job today was to relinquish the past. Our job today was to teach you that you are not those things that you have been. "Behold, I make all things new," sayeth the Christ. And all things are new in frequency as you accept embodiment in the higher realms.

Now your experiences of the physical plane will need to begin to express themselves. We want to give you a little exercise right now in your new abilities and these will take shape in time. And as you continue to work with this text and with these exercises, you will come back to them and find that you have been refined in your work as you have progressed.

But we would like you to imagine three people, one at a time, that you know. And we would like you to imagine tuning in to them in frequency. First one. And then see what you feel, see what you see, see what you know, see what you hear. And then another, and then another.

As you compare these frequencies and the feelings that they assume in you, you will begin to know the differentials between the energy fields of each one. And as you do this, you will create a knowing, and you will begin to create a vocabulary using your own energy fields as the basis. Paul used to hear a certain word whenever he was feeling someone who has suffered a certain form of abuse, or he would taste alcohol in his mouth or feel dizzy when he was tuning in to someone who may have had a problem with alcohol. You will each find your own ways of expressing this. And as you build your vocabulary, you can become adept at creating a new understanding of what you know and how you access your knowing. This can be done by you.

As you walk down the street, claim, "I am Word through all that I see before me," and be in your majesty and be in your manifestation. Be in your deliverance by knowing what you are. And as you do this, you realign the frequencies of all you pass. You are not doing magic. Your energy field is saying, "Yes, here I am. It can be done. You can incarnate as your Divine Self and be in the majesty of the river and the sea of love. You can, you can, you can."

It is all unspoken, but you are giving permission in your radiance for others to do the same. And as you walk forward, those who require your frequency, or the demonstration of your knowing, will be brought forth in clear ways for you to see and meet and bless. This is all wonderful. This is all knowing. And this is the passage that you have taken.

As you enter the sea, your lives become one with that which you exist in. You accept yourself in Divine Flow.

"I am knowing myself in my own knowing of Divine Flow. I am now in frequency and I am flowing in frequency and that which is before me is made known in perfection. And I am knowing how to deal with all that I experience. I am an expression of the Divine moving in Divine Knowing. Word I am Word through this intention. Word I am Word."

As each individual realizes his potential, each one calls to him the others. And as this happens, the planetary frequency begins to shift upwards. It is what happens. The Christmas tree is lit and the light is bright and it is all quite wonderful to see. However, you all have questions about what this means, and what is happening on this plane now on an experiential level, where you see war, where you see suffering.

This is the last time this planet will be aligned to those vibrations. This is what is being changed. There is a new dawn coming where such things will no longer be aligned to this frequency and consequently there will be ways that these behaviors will be changed. And this will be out-pictured for many in the coming years. But do understand, please, that your requirement to be realigned is part of the solution here. This is no whimsy. This is no exercise in religiosity. Nor is it an exercise in ego. To say that you are the Christ is your truth, and to say that your brother is is the truth. And to say that the one you have perceived to be your enemy is is the truth. All are this thing. Now once you get it, and when we say, "get it," we mean know, capital "K," Know, there is no other reality. So as you assume this knowing, you are the solution. And you are the blessed one that can incur change.

Now understand, please, that change happens at a level of frequency and thought before it is acted upon in knowing in the active way that you would assume when you take on a task or a mission. For some of you, your work is going to be collective work, and we will anticipate that there will be those of you who will sit in groups and radiate frequency for the health and well-being of others. And we would assume that there will be those of you that will hold this planet in a perfect vision of light that will sustain it through the trials to come.

You all have choices, and the choice to be this in your knowing supports the global change and it aligns you to the higher frequency. If you would recall, we gave you an example earlier in this text of a field where people were throwing rocks at one another. And when you stay in low frequency, you are hit or struck by those rocks that are thrown. But as you rise in frequency and you hold a new vision for your lives, your ascension, as it were, carries you above that lower level of impactfulness and it stops becoming your experience. So we are not saying that bodies will not be harmed if somebody tosses a rock at it, but we will say to you that you will not be present for the rock throwing. Your consciousness will have decreed you be elsewhere for that little demonstration of low-level exchange.

As you choose to become one with Source, your experience has to reflect that. That is the law of metaphysics. You cannot be what you are not. And in consciousness, that is where your knowing kicks in and your physical reality has to transform in kind.

Now we thank you for this chapter, which we will call "Manifestation," and we will talk tomorrow about the world and love and the vision to come. We thank you both for your time and for your willingess to be present for this teaching. Thank you and goodbye.

Stop now, please.

EIGHTEEN

THE ANSWER

Day Twenty-Six

We're going to listen to the needs of those who read the book today. And the questions that will be asked and answered will be by us in methodology. "How do I do this? How do I do that? What happens when?"

Now each of you are students of this *Book of Love and Creation*. You have taken the time so far to review what you have read, to consider it, and now we are in the home stretch. We will have one more chapter to teach you in, and then we will have a moment at the end to reflect upon the teachings and guide you forward towards your next steps of embodiment. But today we want to give you answers to those questions that you may have been wondering about.

Your choices up until today have been born out of the information that you had available to you. And now you have more information and consequently your choices have changed. So we want to adhere to the process so far that you are in choice, always, always, always, and if you elect at any moment to grapple with the lower frequency, you can always elect to release it and move to the higher. That is the choice you have now that you know you can.

How long does it take me to become aware of frequency?
You are already aware of frequency; you just don't know it. And the passage to becoming clairsentient is a passage of awareness. If you don't imagine what it feels like to stand in the wind, you will have a new experience of the wind the first time you stand in it. So there's really nothing for you to do except to align to the fact that the ability is inherent in all men and women in frequency. And your choice today is to begin to attune to it and to learn from it as it teaches you.

I've been reading this book so far, and I can't feel it. Is there something wrong with me?
Absolutely not. There is nothing wrong with you. You just have a ways to go still. You are still learning to enhance your own frequency to the level where you are able to feel comfortably and stand in your knowing.

We would like you to try something with us. Several inches above the body, we will say about five inches, there is a small energy shelf where you can feel the frequency that emits from the lower chakras. And the lower chakras, we will say, are the ones that adhere to the primary chakra system, which is in the body. You have seven of them, of the major ones, from the crown center to the root at the base of the spine. And, of course, you have others as well, outside of the physical self, above the crown and adhering to some of the organs in the body. If you would, place your hand now over the heart center about five inches off of the body and feel as if you have a small shelf there. Feel the body, feel the shelf, and see what you feel emerging from the heart. This would be of benefit to you to feel.

Now when you feel frequency with your hand, and we recommend you place your left hand above you, you can feel the movement of the frequency. If you move above and below the heart center, which is between your breasts, you will feel the difference when your hand is no longer moving around and above the heart chakra and is no longer feeling the release of frequency there. This is a way to begin to learn, but please do understand that this work in attunement to frequency takes time and you are on the road already. There is nothing wrong with you.

Now we want to teach you something. Imagine, for a moment, that you are sitting under a tree and that the tree is flowering. As the tree is flowering, you begin to imagine that the chakras in your body, from the lower center to the higher, are all beginning to open and flower as well. And in this new attunement, "I am Word through my being," you set this intention:

"I am now choosing to balance all of my energy centers in Divine Love. I am Word through this intention. Word I am Word."

And as we do this with you, we realign your energy centers to support you in harmony, in balance, and in understanding: "I am Word."

Now the next question we would answer:

Where do I go when I die?
When you die, when the physical body is no longer required for this journey, you return to Source and you return to learn, to learn, to learn, to learn what is required for your next mission. As you ascend, you have many lifetimes and you learn through them each what you are required to know in order to move upwards and to return to the heart of God, as it were. When one returns to com-

pleteness in ascension, one is living in that heart and one is demonstrating this through their knowing.

Now the old paradigm told you that you were not allowed to align to the frequency of Divine Love in body and this was reserved for this passage into the afterlife. We will explain this to you: While it is true that once you release the physical body you stand in, you move dimensionally and then you align to light in a new way, you can still do this in form. We are not bypassing physical reality when we take you through this process; we are incorporating it. We are coming into form, as it were. The difference was that the balloon had to leave the atmosphere, as it were, in order to go someplace, and now the balloon does not. It can still fly. The atmosphere has changed and, in a way we can say, it has come to you.

Now your dealings with the occult, which of course means the unknown, have given you all kinds of ideas of what might be there in an afterlife. And we will move the energies for you in the way that we can in order to support you in your gaining your own knowing of what this might be without your being reasoned with through fear.

You understand already that on a very basic level, everything is frequency, everything is vibrating, and that there are higher and lower frequencies. As you ascend in consciousness, you realign to the new frequency "I am Word," and that becomes your home base. And as you move on to other lives, that is incorporated. This is the last lifetime for some of you before you move into consciousness and have no requirement to come back into form. But most people are still on their journeys and this level of ascension that we are gifting you with does not preclude your learning in new lives.

Every teaching you get in this lifetime is an opportunity for you to move forward to the next one. And as you grow and learn, you create new consciousness that you can then work with.

Our next question has to do with beliefs and God. Now there is no difference, frankly, between the Godheads that you have embellished and worshipped throughout time except the qualities you have invested them with. If you have an angry God that will smite people, then that is the experience of your God and then that becomes your reality.

As you move into consciousness and outside of the duality of good and bad, black and white, you can begin to learn that anything that would be held outside of the Christ, outside of the love of God, cannot be God. So everything must be included. What you would hold outside of the Christ in frequency is what must be reclaimed in love. So judgment of others, judgment of self, all must be unified, healed, and brought into the light. The Christ consciousness that you are inhabited as holds all and does not exclude anyone.

The other Gods, you can see, are there for those who require them. You cannot judge someone else's God. All God is one God with a different name. As we go into unity as a group of people, as an energy frequency, as a life, we come into unity with you and all things come into oneness. It cannot be otherwise.

Now the requirements for your growth really mean that you stay aware, you stay in your knowing, and you stay in congruence with your own Divine Self. We would like you to understand something. The reason you have come into knowing is not to make you better, is not to teach you new things; it's to *be* knowing, to inhabit *as* knowing. And the process of becoming this in form is not always graceful. The resistance can occur, the periods of unknowing or disillusionment that we spoke of can occur, and beyond that your own requirements for needs from the past self, those things you have used to self-identify with, will continue to occur until you no longer require them. So we are asking you, please, to be patient with yourselves in this process of realignment and of ascension.

Is this happening to everyone and how?
It is happening to everyone, not through the reading of this text, but through the realignment of the frequencies on this plane. It is in process now, and much of what you see out-pictured in your lives as change is the result of the new paradigm coming in to hold itself and the requirements of the matrix of fear moving out. This is a change, as it were, in consciousness that will be out-pictured in your physical landscape.

Does this mean the physical landscape will change?
It does. It actually does. As it's required to benefit you. Now we will not talk in this book about catastrophe, nor will we teach you that there is apocalypse. We said earlier in this text that that is something that is actually inborn within man. And that man actually has opportunity now to become one in Divine Love. And as that is moving, all is moving forward. To get caught up in predictive work is actually to adhere to old systems of fear. We will teach you in our way. And to decide today that there is only promise before you, that there is only love, will support you as changes occur.

You don't always see the finished product when an artwork is in progress. And until it is completed, it may look quite messy. But please understand that what is being reformed is being reformed in congruence of the needs of those here. And as those needs evolve, what you will see around you will be changing.

Why don't I know anything? Why do I feel like I don't know?
Well, that's an odd question, but what you are really saying is, "Am I not in my knowing?" The first thing we would recommend to you to anchor your knowing is to find areas of your lives where

you do have certainty— "I know what my name is," "I know what I look like when I see my face in the mirror"—and see those things before you that you can ground with, that you can say, "Yes, I know this thing."

As you anchor your knowing in simple ways, you can allow that knowing, then, to extend into the higher frequencies. It's really very simple. You know already, you *think* you don't know. And as you think you don't know, you create with that. So get in the habit of knowing. And in order to do that, get what you know already and learn how that feels. That will support you in realigning outward in your knowing.

Where is my soul mate? I can't seem to find him or her.
Well, if you haven't found him or her, he or she has not arrived yet. But what you are really speaking of, again, is your own manifestation. And perhaps what you really need to be looking at is what you can hold. Also, you must ask yourself if what you are really seeking is a kind of love and not true love, as we have reasoned with you.

Now there is nothing wrong, as we have said, in being partnered. However, when you decide that there is only one person for you to give your love to, and he or she must resemble a certain kind of thing, you are actually creating an obstruction to all the love that would be available for you. But for those of you who are requiring the need for a partner, we can support you in this: Once you accept yourself as whole, you can then enjoin in another's frequency in partnership. When you are requiring somebody else to create you in wholeness, you are not really ready to be in that experience of conjoined venture. Now we will not teach you in this text how to get a date. But we will teach you that once you are in the frequency of love, you are aligned with love, and what you call forth to you will be in love.

Now our teaching today in these questions, of course, will run the gamut. But we have an agenda here, whether you know it or not. As you begin to ask questions and place them before you in consciousness, we want you to know that you can get the answers you seek yourself. You are going to become your own authority in consciousness and that is where we are taking you today in this chapter.

> "I am now stating this intention: I am now choosing to recognize myself as inherently knowing that information I require in order to move forward in consciousness. I am now accepting myself as wisdom. I am now knowing myself in my wisdom. Word I am Word through this intention. Word I am Word."

Now wisdom, we will say, moves far beyond the intellect and knowing is encompassed within it. But to be wise requires you to be in choice and usually demands discernment. So while you can know that what is on the counter looks like a toaster, in your wisdom you will know how to operate it. You will know what to with the knowledge that you seek *in your wisdom.*

Now when we teach you, we work with you on several levels. We work with you in the knowing that you have, and we recognize the knowing that you will come to. We are ahead of the game, as it were. When you have a toddler that is learning to speak new words, the parent recognizes already that there will be sentences coming soon. So we see you each at the stage of development that you are at and understand where you will be through the practice of this work.

So that is the next question:

*Where will I be in the practice of this work? Where will it
take me?*

Where this work will take you is where you are required to go, for
you, for your own soul's choices to be recognized and met *by you* in
congruence with your own Divine Knowing. Not everybody ends
up in the same place. Everybody goes where their soul's journeys
require them. How do I know my soul's journey? Because I am on
it, I am attuned to its frequency, and I am in my knowing. Do you
understand this?

The groups that are working together on this plane to shift
energy have made arrangements to work this way. Individuals who
are on their path, that are on their own adventures, are carried to
where they are needed to be in order to do this work in the way that
is most appropriate for them. You each have gifts here and expect
that they will be used. Nothing you have been gifted with will be
wasted or ignored. Your gifts come to you as you require them.

So if you find out in a year that you need to move someplace
because that is where your heart is taking you, you will trust that
your work will be made known to you. So you are the embodiment
of this frequency and how you work with it will be in your
knowing.

"I am not fearful of the choices before me. I am trusting completely that I am in my worth and that I am standing in my
knowing as a Divine Being. I am Word through this knowing. I
am Word through this intention. Word I am Word."

What will happen to me when I change?

Well, that is a good question. You have been changing your whole
life. You should be used to it by now. But what we have taught you

here is about frequency, is about love, is about creation and manifestation. So who you become is the person who can work with
these new ideals and can learn to work with the choices that they
call to them. You are who you are on a deeper level and you are
expressing yourself in a new way through the recognition of the
abilities that you have. Your opportunities will be gifted to you as
you move forward.

Now the requirements of the time for everyone is to be in amplification of frequency, which means that you must become what you
say you are in vibration. As you work with this consciously, you call
to you the others who would be resonating in similar frequency.
These are your fellow journeyers, and we recognize each other
through our light.

So we say to you each, it will be to your benefit through these
times of change to join energies with those who are like-minded,
those who are on a conscious path, those who are realigning themselves to the new paradigm of consciousness that is here now, operating well and emerging gradually as the new name "I am Word," "I
am an aspect of the Creator," in whatever language you wish to
give it.

Those who are on the journey and aware of it have much to
teach each other. Sharing the information of your own development spiritually can only enhance your own knowing. As you get
the affirmation from your brother that he or she is having similar
knowing, similar experience, similar concerns about the obstacles
on the path, you can begin to work together to support one another
in transference and in choice. We would recognize you by your
light. You will recognize your brothers through the same means.

"I am now choosing to recognize the fellow travelers who I will
be working with. And I will be brought to them in divine order

as is required for my highest good. I am Word through this
intention. Word I am Word."

*What is next for me? What is my next job, or my next activity,
the next thing I am meant to do?*
Well, you're always told this and you are always choosing this. You
have been gifted with this text as a way of accessing that information. Do not assume that when this text is over, the teaching is finished. So much of this teaching has been about imprinting you on a
causal level with the systems that would align you to your own
soul's path, to your own knowing of what you need to do to realize
yourself in completeness. As you do this, your choices are clear and
you do not need to ask because you know. "I am Word through my
knowing. Word I am Word."

Our responsibility to you as teachers of this text is to remember
you, to remember who you are, why you are here and what your
jobs are as you move forward to claim them. Yes, indeed, there is
work to be done. There is great work to be done.

The planet, right now, is in its shift. As you recognize this, as
you choose to redefine your lives to work in congruence with your
Divine Selves, you assist the planet in its evolution in love. We will
do some work now with the planet, and we will do this with you.

"I am now choosing to make this decision: I am worthy of my
work here on this planet. And as I know this, I prosper in my
work. As I prosper in my work, I make my work available to
others. As I make my work available to others, the energy of my
work in frequency is magnified, and I make the choice to illumine myself in visibility to be of service to those who would be
called to me. As I choose this service, in whatever form it takes,

I become a light for others. And as I become a light for others, I move in to take my rightful place in this new movement of Christ consciousness. I have inhabited myself in my own knowing and I hold the planet in the frequency of love. I am Word through all that I see before me. Word I am Word."

In your mind's eye, imagine right now that you are holding the planet in love. Your own choice is to serve in this regard, and you are aligning your own frequency to support those on the planet who are waking up to their own divine potential.

"I am now accepting myself as one who serves the light. I am Word through this intention. Word I am Word."

What will become of this planet?
This planet has its choices to make. However, we will explain this to you. Do not confuse it with "the earth." When we speak of the planet, we speak of planetary consciousness and all that lives here. The earth, as an organism, will stand in its health because it will not allow itself to be destroyed. The earth will be here, we promise you that.

How you choose to inhabit this earth, how you choose to participate in its healing, is your conscious action. As you become active in this awareness, you assist others in doing the same. But we promise you this: The planet will be here. Your choice, as its inhabitants, is to remember that you are in co-creation with it, but you are not the ruler. Your belief that you rule the elements in this regard without regard to the requirements of the organism you are on and living in is the problem. Once you become aware and working in congruence with your Divine Self, you automatically go into congruence with the planetary needs, and the earth then responds accordingly. You are not in dominion without agreement, and the earth is a living thing, and she will require her own needs be met as well.

The vibration on the planet and the vibration of the earth is in ascension. It is lifting in frequency. Those things that vibrate at lower frequency will not be held here much longer. That is what is happening. You will experience this as a new world that will emerge in its own time. You are the first generation that will be experiencing this. There will be others to follow, and they will be illumined.

The teachings that we are giving you here, in this text, believe it or not, will be taken for granted soon. Telepathy is a natural evolution of the species. When we teach you to tune in and listen to your brother, we are teaching you telepathy, and it will come to you in time and probably quicker than you think. But those who are being born now are not born in the level of resistance that others have been. They are coming into their own awareness very rapidly and they are here to herald a new dawn.

What is the new dawn?
The new dawn is the acclimation to the higher frequencies. And what is transpired through this process is a recreation of ecosystems, of political paradigms, of structures of governances and structures of behavior. All of these things that we just mentioned are things that are impacted and have been created through consciousness. So they can be recreated through the new consciousness. And that is what is happening here. As the new replaces the old, the old has a little angry fit on its way out, and there can be chaos at times as the old is replaced by the new.

If you can imagine for a moment that you are replacing all the furniture in your house, and the new is coming in as the old is going out, you can imagine quite a mess, can't you? In some ways, that is what is happening here.

What about war? What about these things? What do I do about them?

In fact, you are doing what you need to do about them right now. You are rising in consciousness. Now if you choose to, we would recommend that you hold these places where there is war in Divine Love.

> "I am now choosing to see the inherent peace in this place on the earth. I am Word through all that I see before me."

However you wish to claim it, that is an active thing that you can do. However, your choice to rise, as we have said many times, has a much larger impact on the matrix of this planet than you can assume. And as you lift, you give permission to others to do the same. And that will change everything. "I am Word through all that I see before me" brings the frequency of the Word to that which you see before you. If you haven't tried it yet, please do. This is the work of the book.

What happens when I do this? When I call forth the Word in all that I see before me?

You bring congruency. You realign the frequency. You bring the energy of Divine Light, the Word in action, to all that you see before you. You recognize that place, that thing, that which is in your vision with the eyes of the Christ, and you let the frequency do its work. When you state this, you may have a physical response; you may feel as if your body is shifting or the frequency around you is lifting. In fact, that is what is happening. You are lifting.

Now we want to offer you something. You are each reading this book and you are each in passage with it. As you are in passage, you are acclimating your own frequency. As you acclimate your own frequency, you begin to realign it, and you can be of support to others.

When we ask you this, we want you think for a moment before saying "Yes." But if you wish to, you can allow your energy frequency to be in service to the other readers of this text who may require support. And all you have to do is say, "Yes."

"Yes, I am willing to allow myself to support others in their conscious awareness and in the lifting of their frequency."

And if you say, "Yes," then others can then call on you.

"I am now calling on the energies of those who are working with this text in light to support me on your journey. Word I am Word,"

will then call to you more light when you require it.

Now we work with each of you. You are being talked to groupwise and individually through the reading of this text, and through this process of learning you begin to know things. However, you are being held through this process and we want to remind you of this again. When you require our frequency, you must request it. We do not come and support you without knowing that we are welcome. We are serving you in this regard. We will stand and watch, we will lend a hand, we will support you in shifting your frequency as required, but we will not be invasive, nor will we intrude. But if you wish to be supported in this work, you simply have to ask and we will support you.

"I am Word through all that I see before me."

We will continue with this chapter tomorrow. We thank you for your attentions. I am Word.

Stop now, please.

Day Twenty-Seven

We'll help you through this time, as you require it. The transitioning from one state of consciousness to another requires that you transition yourself in your experience, and sometimes the changes are not graceful or require you to forgo the things that you normally would have gone to as a way to anchor the self in experience. What we mean by this is that when you have a transition from one consciousness to the next, you have to remember that what you have used to support you or to self-identify may not be there in the new frequency. And the uncomfortability that ensues is really, simply, about the unsteadiness of the new transition.

So we want to explain to you that the merit of working with this text is great achievement in transitioning. However, the issue that you will contend with as the result of achieving this is relinquishing the old.

Now to an extent, the way that we have structured this text has been to support you, initially, in re-identifying those areas of your life where you were out of momentum with your own frequency because you were in agreement with controlling forces, or structures, or beliefs. And as you understood them, you were asked to begin to dismantle them and then realign to love, step into the river and begin to flow, and understand those things that would realign you in congruence to that frequency.

We have taught you through illustration and through decree wherein you change your own frequency by calling forth the frequency of the Word into your own energy field with the decision to make something into matter, into the material, through your consciousness. And by this we mean change your thinking, change your frequency, so that your experience may change.

In this final section we have begun to regroup and to create a system of achievement in manifestation. And the work of this today is to re-decide your merit, your choice, and your willingness to stay the course. And the course is as follows:

"Am I now willing to allow myself to become who and what I am in responsibility to my own name, I am Word, I am Word, I am Word? If I am choosing to say yes to this, I call into myself the promise of the Christ, of the Creative Self to align me to this choice in all aspects of my life. And that makes me in knowing the one who claims himself, herself, in 'I am knowing I am Word.' As I know this, I make myself known and my frequency inhabits me in Divine Knowing in its creations. I am now chosen. I am now choosing. And I accept the responsibility of my choice."

As this is said, you call to you the choice and the ramifications of the choice that will then change your life, as it's required to bring forth this in full creation. It does not happen without your okay and it does not happen without your claiming your responsibility for it. We do not wave a magic wand. However, we do call to you those things on an experiential level that you will need to manifest this, and these are the gifts of the spirit, as you understand them.

We do not align you to your own telepathic ability for the invasion of others' minds. Nor do we gift you with clairsentience to understand someone's weakness for exploitation. We give you the gifts in manifestation in order to know yourself in dominion. In dominion as the Christed One come home into his own knowing, into her own knowing. Everyone is this, we say this again. You are not peculiar or special. You are just getting there a little quicker through your own choice.

"I am accepting the choice and the responsibility of the choice to call myself into manifestation as my own Divine Self. I say yes! I say yes! I say yes! Word I am Word through this intention. Word I am Word."

The causal body in your auric field will connect up and align in perfection to that which it is come from! And this acknowledgment in union will call to it the powers of emissaries of the Christ to bring this to be! This is happening now. This is the joy and this is the miracle that you are promised. This happens very quickly. The manifestation of it takes time, but the action of it is now in process. The linkup is here. It is being done. It is in choice. It is in your acceptance. And now it is so! It is so! It is so!

We gift you with the presence of the love of the Creator. We gift you with the knowledge of yourself as one with All That Is. And we honor you in your endeavors as a seeker who has come into the knowing that he requires to complete his journey here.

"I am knowing *you* as the Word," sayeth the Christ. "I am knowing you in your beauty, in your wonder, and in your truth." And our joy for you that this miracle is occurring is great. We have waited. We have waited. We have waited. And we are claiming it now:

"I see before me the New Jerusalem. I see before me the Kingdom of God anchored on this plane. I see before me the beauty
of all that is created. And I accept it in my dominion and in
my love."

We are choosing you, we are accepting you, and we live with you
now in frequency. As the choice was made, the realignment was
done. And this was done in the higher frequencies. The benefits of
this will be grand and they will be experienced. They will be understood and they will be changing you.

You have listened to us speak now for four weeks of dictation.
You have taken the words down on the page. You have read them.
You have discussed them. You have thought about them. But you
have not known what they mean.

What does this mean? will be the question now.

What this means is, is that you have changed your lives. And
you have accepted yourselves as what and who you were intended
to be. And in this doing, the mountain has been climbed. And the
mountain before you in consciousness was a big one. Now it is not
a passive experience, you see. You have not taken an easy path. And
for those of you who might be thinking, "Oh, how lovely, I read a
book and I am ascended in consciousness," will have a bit of a rude
awakening. Because you have to do the work. It is claimed in frequency. But many are called and everyone is chosen, eventually.
But you must engage in the work. You must do the work. You must
decide yourselves the ability and the calling of the requirements
that will now come to you.

Paul is wondering, *"Many are called but few are chosen"* is the
verse he knows. Is that no longer so?

Everyone is called, everyone is chosen to their own alignment,
to their own Divine Selves. However, the achievement of this is not

coerced, nor is it claimed for you outside of alignment and agreement with your own soul's worth and choice. So you see, the door is open to all, the hand reaches to beckon, the party is inside, but there are many still who, although they have an awareness of this, decide for this time, at least, to stay in the dark, to let the light be reflected by others. And this is because they are frightened of what would happen if they aligned themselves to the light.

This does not require a belief in God, you know. The light has no denomination, and we could say light as easily as God. But the personification of consciousness, which we will claim as God in choice, gifts you with a different understanding. You cannot appeal to the light in the same way as you can to something that you have ascribed consciousness to. Now light is consciousness. That is what it is. However, those of you who would still prefer to wait outside will come in eventually, in your own language, on your own terms, when you realize finally that the options do not support you in staying outside of the light.

Why would someone elect to stay out of the light? That is the next question.

Fear, of course, as we have stated. But denial of the self, the belief that the self cannot be loved, the belief that the self is damned for whatever crazy reason, the belief that one will be lied to, betrayed if one offers himself, herself to the love of God, who relinquishes those beliefs on the altar, as it were, who fear then that they will have nothing. Many, many, many, come to the altar in faith and turn away out of shame.

We want to heal you of shame now, and we want to do this very quickly. Shame, as we have stated, is like rolling in a mud puddle. And those of who you incur shame have a tendency to wish to throw yourself back into that puddle again and again in this way because it reminds you of something that you believed once that was not so in love.

Now we do this with you:

"I am now choosing to reclaim myself on all levels from the patterns, from the beliefs of shame that I may be holding anywhere in my energy field, in my memory, in my body, in my knowing. I am now choosing to relinquish the fear of dismantling this pattern of shame of myself, my body, my actions, and my being. I am now accepting myself as liberated from shame and I attune now to the frequency of Divine Love who will clean me of it."

What will happen in this clearing is as follows:

We ask you each now to receive through the top of the head a golden light, a golden light of brilliance and warmth. And we ask you to allow this light to come through the being that you are, through you, around you, above and below. We allow this light to come to you and accept you in your perfection. And as this happens, any belief, any requirement, any acceptance of the pattern of shame that needs to be transmuted will be cleared for you.

"I am Word through this intention to be cleaned of shame and restored once and for all to my knowing of my own worth in love. Word I am Word through this intention. Word I am Word."

Let it come, let it come, let it come.

As this is transformed for you, your choices change again. Anything that would stop you now from offering yourself to your Creator, to your Divine Self, to that aspect of yourself that you can admit and accept as the Christed One, the Creative Divine Self, anything and everything that you can say yes to in light, we would ask you then if you can offer yourselves and accept it as the gift that it is.

When one is surrendered in the light, one accepts the light and the light works with you. This is choice. And it is the benefit. So yes, everyone is called, everyone is chosen, and in time, all will stand before the altar. And please understand this, the altar is consciousness, it is that, that surrender to the light in consciousness. And as all stand, all are healed. You have come a little faster. If you were attracted to this text, if you purchased it and have made it this far, you have become attuned in Word. And this is the frequency that will lift you and align you as is required to support you in this journey.

Our teaching for today and in the prior chapter is called "The Answer." And we will talk about questions again for a few moments. Your responsibility is to change yourself. How is this done? Every day, as you are required to do your work—"I am Word through that that I see before me," "I am Word through my knowing," "I am Word through my body"—you are in responsibility.

Every day you accept yourself as an aspect of the Divine, you are in your responsibility. When you are in your knowing, you are impelled to act and you choose those actions wisely. As you transition from one state of consciousness to the next, you accept the fact that there is turbulence at times as you move upwards. You accept the fact that what you expected to be able to hold to you may not be there, and that something else will come in its place that is appropriate to your new state of being. And as you choose this, your ascension comes to you.

Do I keep my body when I ascend?
Well, this is an interesting question. And we will say to you that there are those that have ascended in body, which essentially means that the body itself has come into a new alignment, that it can harbor frequency at such a level that it can come and go. They are no longer tethered in form, but the body can remain a vehicle for

transit, as it is required. There have been some and there will be more. But your body right now is the vehicle through which you are experiencing your ascension on this plane. So please understand right now that it's not about being lifted in body to heaven, although that is exactly what is happening.

There has been a belief incurred in something called a rapture, where people are lifted in their bodies from their offices and from their cars and all kinds of mayhem ensues. This is a complete mis-interpretation of ascension. What is truly ascending is you, in your frequency and consciousness, and as this happens the body has to be receptive for this as well. The apt metaphor here, though, is that there are some who will ascend in frequency and that there are others who will not. And in Christianity, the statement has been made that this has to do with an allegiance to the Christ through Jesus. Now that is one way that a man or a woman can enter the Kingdom. But the Christ, of course, has no denomination. The Christ, in truth, is the indwelling God within each man and woman that is awakened in Divine Knowing through this action, "I am Word."

There are other ways, of course, to awaken the Christ. It is being awakened in languages across the globe. But the ascension we speak of in this light is a transition of consciousness. The new world that will be coming is a recreation of the existing world in higher frequency. It is as if the veil that has been permeated and is dissolv-ing will be swept away and you will be aligning to the frequency that will become available. Now this incurs a dismantling of exist-ing structure. And the world to come, as we have stated, cannot hold the lower frequency of domain through control of others and through the matrix of fear. So the realignment of this life, this space, this planet through these changes will require a new response from all who live on it in order to change these things.

Now Paul wonders, when we talk about these things, are we

talking about cataclysm? Cataclysm, frankly, is a very grand word to call change. And some things that are cataclysmic are very quiet and happen within the being with profound change. So you don't have to see everything out-pictured in cataclysm to go through your own creations or recreations as you change your consciousness. Is cataclysm required? No. May it happen? In some ways, as required, to support the shift. But this is not necessarily something that you need to see out-pictured in your physical reality. It is an opportunity, here, presented to support you in transforming in love. And we gift you with this option now:

> "I am now choosing to align myself to the new grid of Divine
> Light that is present now on this plane. And I support the action
> of the light in achieving its mission to bring light to all things
> in love and in peace. I am Word through this intention. Word I
> am Word."

This is the call to you, then, to speak your truth and to support this transition in love. It does not have to be hard. It may not be easy. And sometimes change is not easy at all. But it is happening. It is in process. And the escalation will be continuing, rapidly, in the years to come.

Understand please that this is the threshold of the New Age. You can say "Aquarius," you can say the "years of peace," and you can say whatever you like. But you stand on this threshold now with anticipation of what can come. And we speak to you in love when we say what can come, finally, you will be party to in your creations. Mankind has created much in fear. And that which is created must be un-created, must be transformed in some way for the energy to be released and realigned to love.

We understand, sometimes, that the only way people learn is through seeing the evidence of their own ignorance or the actions that have been made in fear. And we cannot stop what one chooses through their free will. But we will say this: The consciousness of this plane is light, is becoming light. And the reaction from the negativity, from those aspects that would seek to maintain their control, will become pronounced as they are released.

We do not need to speak of biblical prophecy. Much of that was done in symbol and the symbols were sealed. Their true meaning will be made known, but what has been interpreted is truthful and is wrong-minded. So we cannot go there today, although we expect to address it eventually in a text we will write someday. But today we want you to say that this is the beginning of a new dawn. This is the beginning of a new life. This is the beginning of change on a deep and profound level that will continue as this time moves forward.

"I am Word through this knowing of myself as on the brink of great change and that the change is wondrous to behold. Word I am Word through this intention. Word I am Word."

Why was I born?
That is the next question. You were born to come into yourselves as knowing yourselves as loved, and as conscious active participants in your creation. You were born to stand in your knowing, to accept yourself as loved, and to see your fellows in their own perfection. You were born to create wonder, to live a life of splendor and of joy. You were created to come into your own knowing in the Son-ship of your own divinity and to claim it in full experience. You were born to say, "I am Word," in whatever language you choose, in whatever vocabulary is truthful to you. You were chosen, you are choosing, all are. "I am Word through all that I see before me."

We are choosing you today to call to yourselves those things you need to move forward on this journey.

Imagine yourself, right now, standing in a room. It is a gateway room. It is a room that leads you to a new room that has never been seen before, that has never been experienced. And what is beyond the threshold is only in your imagination. Around you on the floor is the baggage that you have kept for the journey. And you change your mind and realize that all you need before you will be provided, so you can leave the baggage behind. You can leave it all there in the room. And you stand now in the threshold of this new door. And the door opens and you walk forward and you are carried in wonder to the sea of love.

I am Word. I am Word. I am Word.

We will speak to you again tomorrow. Thank you both and stop.

NINETEEN

DOMINION IN LOVE

Day Twenty-Eight

Today is the day of celebration. The passage has been completed and the teaching is being done in the way to bring this work into flowering. You have all taken a chance in your choices, and you have chosen this. It has chosen you as well and the force of the work that you have contended with, that you have brought through you, that you have made so in manifestation, is what we celebrate. You are the ones who will go forward in light and you will call to you that which you need to renew yourselves as you go forward. Love comes to you and you become love.

Now you ask yourselves, "What does it mean to be this thing that I am now? I claim, 'I am Word.' Am I different in truth? Have I just created a construct?" Well, you have created a construct, but the construct is in your energy field. If you can imagine that you are now a vehicle of love and that is what you were intended to be and you have simply chosen it, called it into being in decree, in knowing, and saying, "I am Word," then you can accept that this is a truth.

Your choices, throughout the lives you have lived, have been to bring you into recognition and reunification with your Divine Selves. That is a fact. And this text has been a benefit to that occurrence and will continue to be as you continue to work with it. The belief that you have that you are allowed this is, in fact, what makes this be what it is: a transitioning from a lower consciousness to a higher frequency. And as you inhabit yourself in the higher frequency, everything around you is made new: "Behold I make all things new."

Now the attitude that you must require of yourselves is one of grace and welcoming. This is the new intention:

> "I am now choosing to see the world around me with grace and
> with thanks. I am now blessing all that I see and becoming what
> I am in tandem with the landscape I now inhabit. I am in con-
> gruence with my own Divine Knowing and therefore I am acti-
> vating myself in perfect ways to be and to do what I am required
> to do."

Now today we need to give you a final teaching. And this teaching has to do with love and the creation of love. We have called this text *The Book of Love and Creation* for a reason. And the creation of love is what we wish to teach you today.

To stand in your knowing—"I am Word, I am an aspect of the divine"—and then to align yourselves to the sea of love—"I am now in the flow of love, I am in the river, I am in the sea, I am surrounded by, I am included in, I am one with love, love, love"—that is the thing you have chosen.

To create from this place is to create more love. We have told you again and again: Fear creates fear, but love creates love. And this must now be your intention:

"I am now choosing to create love in all that I do and my thoughts will be manifestations of love. I am Word through this intention. Word I am Word."

Now today we bring you into your own knowing of yourself as the Christed One, as the Creative Self, as the Divine Self in your manifestations. You are creating in love because this is who you have become. And this decision to be this has been made of your own free will and in love. So today we call to you all that you require to be this in fullness.

"I am now choosing to be aligned to Divine Love in completion. I am now accepting myself in requirement of Divine Love and as I do this, I accept it and I expect it. I am choosing it and as I choose love I bring to me love. I am Word through this intention. Word I am Word."

Your designs of your lives must now alter to improve, to require the love that you have demanded. Now demanding love, we will say, is a more than acceptable thing to demand. It is the truth of what you are. It is what everything is in frequency when you move forward with it, so you can claim it in your dominion. To say, "I don't deserve it" or "Love will come when loves wants to come," is to lie to the self. Love is ever present. Love is a frequency. And you are calling to you to be in reception, to be in congruence, to be in availability to the sea of love.

Everything in your life will align to this through your choices to remain in frequency. Now you don't have to worry about this: "What if something terrible happens?" "What if I fear this?" "What if that happens and I can't maintain my frequency?" The frequency is always ever present. You are the one who moves up and down and in and out. And this book has given you the tools to return there, as you require it. You cannot use yourself as an example of what not to do. You simply have to do it. So if something occurs that you cannot handle in frequency and you step to the riverbank and you catch your breath, at least you know now that you're there and what is required to get you back in the water, as it were.

This becomes very simple in time. It's really a question of monitoring the self and maintaining the self. As the self continues onward, you will encounter more and more things that have impeded you. And as you encounter them, you now have the availability to them to transform them, and to realign yourselves to continue on the journey you have started. "Am I in the ocean?" "Am I in the sea?" Yes, yes, yes, you are. We left you there at the end of the last chapter and we left you there for a reason.

You are now in the sea of love. You never were not in it. You only believed you could not be. But those things that tether you to the shore have been cleared to the extent that you can accept yourself as becoming one with the self in this frequency of love. It is not magical. It is the decision that you made.

As you decide to change something and you do this from a truthful place, you call to you the Universal Power to support you in the change. Every change happens that way: "It's time to move to a new home," and suddenly everything comes to you to make that choice a reality. Anything that you can imagine that you have decided, and we underline *decided*, has called to it the response to allow this change to become so. You don't always grab it. You don't always change. Sometimes you back away. But if the decision is made, the choice has been made. And when the choice has been made, you change to align to the choice and your circumstances, your reality, as it were, has changed as well to support it. So there is nothing very mystical about this. We say to you that the higher vibration has always been here. It's always been accepted that you could be in love, we are simply telling you that is where you are meant to be. So choose it. And if you stop choosing it, choose it again and it will come back once you decide that the obstacle to love, whatever it may be, can and will be contended with.

When you decide that an obstacle can be cleared, it can be cleared. And nothing, nothing, nothing is larger than Source, your Creator, and the ability of your Creator to support you in change is quite amazing. But you need to call on it and you need to claim it as so. As you claim it, you accept the truth of the claim and then the work begins in earnest. You are in the sea of love.

Higher frequency is always present. You always have the choice of realigning the self. This has not been a contest. This has not been anything other than a manifestation of the requests of those who have called us in the higher frequencies to say, "Help, we need instruction, we need a system, we have been lost, and we understand that we have made it much harder for ourselves than it's required to be. So what can we do?"

You can do this:

"I am Word through my body. Word I am Word.

I am Word through my frequency. Word I am Word.

I am Word through my knowing of myself as Word.

I am Word through those I see before me. Word I am Word.

I am Word through all that I see before me. Word I am Word.

I am Word through my love. Word I am Word."

And you continue the list as long as you like to. Your own divinity is what is present and what is working with you. That aspect of the self that is created in light that seeks to inhabit you in consciousness is what you are working with, and we are here as well, supporting this passage. We do the work, we are doing it now, and we only ask that you do the same.

The responsibility to the reader now is to keep it up, to choose it each morning upon awakening. Your frequency, of course, is your own choice and you can choose to stay low. But understand, everyone, there really is no need. You have a habit of hanging out in lower frequency. You will be invited back there, we promise you, but you do not have to stick around.

When you lift, you give permission for others to do the same. In time we would like to write a textbook, a simple way of instructive teaching that would be only open to those who require a simple level of exercise: "On day one you do this, on day two you do that." But this book is the book that was required to take you to a level of your own acceptance of your own divinity, and that was what was required of us. The responsibility now is yours to do with this what you will.

The changes that you will expect will be changes in frequency. If you don't do the exercises, you will not know if they work. If you don't get a partner, you will not get the feedback you require. If you don't take the walks and see those before you in their love and beauty, you will not be able to praise your brother, and then they will not reflect to you the love that you are gifting them with. So we ask you, please, choose it and then accept it, and then do the work and we will support you as we can.

The love that you have in your heart today is nourishing you. Everyone has it. And the nourishment of the heart in the frequency of love is a joy. Can you imagine now existing in this frequency all the time? It is possible, but it is action that is required, that happens when you choose it. You are not passive anymore to your experience here. You have been taught that the key to knowing is you and your choice to know and to accept it as the promise of the Christed Self come into form. As you have chosen these things, you have been given opportunities to experience them, to have your own experience of them, and that has been required by us to make this teaching truthful. We do not wave a wand and send you home with false information.

Everything we have taught you here we have taught through practice. This is what we do, this is how we live, this is how we have ascended in our consciousness. The practice of operating as the divine in recognition of the divinity of all things is the work here. It is the code that will lift you up the ladder of the light. It is the truth, so you may as well work with it.

There will be naysayers, of course. There will be those that say it is a sacrilege to say that man can ascend to the level of consciousness where he or she can self-identify at a level of Christ Self, Creative Self, Divine Self. We would say that those people who would say this have a real intention of keeping you from your own knowing for whatever reasons they have. For someone to tell another that they are not divine is to deny the God within them, and to do that we would say is a sacrilege. All we are teaching you is that this can be realized, this can be done, this can be chosen, and, as you commit to it, you have called forth the teaching that was required to help you to get there.

This is not the only book that will be written by Light Beings to support you. There will be books written in many cultures under many names. Some will be inspired, some will be channeled, some will be the product of a lifetime of work put into a text for the benefit of the new mind. But we will all be teaching you the same thing:

The planetary shift that is being incurred, that is under way, offers a grand opportunity for humanity to transform itself, but this is a choice at this juncture, to do this. The opportunity is here. We are all throwing you all the rope to grab onto to allow you to lift in consciousness. And we do this not just for the benefit of the individual but for the entire human race, who we hold in love.

Now we offer you this. As you work on this text, you must expect that there will be times that you wish to throw it out the window and walk away for good. This is actually good. This is actually good for you. And what it really means is you are practicing your own knowing, and your knowing finally must be the testament to how well this work has supported you. But when you want to walk around the block, or you want to say, "This can't be so," that simply means that you are being challenged to expand your consciousness and the resistance you are experiencing is a time of growth. When one is in growth, one sometimes feels growing pains. And when one is reaching upwards and doesn't know what is there, sometimes one gets confused. So we ask you quite simply to be in your process as it comes and to accept it.

We would recommend that you work on this book with a fellow at times to touch base, to speak of your experience, because this will realign you to the intention to learn, and the learning of this text, frankly, is not a solitary act. It's about your engagement not only with the self, but with the entire world around you. So, yes, get the support, as you require it. You are being taught by us, but you will be teaching others in time through your own knowing. Your own knowing, finally, is paramount. You can go kicking and screaming to the altar in consciousness, but it's not required. You are coming of your own free will to your knowing of yourself as a Divine Being in manifestation.

We told you yesterday that this is not about floating up into the clouds. That is a falsity. What is truly happening is, heaven is here. You are in it as you align to the higher consciousness. There are other realms, other dimensional experiences beyond the one that is coming to you, but the re-acclimation to Higher Source in embodiment is the process this planet is engaging in. The frequency is lifting, all are lifting, and the matrix of fear and control is being dispersed and will have its little fight as it can to maintain itself as an organism. However, we see the image of a plastic belt that is breaking because it cannot sustain the growth around it, and that is really what is happening here. The matrix of fear is being brought about in creation to complete itself and to fall apart, as it were, because it cannot sustain the frequency that is now present and operative.

We are gifted by you. We are gifted by your endeavors and we are gifted by your willingness to learn. As you choose new things to learn, you call them to you to experience, and on that level this text has been, and will continue to be, an experiential one. It is nothing to tell someone that you are experiencing energy in a new way if, in fact, you are not. But you will, we say—through choice, through alignment, and through the ability to claim this as your own birthright.

Everybody here has the ability, inherently, to see, to hear, to feel frequency. That is part of what you do anyway every day. The difference here, in this text, is we wish you to have the experience of it so you can begin to accept yourself as an energy being. And as that happens, the constructs of control cannot control you in the same way because you begin to see them for what they are. They are illusion; they are there to do their work. But your work, we say, in manifestation of the self will be grand and will not align to it.

We would like to teach you today about listening in a different way. And we want you to listen to yourselves as the one in authority. As the one who can say, "I am in my responsibility when I do my work." And that, quite simply, means you have to become very aware of when you are not, when you are acting unconsciously, or when you are in your fear. Most of you operate this way all the time and then don't notice it. But the responsibility of being in dominion—and that is the title of this chapter, "Dominion in Love"—is to be aware of all these things. When you are feeding yourself food that you needn't, when you are taking a train when you should be walking, when you are yelling when you should be laughing, when you are resting when you should be at play, become aware of yourselves.

Now Paul is questioning the word "should," which he has alarms with. And we will explain what we mean. We have said to you before you always have a high choice and a low choice. The high choice lifts your frequency; the low choice diminishes it. So we say "should" to imply, "We encourage you to take the high choice." When you are in your fear and you are working on it to lift you out of it, you are in the high choice. When you are "freaking out," as they say, you are probably feeding the energy of fear and creating from that place. And when you create in fear, you have to dismantle those creations. So we are giving you a little timesaver by saying, "Choose the higher." Your willingness to be on your path is supported by the universe. That is the choice you make when you go forward in your knowing. The Universe always greets the application for growth. That is the nature of life. And stagnation and fear is not the choice that is supported, so we would bring you to this knowing:

> "I am now choosing to know that all the paths that I am now taking will lead me to higher frequency and that I am being supported in this choice by my Creator, by the Universe, and by my own Divine Knowing. I am Word through this intention. Word I am Word."

We would like to sing your praises for a little bit because who you are is a Divine Being and we see you as such. Even when you are a toddler in consciousness, the consciousness is still brilliant, and you are returning in your own way to your own self, as you were first born. The Divine Being that you are that you forgot you were is being reclaimed, and this is cause for celebration.

We will teach you more tomorrow. And today we will say to you: We stand beside you in your choices to flower.

We stand beside you in your awareness of yourselves as Divine
   Beings.
We stand beside you in love and in cherishing the beauty of you.
And your choices will now be reflected in love.
I am Word through this intention for the reader. Word I am
   Word.

Thank you and stop.

Day Twenty-Nine

The choices that come in your demonstrations through your knowing will be catapulting you in ways you cannot envision yet. Your
jobs will be to adhere to your own requirements for your lives in
congruence with this knowing. Now knowing, again, is not about
your intellect, and that will be the trap for many of you to excise
yourselves from. This is about your knowing at a much deeper level.

When we say "catapult," the image is of you flying through the
air to your new destinies. You will be moving quickly. Now how
this all happens is done in consult with your soul. We have to
explain this to you. Once your knowing is inhabiting you, you
enter into discourse with yourself on a much deeper level than perhaps you have to date. And what this brings you is information
about what you require to adhere to your soul's knowing and path.
And this may require a new way of supporting yourself or living
your life that will bring you to your self in higher frequency.
You cannot hold onto the old when it no longer reflects what
you have become.

Now this is where trust comes into play, and the true knowing
of the self will never lead you wrong. It cannot happen. You cannot

be deceived by your knowing at this level. So the choices that you will then make will be clear for you to do so as you manifest them.

Now when you want something—and you need to know this—you must still put it to the test because your old habits stick with you and must not be coming to run the show when they would like to. It can be very simple—"I want what I always had because I cannot imagine differently"—or it can be much more complex. When you decide that you have decided something for your highest good because it serves you in another way to promote the ego self, then you have to watch it.

So now we have to ask you, are you willing to come into your knowing in this way without fear of what can come to you? This is important. It requires you to stake a claim to your own divinity that will require you to leave the comfort of your known self. It will require you to discard the emblems, the amulets, the tokens of a life that are no longer true to who you are. They will lead you to the past. If you go to the future, you will be going naked. You will not be carrying with you those ways of self-identification that you have relied on. When you think of this, and you think of being in the ocean, you think of yourselves as named, and by naked we mean in spirit, and without things that would be tethering you and bringing you down. You want to remain light and you want to be led by the current of love in your knowing.

So when you believe that you can still sit behind your desk and do work that you know is no longer in congruence to who you have evolved into, you must align to the possibility that you will be taken elsewhere where your abilities can shine. And you can be participatory in this. It's not about quitting anything, necessarily; it's about letting yourself be moved by the current, if you wish, and the knowing that you have incurred.

When you hold onto the desk and the current is trying to move you away, you have a really silly picture. But when you allow yourself to release what you hold to because you believe it is your security, or you know that without it you will be frightened, you have to let go. Those things that you hold on to that keep you in place that no longer support you will be released by you on a soul level, so you must learn to expect it. This can include relationships, and it will include the way you have lived your lives.

Earlier in this text we spoke about relationships in love, and the kind of love that we spoke of, "I am in love," had to do with the recognition of the divinity in all, and that still holds true. However, many of you still are tied, are bound in relationships that are not healing you or are not supporting you in your growth. And we promise you that as you continue to do this work and escalate in frequency, those things that are operating at lower frequency will not be able to stay. It will become uncomfortable or impossible. You may not be the one who releases it; the lower frequency may release on its own.

Imagine, again, that you are a ship and you are tethered to a shore. The farther the ship moves out to sea, the farther it moves away from the dock it was tethered to. Eventually the binding will break. It can no longer be held. The current has moved the ship downstream, as it were.

So be prepared, everybody. Now when you face these things and you receive the knowing of why things are happening, your first impulse may be to say, "Aha! More growth. I see what's happening," and the second impulse may be, "Oh no! I can't lose that. I can't lose him or her. Or that station, or that profession, or that thing I have believed myself to be." And of course you can understand that that is the ego's way, seeking to control you. If you believe truly that if you lose what you have you will not have something new to replace it at a higher frequency, that will be what you create with. So you must remain open. When your hands are open, you can receive. When they are clenching tightly, they cannot. And you must be prepared for your own willingness to be called upon in the face of fear.

When you are embarking on great change, you have a mission before you, and that is to face the change with gratitude, with welcoming, with an open mind and an open heart, because then you can be taken to someplace wonderful. When you are frightened of the journey, you hide from everything or you wish to remain only in the comfortability of the known, and we say to you in truth, that is no longer possible, it cannot be held. And not just for you, but for anyone.

The transition on this planet into frequency is calling everything to the light. That which has been hidden will be revealed. That which has been kept in darkness will be brought to the light, and this happens on the level of the individual. It happens in the level of government and culture and society, and this will be happening again and again and again.

Now of course, if you have a secret that you have been invested in hiding, you will try to cover as opposed to do the easy thing and the truthful thing, which is, allow the release to come. Now we are not telling you you are going to be exposed or suddenly there will be an opening of knowledge that everyone will see about a structure or a governmental operation. We are giving you a description about what is happening already.

Those systems that have not been in alignment with the light are being exposed to the light. They may make a last-ditch effort to retain their control. Ultimately, regardless of what you see before you out-pictured in the physical realm, all things are being brought to the light and what you perceive as strange, or as frightening, or as something new that you cannot identify, is all part of this process of transformation.

"As within, so without"—this happens on the macrocosmic and microcosmic level. Everything is in transformation and will con-

tinue to be so. So if you can imagine the man who holds on to the
corners of his desk for dear life to hold on to a system of the known
when his soul would bring him to a higher place, you have a good
metaphor for how many people and how many structures are seeking to maintain the known out of the fear of the changes that are
coming.

Now everybody, get this: You don't have to fight. You can allow.
Allow, allow, allow. And then the transformation comes so rapidly
that you don't have to worry about it. The time you spend worrying
about what will become of you if this or that happened is time that
is wasted. It has never gained you anything, nor will it ever, except
that you create from your worry and then you have to contend with
those structures that you have built.

So we offer you this:

As you release your attachment to habit, to the known, to a status quo that may not be servicing, you realign it to the new requirements that you will call to. When your heart is open, when you are
in your knowing, you are in congruence. The Divine Will, your
soul's knowing, and your own being can all be operating in tandem
and then you are set on the right road and you will know.

Choices come to every man and women, and as you decide
things you create new paths. When you are in confusion about
your path, you choose the high one. When you don't know what to
do, reclaim your knowing and then trust. When you see before you
a new opportunity for growth, align to it in wonder. It has been
presented to you to choose. And when you are coming from your
knowing, you will choose in truth that which is good for you.

We teach you today about the requirements of this text if you
have engaged with it in truth. If you have read the text every night
before sleeping and then watched TV and then forgotten about it,
you cannot expect the benefits to be incurred, other than the consciousness shifting to allow for the possibility of great change. If in

fact you have done the text as a manual, and we would like to say we consider this to be a manual in love and creation, you will invoke great change. And when you choose it, it is called to you and then this becomes your experience.

Your trajectory, as we have said, is to be catapulted into your new knowing and the experiences that will be required for you to establish yourselves in your knowing in a new way. Each day when you awaken, we request that you say the following:

> "I am now choosing to align my energy systems to the highest frequency available to me. And I align myself to my own Divine Knowing and to the love and to the frequency of love that I now exist in. I am Word through this intention. Word I am Word."

If you say this, you will be acclimating your energy field to a higher frequency and setting an intention that this is the course and the trajectory that you will take. Until you become habituated in raising your frequency, you are going to have to monitor it carefully. And this means knowing when you go down and return to the old ways of thinking that have not supported you and when you are choosing the new.

As you move through these changes, you become more adept. And as you become more adept, you spend far less time in lower frequency. And as that is the case, your reality has to conform. It's really that simple.

The changes that you have chosen are all to bring you into dominion of your own knowing and your own life's worth. You are the Divine Self in truth. That is who you have always been and we are teaching you to be, to say, "I am Word," which is to lay claim to the Divine Son-ship, your own aspect of God as the truth of who you are. As you know this, you lay claim to your own inheritance as a Divine Being which is inclusive of the gifts of the spirit. The gifts of the spirit are given to you in love and they are meant to be used in love. You all have eyes to see and everyone has forgotten what a gift that is on a daily basis. So clairvoyant sight, which is enhanced seeing, is just another level of who you are and what you can do as you raise your frequency.

The triumph of the self, of the Divine Self in fortitude, is grand. And the choice to be in your knowing is a great one. Again and again and again we have taught you that who you are is the light, and who you are is a creation of God in a body. And the process of embodiment, of incarnating as yourself, as your Divine Self, is the action of this text.

What will happen next, and what will happen after that?
We would like to teach you something. As this journey goes on, many, many, many will be joining you in their own ways. And the collective awareness of divinity, the collective shame in not knowing the beauty of the brother, will be releasing as people become awakened to their own accessibility to this information in the perfect way that will speak to their knowing, and this again happens on a planetary level.

As more and more people awaken to themselves, they have to awaken to the beauty of their brothers, and therein lies the massive change of the great awakening. Every cell in this organism that is you and is this planet in consciousness is alive with God, and the recognition of this is what will teach you on a moment-to-moment level who and what you are, and who and what your brother is. As you take the responsibility to do this work, you awaken the self. And your brother is awakened and his brother and his brother and his brother. And the mass awakening to the light will be something glorious to behold.

As many people in their knowing hold a truth, the planetary

truth must change. When many people hold a vision for how this world can be, this world must be transformed. The choices that are made in knowing are high choices. The choices that are made in fear are low choices. War is a low choice. It has always been a low choice. Love is a high choice and it is the only real truth.

The ascension of this planet and of all who inhabit it is the truth of this teaching, and as we awaken you we know, and we underline *know,* that you will be calling your brothers, your sisters to their own awakening. And as you sing your song, "I am Word. I am an aspect of the Creator in form," you resonate in this and the resonance of that is carried out as a beautiful note that will call to it the awakening others. This is happening now, you have chosen it, and we stand beside you and sing your praises with you as you claim your truth: "I am that I am. I am Word. I am Word. I am Word."

Our teaching is completing. And our actions now will be to stop this text and to begin to teach those who would follow it. Our decision to come here and to tutor was taken seriously, and as the student is serious, so will the level of assistance that will be brought to the student. No request for spiritual growth is ever denied. But do know that those obstacles to growth will be made apparent and there is no reason to run when the going gets tough. That is all the more reason to accept the fact that you are on this trajectory.

As we continue this text in our final section, we will remember what we have taught to you and we will sing to you in frequency. And what this really means is that we will give you a teaching that is not in words, but is in an all-encompassing "I Am." As you accept this in your frequency, you will be received by it and you will go into oneness. That final section will be accepted by channel Friday this week. Until that time, we wish you to each remember the work so far and to accept it in its love.

I am Word. I am Word. I am Word.

Thank you and stop.

EPILOGUE

Day Thirty

We would like to address the worries of the reader, who might believe that they have engaged in something that will not bring them to the level of enlightenment that they seek. In fact, that is a way fear works to withhold you from the good that you have claimed. And we ask you now to remember, every way you can, that the essence of this teaching is your own truth in the Christ promise of Divine Selfhood, and everything else that could present itself to you is a fallacy.

Of course you cannot be other than you are, and in truth this is who you are, and have been, and will continue to be. But it is through the process of re-identifying the self in this way that permits the frequency to shift, and all of the exercises we have offered you thus far have been prepared for you in order to bring you to this next station of your evolution. The planet is changing and you are of the planet. All are rising.

We said before we took a break that we wanted to gift you with an exercise that was in frequency that would actually bypass the intellectual self and support the self in many ways as an anchor of unity for the reader to prepare herself, himself, as they continue on, and we will offer this to you now:

"I am now knowing myself in my oneness with my Creator."

Now this simple statement actually carries with it magnificence. And we want to show you what we mean:

Your essence of yourself is a piece of the Creator, and the self that remembers the self as an aspect of this seeks to reunite in completeness with the Source of All That Is. That is the journey to the heart of the Creator that is established in you. Your return is set. However, we want you to understand that this can be accessed in body.

"I am now choosing to reunite my causal body, my own Divine Self, with the heart of God. I am Word through this intention. Word I am Word."

This will allow. Now if you allow this in your own way to be your meditation, the amplification of the Divine Self within you, in conjunction with the Creator, the idea of union will become a simple exercise in re-membrance. There is no magic here, there is only truth. The work of this text is remarkably simple when one accepts it as a simple action. And we wish you to do this with us:

"I am now knowing myself as in the Creator's Love. I am now knowing myself as at one with the God that created me. I am now accepting my will in alignment with the will of the Creator and I am remembering myself as an aspect of God in love, in alignment, and in wonder. I am Word through this intention. Word I am Word."

Our corrections of your energy fields are a continual action. To be re-membered requires support and it also requires some discipline in monitoring your consciousness and staying the course when it feels as if you are not moving forward. It is really impossible, finally, not to move forward in these exercises and the decrees will be established within you, within your energy frequency, and brought into form through your actions. It is through these actions that the work completes itself.

We decided this week to wait four days before continuing this exercise with the reader. And the reason for this was so that the channel could acclimate to the frequency we have thus far brought him. And it has worked, to the extent that he has realigned his energy field in a beautiful way that will allow for the support of others. As each of you embark on this in truth, this will be the impact on your field as well, and you will be offered the opportunities to regard the self as the one in her knowing, in his knowing, as you continue on your journeys.

As you claim these opportunities, you offer yourself in regard to service to love. And as you serve in love, you serve the Creator. There is no religion here. There is only love, there is only love, there is only love.

We are grateful to you each for your endeavors. We are blessed to be a participant on the road ahead. We will greet you at the stations you stop at and we will see you, we promise, in the light. We are in the sea of love, and you are joined with us in your intention to be here.

We gratefully attune you now to the words, "I Am That I Am." We would ask you to take a moment to receive this attunement in awareness of yourself as part of the Divine Plan unfolding in its perfection. Receive, please, the Word through the crown center and allow it to move through your entire being in perfection.

I am that I am. I am Word. I am Word. I am Word.

We call to you each the Emissaries of Light. We call to you each those who serve the Christ. We call to you each the truth of your knowing come forth in fruition of the Divine Plan. We call to you each the miracle of your birth and of your awakening. We bring to you the angels, the servers, the teachers who would herald your awakening. And we remind you now that you are never, never, never without love.

We gift you with this, precious one, in all of your love and beauty. We are with you now in energy. We are with you now in creation. And we say to you this:

I am Word.

ACKNOWLEDGMENTS

Tim Chambers, Mitch Horowitz, Amy Hughes, Jeannette Meek, Victoria Nelson, Alan Steinfeld, and the members of the Thursday Night Energy Group.

ABOUT THE AUTHOR

Paul Selig was born in New York City. He attended New York University and received his master's degree from Yale. He had a spiritual experience in 1987 that left him clairvoyant. As a way to gain a context for what he was beginning to experience, he studied a form of energy healing. He began to "hear" for his clients, and much of his work now is as a clairaudient, empath, and conscious channel. He has led channeled energy groups for many years. He lives in New York City where he maintains a practice as an intuitive. Also a noted playwright and educator, Paul directs the Master of Fine Arts in Creative Writing Program at Goddard College and teaches at New York University. His website is www.paulselig.com.

If you enjoyed this book, visit

www.tarcherbooks.com

and sign up for Tarcher's e-newsletter to receive
special offers, giveaway promotions, and
information on hot upcoming releases.

TARCHER
PENGUIN

Great Lives Begin with Great Ideas

If you would like to place a bulk order
of this book, call 1-800-847-5515.